MALICE AFORETHOUGHT

MALICE AFORETHOUGHT

The History of Booby Traps
from World War One to Vietnam

Ian Jones, MBE

Greenhill Books, London
Stackpole Books, Pennsylvania

Greenhill Books

Malice Aforethought: The History of Booby Traps from World War One to Vietnam
First published 2004 by
Greenhill Books, Lionel Leventhal Limited
Park House, 1 Russell Gardens,
London NW11 9NN
www.greenhillbooks.com
and
Stackpole Books, 5067 Ritter Road,
Mechanicsburg, PA 17055, USA

British Library Cataloguing in Publication Data
Jones, Ian
Malice aforethought : the history of booby traps
1. Booby traps – History – 20th century
I. Title
623.4'514

ISBN 1-85367-613-6

Library of Congress Cataloging-in-Publication data available

Typeset by Servis Filmsetting Limited, Manchester
Printed and bound by Creative Print and Design (Wales), Ebbw Vale

Contents

Illustrations

7

Aden: The results of an explosion of a booby trap on a motorcycle
A selection of non-explosive traps in Vietnam
A Viet Cong tunnel complex located during operation Cedar Falls, 1967

Acknowledgements

In the writing of this book I have relied on a large number of people for help, advice and information. I am particularly indebted to the following:

The staff of The Royal Engineers Library at Chatham, The Imperial War Museum Library, The MoD Library and the National Archive at Kew.

Mike Pugh and Sandy Sanderson of the Explosive Ordnance Disposal Technical Information Centre for their in-depth knowledge and their assistance with tracking down details of devices and people.

Lieutenant Colonel J McLennan, Controller of the Royal Engineers' Association, who put me in touch with many ex-Sappers, in particular Ron Harris and Reg Journet of the bomb disposal branch. They both provided much needed information and Reg also showed me his pictures of booby traps in Italy – some of which are reproduced in this book.

Sid Leader from 18 Bomb Disposal Company RE for his wealth of first-hand information about operations in North Africa. He defused his first bomb with a clasp knife and subsequently undertook many more hazardous operations until the end of the war.

David List, whom I met via a seat number at Kew, explained the workings of the files at the Public Record Office to me, and in particular he suggested that a good place to get details of booby traps was from enemy Explosive Ordnance Disposal (EOD) reports of recovered devices.

Lieutenant Colonel (retd) Philip Robinson both for information and for pointing out documents at the Public Record Office for me to read.

Andy Hoad, Mark Seaman, Peter Chamberlain, Mark Khan, Jamie Adam, Hugh Furse and John Harding for their time and expertise.

Liz Labbett for translating German documents. Tony Debski for drawing the pictures of the Viet Cong non-explosive traps from poor-quality photographs and sketches.

Cliff Cadman and the staff at the Metropolitan Police Explosives Office for their patience, and Tony Ashforth for preventing my lap-top computer from being thrown out of the window on more than one occasion.

Bob Leienedecker in the USA, who knows more about Explosive

Ordnance than anyone I know as a result of his operational work in Vietnam and his years providing EOD intelligence for the US armed forces. When I had all but despaired of tracing a 1970s American report on mines and booby traps from the Second World War to the end of the Vietnam War, Bob turned up in my office one day bearing a small package containing some useful US documents but more importantly a microfiche of the mine warfare report I needed. For that I am eternally grateful.

Mike Hibberd, who recently retired from the Imperial War Museum, for his much needed direction and assistance, particularly in the early days of the project.

Norman Bonney for his invaluable input regarding the SOE and for his detailed knowledge of devices and munitions. Without his help I would still be researching now.

As always any errors or omissions remain my responsibility. Finally I must thank Catherine, my wife, for editing the manuscript; without her, all my efforts would have come to nothing.

Ian Jones

INTRODUCTION
A Savage Practical Joke

Booby – A name applied to those species of bird, genus Sula. They owe their common name to their seemingly stupid behaviour in allowing themselves to be caught by hand.
              The Hamsworth Encyclopaedia, volume II, 1906

It has proved impossible to establish exactly how and when the behaviour of an innocent but stupid bird became synonymous with the deployment and use of explosive traps. In most, but not all, cases stupidity has nothing to do with the success of such a device. It is the cunningly conceived and carefully laid trap that catches out and kills the unwary soldier. In Italy in 1943 British troops came upon a highly desirable billet abandoned by the retreating Germans, its front door invitingly half open. Entering cautiously through a window, to avoid the likely booby trap, the troops approached the front door from inside and found attached to it the expected explosive charge apparently designed to function when the door was moved. They left the house and attached a line to the doorknob of the front door. They retreated across the road to a conveniently sited slit trench and pulled the line. A second trap hidden in the trench and connected to the door exploded and killed them all.[1] This fiendish and lethal attack illustrates the effectiveness of booby traps and the ingenuity with which they can be laid.

Both non-explosive and explosive traps have been around for a long time and some people seem to derive a perverse pleasure from their use. Booby traps were developed not long after the invention of the wheellock mechanism for small arms early in the 16th century. The new system opened the possibility of firing charges at a distance by a spring operating a lock, or a lock-operated clockwork device, the second mechanism giving birth to the time bomb or 'infernal machine'. This use was mentioned in a work written by Samuel Zimmermann of Augsburg in 1573 which, although it mainly dealt with fireworks, included the mischievous use of explosives. He made several contraptions operated by concealed springs or hidden string. It was recorded that:

The device can be applied to such pleasing purposes as to make a
stool or a chair with such a spring fire-work inside it, so that anyone
sitting on it will be shot or else terribly burnt. Similarly, one can lay
in the street what looks like a purse of gold, upon taking up which
anyone is at once shot.[2]

Further devices were recorded in the 16th century: there were packets,
boxes and chests, which were filled with gunpowder but were supposed to
contain valuables, and which exploded on opening. One booby-trapped
chest was used in the siege of Psków in 1581. This was sent as a gift to the
Russian defender Ivan Petrovich Shuiskii and when opened by a few of his
companions it exploded and killed them.

In Britain flintlock trap-guns were used for the protection of land and
property. They were designed to shoot automatically at men and animals
that came into their line of fire. The system used a double flintlock initiation system and a short-barrelled gun, which was mounted on a pivot allowing it to swivel. Several lines were spread out from the gun to cover a large
area and fixed close to the ground. When a line was caught and drawn taut,
it swivelled the gun towards the unsuspecting victim and fired. Spring guns
of a similar kind were used to deter poachers. They were outlawed in the
1820s but some estates displayed notices warning of such devices long after
they were declared illegal.

A definition which catches the evil nature of a booby trap is:

A booby trap is a cunning contrivance, usually of an explosive and
lethal nature, designed to catch the unwary enemy; a savage practical joke. The essence of a good booby trap is low cunning spiced
with variety.[3]

Psychologically, there is something very emotive about the use of these
devices. They can have a profound effect on soldiers' behaviour. They
evoke feelings of fear, anger, resentment and revulsion; similar emotions in
many respects to those felt about snipers who target the unwary or unlucky.
It is the new or inexperienced soldier who exposes himself too long, lingers
in the wrong place, or goes to help a dying colleague who becomes the
sniper's prey. One almost always feels sorry for the victim because he is an
individual who has been selected from the masses and killed. In most armies
snipers are elite hunters, carefully selected and trained and expert marksmen. That the ordinary soldier resents them is without question.
Surrendering snipers often forfeit their lives. The same emotions can be
evoked by booby traps where the unsuspecting victim, who may have just
survived a gruelling battle or is resting out of the front line, is suddenly
killed or maimed as a result of his own action when he disturbs an unseen

device. Worse still, those that go to his assistance may also be targeted and finish up as victims of other devices. The indiscriminate use of mines and booby traps is another facet of war, which devalues or debases human feelings. It is irrefutable that maintaining morale is a vital factor in war and anything which chips away at this is bound to have an adverse effect on operational effectiveness. Booby traps however are not decisive weapons of war, like an armoured thrust or infantry assault, and this should be borne in mind when reading this text.

There has always been unease about the use of certain types of weapons or ammunition in warfare. The use of dumdum expanding bullets designed to cause massive injury was notably banned at the beginning of the 20th century. More recently concern has been raised over munitions that are designed to be deployed but are not immediately activated. These may remain buried or hidden but still be able to function long after a conflict has finished. Many of these, although not banned outright, are subject to international law, which aims to prevent the use of those that indiscriminately affect both combatants and non-combatants.

The Inhumane Weapons Convention of 1981 aimed to prohibit or restrict the use of certain conventional weapons. Included in these were anti-personnel mines, booby traps and other devices. Booby traps were defined as 'any device or material which is designed, constructed or adapted to kill or injure and which functions unexpectedly when a person disturbs or approaches an apparently harmless object or performs an apparently safe act.' It further defined other devices as 'manually emplaced munitions or devices designed to kill or injure which are actuated by remote control or automatically after a lapse of time.'

Despite the attempted ban, booby traps will almost certainly appear in future conflicts. Sadly in war necessity (perceived or genuine), not humanity, prevails. What is clear is that once a war starts all means will be used to destroy the opposition. Cobden observed in 1862 after the outbreak of the American Civil War that, once started, conflicts inevitably degenerate into gruesome killing matches from which the combatants fight until exhaustion. Succinctly he wrote:

> From the moment the first shot is fired, or the first blow struck in a
> dispute then farewell to all reason and argument; you might as well
> attempt to reason with mad dogs as with men when they have begun
> to spill each others blood in mortal combat.[4]

It must be expected therefore that in any major war or prolonged guerrilla campaign booby traps will be deployed. Many of the switches designed for booby traps are also well suited for use in sabotage operations and vice versa. For example, the daring and highly successful SAS raids on the airfields in North Africa in the 1940s used delayed-action devices to destroy aircraft on the ground. They used specially designed, locally produced bombs; these and some other sabotage devices will be described in the book. The operations themselves however have already been extensively written about and will only be briefly discussed where relevant.

Next it is necessary to address the issue of land mines. Mines are traps, most of which are victim- or target-operated. They rely on their concealment for their effectiveness and tactically are designed to delay, deter, and demoralise enemy troops. However there are a number of features that distinguish mines from booby traps and it is important to understand the differences between the two.

Military land mines are mass-produced, often laid in large numbers, and are by design comparatively safe, simple and easy to deploy. They are purpose-built, normally contained in wood, metal or, more recently, plastic containers and have an in-built initiating system that causes them to function. The most common types of mine are anti-tank mines which will destroy or disable armoured and other vehicles, and anti-personnel mines designed to kill wound or otherwise incapacitate people and animals. There are also some mines which are command-initiated. These are often used in defensive positions or ambushes and are designed to de detonated by a remote observer when the enemy enters the mine's lethal area.

Mines are usually deployed *en masse* to form minefields that provide artificial barriers or obstacles to men or vehicles or both. Minefields, like other obstacles, are not impassable barriers, but unless they are breached will cause casualties and inhibit the movement of troops. Minefields are laid according to the needs of a strategic or tactical position. This book is not concerned with the use of mines in this main role.

Mines can also be used individually or in small numbers and this form of deployment is known as nuisance or harassing mining. This is the act of placing mines in the verges of roads, or among the rubble of demolished bridges or farmyards that must or could be used by the advancing enemy. It requires some premeditated thought on behalf of the layer; clearly it would be pointless sowing nuisance mines in an area the enemy was unlikely to use. The Germans mastered these tactics during the Second World War. The value of this type of mining within the total concept of battle is the same as booby-trapping, that is, to promote caution in the minds of the enemy. It makes them think twice before advancing into new and unknown territory and adds an additional stress to those already strained by the impact of war. When mines are deployed in this fashion they are sometimes laid in conjunction with booby traps where they complement each other. When

German village, mined and booby-trapped, showing; A anti-personnel mines,
B anti-tank mines, C booby traps

mines are used in this manner it is difficult to differentiate them from booby traps and vice versa.

Finally, mines themselves can be booby-trapped; the main reason for this is to prevent them being easily lifted and cleared. The Germans in particular in the Second World War employed this tactic as an effective deterrent to the rapid clearance of their minefields, particularly those that could not be covered by fire.

I intend to examine some of the many novel or unconventional uses of explosive for specific and unusual tasks. This covers original, experimental or improvised applications that do not easily sit in any other category. These range from an ill-conceived, locally planned scheme in Italy to load a sled with explosives and send it down a hill, guided by string, towards German positions, to items like the Giant Panjandrum, a massive rocket-propelled demolition charge.

Excluded from the book are the booby-trap switches that were fitted into conventional aircraft-dropped bombs and sea mines to prevent them being easily defuzed. During the Second World War, the Germans used a number of anti-handling fuzes and fuze attachments. The ZUS 40 anti-withdrawal device for example was added to the base of some normal German bomb fuzes. Any attempt to remove the fuze would result in a secondary detonator initiating the bomb. Details of all these and other similar anti-handling systems are well documented in other works.

Also excluded are the victim-operated switches developed and used in the most recent terrorist campaigns. In Northern Ireland the Provisional IRA made very effective use of improvised booby traps and in some areas, such as South Armagh, caused many casualties. These irregular devices used in terrorist or counter-insurgency campaigns were deployed with skill, cunning and deadly effect. For obvious reasons these latest devices are beyond the scope of this book. It is, however, intended to cover some of the early post-war terrorist campaigns which saw the transition from the use of military booby traps to improvised traps.

Consequently I have decided to limit the scope of the book from the First World War to Vietnam. The starting point reflects the fact that the First World War was the first time that the devices were developed and used in significant numbers. There are two reasons for stopping at the conclusion of the Vietnam War. Firstly, up until the end of the Vietnam War, most booby-trap switches and igniters were fairly simple mechanical or electro-mechanical devices. However, in the last three decades a new breed of sophisticated multi-purpose, multi-sensor electronic switches for use in booby traps has appeared. These have been used in recent conflicts around the world, for example, in the bloody and brutal Balkan wars. These more modern devices will not be described. Secondly, the post-Vietnam world has been dominated by terrorism and the use of improvised explosive devices. These, although fascinating, are beyond the scope of the book which as already stated aims to investigate military booby traps, sabotage devices and the unconventional use of explosives in war.

For those new to this field, a short description of the different types of explosive and their basic methods of operation is necessary. This is important because it limits what can and cannot be done when laying a booby trap.

Everyone is familiar with gunpowder, a low explosive used in fireworks, that simply needs a flame or a spark to get it to explode. Gunpowder's main disadvantage is that it is hygroscopic: if not protected by a waterproof barrier, it rapidly absorbs moisture and becomes impossible to initiate and therefore is rendered ineffective. Cromwell's comment 'Put your trust in God, my boys, and keep your powder dry' is a testament to its susceptibility to the damp. The need to keep gunpowder dry limited its use as the main charge, which might be buried in the ground or exposed to the elements. Some were used as fougasses in Malta in the 18th century and they were encountered in the American Civil War, but it was not really until the advent of high explosives that effective mines and traps could be made.

Most high explosives were discovered in the early to mid 18th century, but were not developed as safe and serviceable stores until the beginning of the 1900s. Military high explosives, for example gun-cotton, need a detonator to get them to function because they are fairly insensitive to shock and heat stimuli. Other explosives, such as TNT, are even less sensitive and need small gun-cotton primers to get them to detonate. Detonators themselves use much more sensitive explosives and come in two varieties known as electrical or plain. Clearly the former require an electrical current to get them to function. The latter, plain detonators, can be set off using a small flash of flame from a low explosive like gunpowder. Plain detonators are almost invariably initiated by a burning fuse. Two basic types of burning fuse are available: safety fuse, which burns at a relatively slow rate, in the order of a metre per 100 seconds, and an instantaneous fuse which, as used in British service, burnt at 30 metres per second. In booby traps, fuse instantaneous was often used to allow an explosive charge to be located some distance from the trap mechanism itself. Finally, the French developed *cordeau detonant* in 1907. This was a lead pipe filled with high explosive which would allow a detonating wave to pass down it. Travelling at some 4,900 metres per second it made fuse instantaneous look slow. This rigid tube was replaced in the mid 1930s with an improved variant of detonating cord, often called Cordtex or Prima Cord. This looks like plastic washing line and is a flexible high-explosive line, which not only allows a detonating wave to pass down it, but it can also be bent round corners or obstructions. As with fuse instantaneous, it can be used to site a charge away from a firing device.

It was only after the development of all these explosives, which were safe, stable and could be deployed in all weather conditions and remain viable, that effective use could be made of mines and booby traps. These traps need some form of firing switch and igniter, a detonator, a main charge, sometimes a small booster charge, and if the firing switch and igniter are separate from the main charge then these must be linked by a quick-burning fuse or detonating cord.

When reading the text it is important that the reader understands some of the mythology that surrounds the use of explosives. Historically when reading about the First World War it must be remembered that most of the soldiers that fought the war did not enter it with same understanding of explosives that we have today. Clearly they would quickly become familiar with the terrifying effects of high explosive as a result of artillery bombardment. But booby traps and mines were novel devices. Conversely all the readers of this book will have grown up with television images of conventional and terrorist bombs. Pictures of explosions and their effects no longer shock and are widely available. Although no less terrifying they are not the new or bewildering devices that they once were. On the contrary, the current generation, used to spectacular special effects of the film industry, often over-rate the power of explosives, which has been exaggerated out of all proportion. With their clever techniques, the special effects practitioners do the most amazing stunts which distort the truth. Cars do not explode when set on fire and hand grenades do not demolish buildings.

Finally I am clear that this is not the full story. I know that both the Germans and the Russians, in the bitter war on the Eastern Front, used booby traps extensively. These are touched upon but not dealt with in detail. Equally there is no reference to the many other wars, for example the French in Algeria. The reason is simply access to and availability of information. I also recognise that a book could be devoted to each of the chapters, or to any of the many brave men who dealt with booby traps, be it in the dimly lit dugouts on the Western Front, on the beaches of Normandy or the dark and dangerous tunnels in Vietnam. While undertaking my research I also discovered a great deal of intriguing information about sabotage and other clandestine activities and could have written much more on the subject. My main aim, however, was always to look at the design, development, deployment and effectiveness of booby traps in a military context and the measures that have been taken to negate their effects and to neutralise them.

Notes

1 Regan, Geoffry, *The Guinness Book of Military Anecdotes*, Guinness Publishing, London, 1992.

2 Partington, JR, *A History of Greek Fire and Gunpowder*, W Heffer and Sons, Cambridge, 1960.
3 Field Engineering and Mine Warfare, pamphlet no. 7: *Booby Traps*, The War Office, October 1952, WO code 8741.
4 Cobden, Richard, *Speeches on Questions of Public Policy*, volume II, page 324.

PART ONE

World War One

CHAPTER ONE

Motivation and Methods

Kill the enemy without scruple and by any means.　　　Ernst Jünger

The First World War was an outstanding example of technology bringing new and murderous weapons to the battlefield. Industrialisation ensured that the weapons – modern rifles, machine-guns, quick-firing and heavy artillery pieces, poison gas, mortars, tanks and aircraft – were delivered to the armies in large numbers. The conflict also saw the development and use of explosives in the form of booby traps, mines, delayed-action devices and mobile charges in significant numbers. However, amid the orgy of destruction, the sheer scale of the fighting and horrendous casualties, the impact of these devices was diminished.

Although they were of no strategic importance, tactically these devices proved to be effective and the seeds were sown for their subsequent development and use. There is some evidence for the limited deployment of non-explosive traps throughout the war. Captain J C Dunn, serving as a Medical Officer with the Royal Welch Fusiliers, wrote on 15 October 1915:

> A trap for our cavalry to tumble into had been made by digging up a road and putting harrows with their spikes uppermost into the holes.[1]

Towards the end, in July 1918, the Americans photographed a mantrap in a gap in a barbed wire obstacle presumably designed to catch an unwary night patrol. There is also evidence to support the early use of devices for exploding mines or hidden charges, often by some form of victim-operated trap. On the Western Front these chiefly consisted of tripwires introduced into barbed wire entanglements. At Beaumont Hamel on 8 October 1915 the German 119 Reserve Regiment recorded a night patrol moving through a British minefield. One of the mines was recovered from a crater for defusing later but it exploded.[2] These traps, however, were liable to be as much of a source of danger to one's own side as the other. The necessity

23

to go out into 'no man's land' at night to patrol and to repair wire damaged by shellfire did not encourage the use of traps.[3] Devices of various natures were used to protect sentry positions and give advance warning of an approaching enemy. Their main use, however, was to cover withdrawals, either after local trench raids or to assist in major operations, for example, the extrication of Allied troops from Gallipoli. On the Western Front it was predominantly the Germans that deployed booby traps, particularly as the tide of war turned against them.

Booby traps made a very definite impression on the individual officers and soldiers that fought in the front line and who came into contact with them. For most men they were new devices. The first significant British report on the subject was entitled 'German Ruses' but the name on subsequent reports was changed to 'Mines and Traps'. In the front line the talk was of traps, mines, booby traps, demolitions, gins, mobile charges, infernal machines and delay devices. They also left their mark on the Royal Engineers who had to locate and disarm them. Many of those that wrote of their experiences, during and after the war, refer to the use of booby traps and their impact, both real and imagined.

The development of new munitions, particularly demolition stores and grenades that could be modified or adapted, enabled the deployment of booby traps in greater numbers as the war progressed. Prior to the introduction of the tank, land mines of various types were employed. These were used in comparatively small numbers, were of improvised designs, were locally manufactured and individually laid. In many respects they were more akin to the booby trap as it is defined today and therefore merit description. After the arrival of the tank, landmines were used to provide barriers by both sides, for example; the German *Falsh* mine was manufactured in the rear areas in significant quantities. These mines meet the modern definition of anti-tank mines and are beyond the scope of this book.

Like all wars, the First World War failed to match up to the expectations of those who went cheerfully off to the front in 1914. What was supposed to be a patriotic, honourable and glorious opportunity to fight for one's country and be home by Christmas turned into a protracted and bloody clash of arms. The development of the machine-gun and the magazine-fed rifle, and the advent of quick-firing artillery able to deliver shrapnel and high explosive shell, which cut down unprotected cavalry and infantry in droves, forced both sides into trenches. As the troops raced to the coast and casualties mounted it became clear that only the seriously wounded would be home by Christmas.

As always the infantry bore the brunt of the fighting and strategy and tactics were designed to support them. By the end of the first year, excluding the brief period of fraternisation at Christmas, both sides had settled down to a brutal slogging match. As they dug in, all along the front, it became clear that the infantry would need a new range of weapons if they were to survive and fight in the trenches. Accurate and deadly rifle fire, which had been telling in the small conflicts in India and Africa and at the beginning of the war, was no longer effective as the numbers of highly trained marksmen dwindled as a result of casualties. At close quarters the weapons needed were grenades, clubs, pistols and fighting knives. Of these the most important was the hand grenade and these, as will be seen, were well-suited for booby-trapping.

The outlook of the infantry, who manned the front lines, hardened as the illusion of war was shattered by the grim reality of life in the trenches. In all weathers they endured the snipers, machine-guns, artillery and trench mortar fire. They became accustomed to the dreadful sight of the dead and the cries of the wounded. The former were often left out for months in no man's land or, if buried, churned up by artillery fire, slowly decaying and providing a vast breeding ground for rats and flies. In this horrendous carnage life became a common commodity which was easily traded and men overcame their reserve about killing. Lieutenant C Edmonds gave this account of a counter attack:

> I saw straight to the front and a hundred yards away a crowd of men running towards us in grey uniforms. Picking up another rifle I joined him pouring rapid fire into this counter attack. We saw at least one drop, to Walker's rifle I think, and then noticed that they were running with their hands up. Laughing we emptied our magazines into them in spite of that.[4]

Life was cheap and the means of taking it diversified. Methods used to kill, which were previously considered immoral, taboo or in many cases as unchivalrous or simply 'not playing the game', became commonplace. For example, poison gas, a new and terrible weapon was unleashed on the unsuspecting British infantry on 22 April 1915 in the second battle of Ypres when chlorine was discharged from cylinders over the battlefield. As the gas drifted over them, the soldiers' eyes began to sting and their throats tightened. With no protection they were soon fighting for breath, coughing up blood and dying.

Another fearful death came from the classic use of mines. In the tradition of siege warfare miners on both sides tunnelled under each other's lines and laid explosive charges. Initially these were quite small: the first mine, fired by the Germans on 4 December 1914, contained some 660 pounds of explosive.

By 1917 the British had fired a single mine of some 42 tons. When detonated, these destroyed the opposition's trenches and strong points, blowing vast clods of earth and clay into the air. The lucky ones were killed in the blast; others were buried alive, or incarcerated in collapsed dugouts. For those in front line the lessons were clear; it was kill or be killed and any method or means was acceptable – booby traps being no exception.

On the Western Front in the stalemate between major battles, trench raids were used to maintain the offensive spirit. These varied widely in size and complexity from two or three men creeping into no man's land at night to snatch a sentry to whole battalions occupying the enemy's front line trenches for short periods. Sentry duty was therefore a vital but lonely and unenviable task, particularly in wet, freezing conditions. Standing for two hours, in the front line trenches or in a forward listening post with head and shoulders above the parapet with the possibility of being hit by a stray bullet or snatched by an enemy patrol, was nerve-racking and physically exhausting. Very early in the war simple warning systems were devised to protect sentries. For example, Hutchison in his book *Warrior* described how tripwires were used in conjunction with machine-guns to catch unwary enemy patrols:

> The ingenuity of the British soldier is proverbial. In 'No Mans Land' we devised 'booby traps'. The war could not have continued for a week without canned food: and these tins served a dual purpose. They were strung together on tripwires in the most inviting places for enemy patrols, with machine guns trained upon them. Soon as the tins rattled fire was opened up with the machine guns and a patrol hurried down the ditch to bring in the quarry, a prisoner or a corpse. In the first experiment I brought in samples of each.

This according to Hutchison brought a lethal response from the Germans opposite:

> But if the British soldier played with booby traps then the German was not to be denied, for they placed an elaborate explosive dummy in a ditch leading from our lines much used by our own patrols. The decoy proved, as was expected, too much for Jock's curiosity, and we lost two good men as the consequence.[5]

It would seem that the use of booby-trapped dummy figures was a popular ruse with the Germans. In a 1917 publication it was recorded that dummy figures placed 60 yards in front of a German trench were set to explode if moved by a patrol. In another case an upright dummy was found in a shell hole; it had a battery and unspecified firing switch connected to an explosive charge in contact with an unexploded shell. The slightest movement of the dummy would cause the switch to close and detonate the shell.[6] Although not a booby trap, the Germans also used a dummy apparently dressed in a German uniform which was left out in no man's land. When a patrol went out to secure identification of the corpse they were ambushed. In another case the dummy was rigged so that it appeared to be beckoning for assistance.

The same report also detailed mechanical devices, in reality booby traps. These included a bomb buried in a listening post with the handle exposed and giving the appearance of being a half-buried pick. The bomb exploded when the haft was picked up. Bombs were also discovered placed in sandbags on the ground with friction igniters anchored to stakes. If the sandbag were lifted the friction igniter would function causing the charge hidden in the bag to explode. A final example was a flag was placed in the ground, which was connected to a charge on a pole nearby by means of a small rope. Picking up the flag caused the charge to explode.

Captain Herbert W McBride, who served with the Canadian Corps from September 1915 to April 1917, described how one night, alone, he went into no man's land to recover a German flag, which was flying just in front of their trenches. As he approached the flag he noted:

> It was simply a matter of moving forward quietly and cautiously down the outside of the German embankment. There were a lot of tin cans and rubbish which had to be avoided, but in a short time I came to their flag; it was planted right in the midst of an area of what we called 'tripwire'; that is wire strung on stakes which were driven in almost to the ground, the wire, (barbed, of course) sticking up about ankle high. Nasty stuff to get through alright. The Flagstaff was firmly embedded in the ground and was further braced by guy-wires which were anchored in the ground. I managed to unfasten the guy-wires and then pulled the staff out of the ground. Guess I must have overlooked something – some wire connected with an alarm in their trench, or possibly a 'set' rifle or two. At any rate a couple of rifle shots rang out and the bullets came uncomfortably close. I think one hit the stick the flag was fastened to, and I had two pretty severe cuts in my hands which were suspiciously like bullet marks.[7]

After things had quietened down, McBride managed to regain the safety of his own trenches. The flag protected by its tripwires and fixed rifles was a classic case of a 'come on' in which an item, either attractive or provocative, is used as bait to lure the unsuspecting into danger. The use of such lures is a common theme for the booby-trap layer.

The use of grenades that could be adapted to make booby traps, particularly by the Germans, was commonplace towards the end of the war when stocks were readily available. Essentially two basic types of explosive hand grenades were used. Those that employed some form of burning fuse which provided a short delay between throwing and functioning, and percussion grenades which were designed to detonate on impact. Of the two types the former proved to be the most popular. They were safer to use and more reliable than the impact designs. The key components of such a grenade were a simple mechanical arming system, a short delay and an adequate explosive charge. Grenades with these characteristics were easy to adapt for use as booby traps. Wires could be attached to safety pins on the British Mills grenades and they could be laid so that they would function when tripped, or when an object they were attached to was picked up or pulled. German grenades, both the stick and ball types, with friction igniters could be adapted in a similar manner with a wire attached to the igniter and set to function when pulled.

The grenades themselves could be booby-trapped as the intrepid Captain Herbert W McBride described:

> The German potato-masher grenade was rather clumsy to look at but really very handy to use. They had a playful habit of fitting these things with instantaneous fuses and then leaving them lying around in no man's land where one of our men might pick them up. If the poor devil tried to use the thing, he was blown apart the minute he pulled the string.[8]

The Germans also devised traps using grenades to protect their sentries. On 7 December 1916 a Canadian officer, Lieutenant A A McDougall of the Princess Patricia's Light Infantry, was injured when taking part in a small raid against German trenches on Vimy Ridge:

> The raiding party consisted of McDougall, another officer and eight men, whose task was to gain information and most importantly prisoners. At 03:30 hours on a freezing night the raiders crept forward. The two officers went ahead to a position where they could see two sentries, then the other men were ordered forward to provide cover while the post was rushed. McDougall demanded the two men's surrender at pistol point, the sentries raised their hands but at the same time one of them dislodged a grenade on the parapet using a foot-operated mechanism. The grenade exploded and McDougall had both legs badly injured. The covering party immediately dispatched

the sentries and then carried their Lieutenant back to their own lines.[9]

It is not clear what type of grenade was used or how the release system operated and in the final analysis it did nothing to save the luckless sentries. It was, however, clearly effective against the raiding party and prevented the patrol achieving their main aim of capturing prisoners and in addition injured its leader.

In larger-scale raids, where the enemy's front line trenches were occupied, mobile and delayed-action charges were often used. They were designed not only to destroy enemy dugouts and kill their occupants, but also to deter the enemy from rapidly re-occupying their positions and hence give the raiders time to retire. The charges were necessary because grenades, for example the No. 5 (Mills) with their small explosive charges (typically just over 2 ounces) were ineffective, particularly if bomb traps designed to catch and stop grenades rolling down the access stairways were built into the dugouts. In 1916 the Experimental Section of the Royal Engineers was called upon to design a fuse to fit a variety of portable charges. These were typically petrol tins, oil drums, ammunition containers and the standard issue 50-pound ammonal (high explosive) tins. In 1917 a number of trials took place and the conclusions arrived at were that charges of 10–30 pounds had little effect in the dugout shaft itself, and in no case could it be regarded as effectively sealed; that a charge of 20 pounds would kill – or at least incapacitate – all the occupants of a dugout; but with little effort the dugouts could still be used by our men after the charges had been fired.[10] One of the problems with the portable charges was getting them down into the bottom of the dugouts, particularly if the steps into them had corners. To get over this a 'Ferret Bomb' was designed which was round and which would not easily lodge on steps or landings. It consisted of a square box containing 8 pounds of gun-cotton slabs on to which ribs were attached to make it ball-shaped (see illustration overleaf).

The charges were initiated by lengths of ordinary safety fuse wound in various ways to give a maximum time delay of about 20 minutes. However these were not always satisfactory. In the bigger and more complex raids at company or even battalion strength, where command and control were difficult and unexpected enemy actions or casualties could cause delays, 20 minutes was often considered insufficient. The fuse could also prove difficult to light in wet or damp conditions. Finally, even with short delays there was the possibility that the enemy, on re-occupying his positions, could discover the charge by the smell of the burning fuse. It must, however, have been a brave man who would go into a trench or dugout looking for a

FERRET BOMB
XVII Corps 20-10-17.

Weight about 17 lbs, with 8 lbs of guncotton.

(Charge should not be less than 10 lbs. See E-in-C.Fieldwork Notes Nº46.)

View of ribs for top and bottom portions.

Detonator

A

B

This form of charge is very suitable for rolling down dugouts, as it rarely lodges on the steps or landings.

6⅝"

7"

Sketch of box with lid on, in which eight slabs of guncotton are placed.

A ferret bomb

device not knowing how long the fuse had to burn. The Germans had a slightly better system, which was described when miners from 181 Tunnelling Company RE broke into a German tunnelling system in early March 1916. The report into the affair detailed the capture of German mobile charges that were described as follows:

> The enemy mobile charges are as useless as ours except that it is not possible to put out the fuze when lit. It is merely an infernal machine. The long fuze is covered by a wooden case. Inside there is an auto fuze lighter connected to a rope handle 9 inches long. It would be great advantage to have mobile charges of the German pattern ready. They provide a long fuze that cannot be extinguished with out taking the box apart. The automatic fuze lighters are also very useful.[11]

As well as being ahead of the Allies with their grenades and mortars at the start of the war, the Germans were also tactically more aware of the need for the development and deployment of mines and booby traps. They recognised the importance of such devices in impeding and slowing down an advancing enemy even before the first tanks appeared on the battlefield. In 1915 in the German Manual of Demolition (*Sprengvorschrift*) they stated that:

> Land mines are employed on roads likely to be used by the enemy during an advance; on probable sites for batteries and parks; in ground defiladed from the view of German positions; in combination with other obstacles; to increase the difficulties of hostile reconnaissance and destruction of obstacles; and particularly in front of positions in danger of assault. Both observation and contact mines are employed.[12]

The Germans also understood the need to mark the mines in some way to ensure that their own troops did not march over them, but that this should be done in such a manner as not to attract the attention of even a wide-awake enemy. According to Belgian sources, these mines were placed in buildings, under pavements and even in soldier's graves with the corpses over them. The key to these new weapons was the development of a range of percussion, friction and electrical igniters. These, although not designed as booby-trap switches, were reliable, easy to use and suitable for service in most weather conditions. Indeed the German Mechanical Fuse Lighter, a percussion safety fuse initiator, was so efficient that it was copied by the British and issued under the new name of 'Igniter Safety Fuse Percussion Original Pattern'.

By early 1916 the Germans were employing observation mines, contact mines and tripwire mines. The observation mines were electrically fired and could not therefore be sited very far from the position they were intended to defend. They were generally laid in front of permanent or semi-permanent positions, the electrical leads having been laid during the construction of the position. The mines were normally laid in groups of three or more. The charges used and the depth to which they were laid varied. To stop an assault they were laid 12 to 20 inches under the surface, so that the explosive acted directly on the enemy; or 1 to 2 metres deep so that masses of earth were thrown up. Covering the charges with stones sometimes increased the effect. The size of the charges was calculated to ensure that only a shallow trench was formed so as to give no appreciable cover to the advancing enemy. The mines were of course vulnerable to artillery fire that could cut the firing leads.

The contact mines were primitive improvised devices that were the forerunners of modern mines. They were huge by today's standards and, considering that the early models were designed before the arrival of the tank on the battlefield, they had unnecessarily large explosive charges, the figures given ranging from 4–22 pounds of high explosive. This was significantly more than was required to kill a man. Modern anti-personnel mines have only a few ounces of explosive. They were often deployed where trench lines were close together. Single mines were used to block approaches, breaches in obstacles and in ditches or shell holes. The electro-contact mines were similar in construction, but had contact plates on the lid and box, and an electrical initiator. The battery was buried separately near the box, and was not integral to it.

The Germans also deployed tripwire mines; these were fired when the enemy disturbed or cut the wire attached to them. They were considered by the British to be ineffective because the wire was easy to see even in long grass. It must be assumed therefore that the tripwires used in these early traps were much more substantial than those used today. They tended to be used only in front of defensive positions, and were often deployed in or in front of barbed wire entanglements. If used in other locations it was necessary to ensure that the area was covered by fire to prevent the mines being easily neutralised.

The mines were laid using two posts, which were normally placed about 8–9 metres apart. A wire was stretched between them. A third post was driven in the centre of these but set forward slightly. To this was attached a special fuse lighter, which was linked to a buried charge. The wire was attached to the top of the igniter that was under tension; when cut the striker would be released and would fire the mine. Equally, if the tension

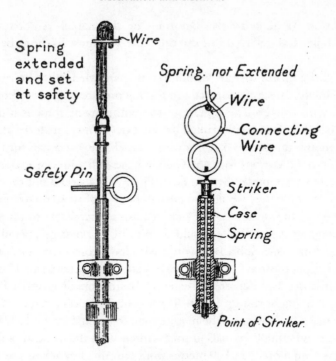

A trip igniter

on the wire was increased it would pull the tripwire from the top of the connecting wire and again fire the mine.

The Germans clearly understood the value of mines and traps and embraced their use whenever circumstances permitted. There is no doubt, however, that the first major use of booby traps and mines accompanied by widespread destruction of stores and livestock was by the British and ANZAC forces at the conclusion of the ill-fated Gallipoli campaign.

The Allied expeditionary force, which had landed in the Dardanelles in April 1915, failed to make the expected gains and in difficult conditions were fought to a standstill by the skilful Turks. Hemmed in close to the beaches in three separate locations, Cape Helles, Anzac and Sulva Bay, the Allied forces clung to their precarious positions. In October, after a change of command, General Monro undertook a detailed review of the military situation. Rapidly he came to the conclusion that an immediate evacuation of Gallipoli was the only sensible military option. Initially Lord Kitchener refused to sign the order permitting the withdrawal. However in November 1915 he visited the peninsula to get first-hand knowledge of the situation. After visiting Cape Helles he went to the positions at Anzac and Sulva Bay. Having seen the conditions for himself the decision was made that the positions at Anzac and Sulva Bay must be abandoned. A decision about Cape Helles was deferred but the outcome was most likely to be a withdrawal.

Of all the phases of war, withdrawal is acknowledged to be one of the most difficult. Breaking contact and leaving prepared defensive positions is fraught with danger. The morale of the withdrawing force is usually at a low ebb and is often accompanied by shortages of men, materiel and stores. If the enemy discovers what is afoot, a rapid follow-up can turn a withdrawal into a disastrous rout. At Gallipoli the difficulties of extracting the force were compounded by two facts. Firstly, they would not only have to break contact but they would also need to be re-embarked on to ships standing offshore, and, secondly, the lack of resources available to lift the force out in one go meant that it would have to be a two-stage operation. The forces at Anzac and Sulva Bay would withdraw from their positions by 20 December but those at Cape Helles would not be evacuated for 17 days after the main force had departed. General Monro himself estimated that the casualty rate might run up to 30–40 per cent of the total force.

The task was enormous: the requirement to evacuate some 134,000 men, 400 guns and 14,000 animals in mid winter, with the Turkish positions in some cases no more than 100 metres from the Allied trenches, was going to need detailed planning. It was made clear from the outset that the withdrawal could only be successful if an elaborate deception scheme was put in place. It would take cunning and Machiavellian ingenuity to invent devices that would send up flares, explode mines and keep up the rifle fire to prevent the Turks guessing at what was happening in the final hours of the evacuation.

The initial planning identified the need to produce defensive obstacles including mines and traps to help delay any Turkish advance should the evacuation be detected. Each division was ordered to produce between 1–200 devices that would be positioned in front of the wire protecting the forward trenches. Further traps were to be used in second and third line positions and to seal routes as the forces departed. No purpose-built devices were available at that time and improvisation was the order of the day. A variety of improvised traps was constructed, many using biscuit tins. 67 Field Company RE recorded the construction of the devices:

> As the only explosive available was ammonal it was of the utmost importance that the cases should be waterproof. The most suitable containers were biscuit tins filled with 30lbs of ammonal. The detonators were taken from T&F grenades inserted with wire from the friction arrangements passed through a small hole made good by

grease. The tin was placed in a wooden box so constructed to leave 3 inches clearance between the tin and the lid, which was fitted with leather back, flaps hinged in an arrangement for igniting the detonator when stepped upon. A second form of mine was made of a lot of wet gun-cotton containing a primer and a detonator from a T&F grenade with the friction device attached to a tripwire.[13]

In trip mines, tins filled with ammonal were used in pairs. These were laid and then connected by fine binding wire, which was fixed into friction igniters in the tins, these igniters being taken from T&F grenades, which were preferred because they were more reliable in action. Laying these mines and traps was difficult and dangerous work. The brightness of the moon and the proximity of Turkish patrols and snipers sometimes less than 60 metres away presented real dangers to those working in no man's land. On the night of 12–13 December, Lieutenant Forbes of the 67 Field Company RE was killed by a gunshot wound to the abdomen while preparing pits for the devices in front of the wire entanglements of the first line positions. In other cases where Turkish patrols were active these had to be dispersed before work could begin.

All along the front the devices were emplaced during the period of 12–18 December 1915. Those in front of the first line were armed on the night of 18–19 December by connecting tripwires and inserting igniters and detonators. Other traps had been prepared for use to block communications trenches and the firing and reserve lines and these were made active by the departing engineers as the infantry abandoned the positions. Sapper officers and Senior NCOs were therefore often the last to leave the lines.

Additionally traps were placed in dugouts and strong points to deter them from being used by an advancing enemy. It had been concluded early on that it would be far too dangerous to back-load many of the stores and provisions as the beaches were overlooked by Turkish observers, any hint of a withdrawal being unacceptable. It was decided that the stores should be destroyed by fire as the last troops left the positions and that booby traps should be laid to use surplus explosive. An example was recorded in the 72 Field Company RE War Diary:

> In the 39 Brigade Area all the remaining Army Service Corps stores were gathered together and booby trapped. In one, a stack of stores and boxes was built around a 60 pounds charge of ammonal. These were arranged so the if any of the boxes was removed the explosive in the centre would detonate.[14]

Many other booby traps were laid:

> The men in the trenches spent the last day turning every dugout into a death trap and most innocent looking things into infernal machines. Some dugouts would blow up when the door was opened. A drafting table had several memorandum books lying on it each with electrical connections to an explosive charge sufficient to destroy a platoon. A gramophone wound up and with a record on, ready to be started was left in one dugout so that the end of the tune meant death to the listeners. Piles of bully beef tins, turned into diabolical engines of destruction, lay scattered about.[15]

On the final night of 19–20 December, all that remained to be done was to withdraw the safety catches from the mines and traps and light the candle arrangements for the destruction of supplies, rations and wells. Fortunately it was a foggy and this was carried out without incident. As the last man left for the waiting ships, at about 4:00 am, the final demolition was fired which was the initiation of a charge of gun-cotton to sever the 'phone end of the sea-to-shore cable.

The German commander of the Turkish Fifth Army fighting in the peninsula, General Linman von Sanders, was taken completely by surprise. According to him, the Turkish troops opposite the positions knew nothing of the withdrawal, until between one and two o'clock in the morning, when a mine was fired creating a large crater. Turkish soldiers advanced according to their standard operating instructions and seized the lip of the crater. They were surprised by the lack of resistance, as normally these craters would be fiercely contested; however, to begin with they advanced no further. When adjoining companies advanced through the fog they again found no resistance apart from a few stray shots. The abandoned trenches were occupied, but attempts to move through them were hindered because obstacles everywhere had to be removed. In many places the Turks tripped or trod on the devices left by the Allies. These exploded causing confusion and casualties and impeded the advance.[16] In this way the rearmost Allied troops gained a good head start on their way to the beaches.

From an Allied point of view it was a remarkable operation, and to everyone's relief the evacuation of Anzac and Sulva Bay was a complete success. There were no casualties at Sulva and only one man injured by a spent bullet in the arm at Anzac. The problem now was the evacuation of the position at Cape Helles, which was finally ordered on 31 December 1916. It is known from the memoirs of Liman Von Sanders that, having failed to crush the forces as they withdrew from Anzac and Sulva Bay, he was determined that this would not happen again at Cape Helles. Plans were made for a rapid advance should the Allies be seen to be withdrawing, which included the preparation of mobile bridges to enable Turkish guns to be quickly got across the Allied trenches.

Again meticulous planning was needed, which included deception and the defensive use of mines and traps. The Engineers were heavily involved in these preparations. The 1/3 Kent Field Company RE devised automatic rifle and flare firing devices and a system for dropping rifle cartridges into braziers so that they would explode as the last elements of the force retreated. They also built and deployed trip mines using grenades and automatic contact mines, which would block any enemy advance.

Some troops were evacuated but on 7 January the Turks launched fierce attacks, which lasted five hours, though they were beaten back. As troops thinned out, on 8 January it was clear that the remaining troops could only hold out for a few hours. However, it was reported that there was no fear of the Turkish infantry because no troops in the world would have got far in the dark across the maze of trenches and barbed wire, especially as they had been laced with hundreds of booby traps. These again were effective and Von Sanders records that in many places the Turkish follow-up was delayed by fields of traps, which caused serious losses.

The expedition to the Dardanelles was a strategic failure. The saving grace was the safe evacuation of the troops and some equipment from the peninsula. This was as a result of sound and detailed planning on the part of the staff who used all the methods of deception at their disposal. Within the plan, the use of traps and mines played their part delaying and discouraging the Turkish soldiers from a rapid follow-up.

Surprisingly, on the Western Front, the British condemned the use of such tactics. In the *History of the Corps of Royal Engineers* in the First World War the Germans are damned for their methods:

> As the Germans fell back, they carried out a most thorough destruction, long prepared and scheduled, and in its executions exceeding all laws and customs of warfare between civilised nations. The mentality of the German race was certainly well exhibited.[17]

This refers to the deployment of booby traps and delay devices in large numbers in early 1917 as they retreated to the *Siegfried Stellung*, more commonly known to the British as the Hindenburg line. They fell back to straighten their line along a stretch of front approximately 20 miles deep and 60 miles long from Arras to Soissons. Code-named '*Alberich*', after Wagner's malicious dwarf, the operation was to include the total destruction and devastation of the area they left behind. The plan required 35 days for the removal of all materiel and artillery and for the execution of the demolitions. Every tree was felled, every road mined, every well fouled, every watercourse dammed, every cellar blown up or made into a death trap with concealed bombs. All supplies or metal were sent back, all rails ripped up, all telephone wire rolled up and everything flammable burned. The area was also sown with hundreds of booby traps. These included hidden explosive charges with delays, traps left in dugouts and trenches, and charges attached to attractive items such as souvenirs. In short the country which the Allies were to advance over was turned into utter desolation.

The first marching day for the withdrawal was 16 March 1917 and the operation was to be complete by 19 March. The programme was modified, however, in the area around the Ancre due to heavy pressure on the German First Army. As the Germans fell back and the Allies advanced the first mines and traps were discovered. In some parts of the line the German pioneer battalions had done such an efficient job that whole areas were laced with traps. Even the German rearguard was wary as the hour to withdraw drew near. Lieutenant Ernst Jünger, a tough battle-hardened German subaltern who fought for sustained periods in the trenches on the Western Front, said:

> When five o'clock came, the hour at which, according to the orders, we were due to evacuate the trench, we quickly blew up the dugouts with bombs, in so far as they were not already provided with infernal machines, some of which we had ingeniously constructed. During the last hours I had not dared touch any box or door or bucket in case I might go up in the air.[18]

The moral justification for such wanton destruction has been much discussed and as recorded earlier condemned in the *History of the Corps of Royal Engineers*. However, the necessity for such actions in total war must be understood. They were well justified by Jünger:

> It seems to me that the gratified approval of armchair warriors and journalists is incomprehensible. When thousands are robbed of their homes, the self-satisfaction of power may at least keep silent. As for the necessity, I have of course as a Prussian officer, no doubt whatsoever. War means the destruction of the enemy without scruple and by any means. War is the harshest of all trades, and the masters of it can only entertain humane feelings so long as they do no harm. It makes no difference that these operations which the situation demanded were not pretty.

On the British side there were some who still harboured old ideas and considered that the use of booby traps was not in keeping with the idea of 'playing the game'. Men who had talked almost amicably about 'old Jerry' now cursed him fiercely. A British officer prisoner, interrogated by a German officer is alleged to have remarked, 'You Germans do not play the game'. The German replied, 'This is not a game. This is war.' And, of course, all is fair in love and war.[19]

The *History of the Great War based on Official Documents* considered that the German use of traps and delayed-action mines was not particularly significant:

> These gins were responsible for a certain number of casualties and caused delays in making use of shelters, but in the main were not strikingly successful.[20]

In his history of the Fifth Army, General Gough made similar assertions when referring to the devices:

> Amongst other attempts to delay our advance, to harass us, and to inflict losses on us, the Germans laid many mines some of considerable magnitude, in places they were likely to catch us. Many of these were exploded by special delay action fuses – several days after the German retreat. In other places they were more in the nature of booby traps. A new shovel would be left lying around amongst a lot of old ones, and some of our men who were keen would pull the new one out of the bundle; or a duckboard was evidently out of place and an enthusiast would pick it up in order to put it straight. Immediately a small mine would explode and two or three of our men might be killed or injured.
>
> These steps did not really delay us or help the Germans much as regards military operations, but they kept alive in our breasts a cordial hatred of our enemy – which was not a very desirable result for the German army to aim at.[21]

It is interesting to contrast these views with those of the advancing infantry who had to occupy the ground that had been abandoned by the Germans. Lieutenant T A M Nash who served with the 16th Battalion Manchester Regiment wrote:

> Booby traps abounded and a large part of our casualties were caused by these slaughter traps.[22]

Another young officer originally with the North Staffordshire Regiment, but serving with the 1st Battalion Grenadier Guards, Lieutenant B L Lawrence, described the advance towards the Seigfreid line:

> As we crossed no mans land we noticed the REs had dug up or wired off a number of land mines which the Boche had laid in the hope that we might set them off when we advanced. There were plenty of dugouts in the trenches that we occupied, but everyone was rather chary of entering them. All sorts of stories of booby traps, explosive dugouts, and so on were in circulation, and some of them were only too true. The battalion we relieved had had several casualties; in one case a man found a full rum jar, which, on being uncorked, exploded. In another case a man picked up a spade, which set off a mine. And of course there were several cases of souvenirs such as helmets, which detonated bombs when you touched them.[23]

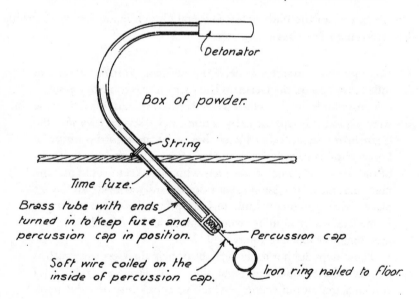

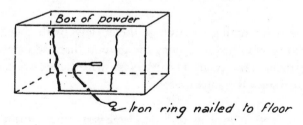

A box trap

Other ranks to wrote of their fears of traps. George Coppard, a corporal in the Machine Gun Corps, wrote:

> There was a German artillery dugout behind the ridge where our guns were; before I investigated I lobbed a Mills bomb down the steps. I descended and found a dead Jerry at the bottom, but he was cold. There was a large supply of black bread there but we had a nausea about the stuff and although ravenous we didn't touch it. I was canny about touching anything in case of booby traps. A choice souvenir could well tempt me to a sticky end.[24]

Another soldier, John F Tucker, who fought with the London Kensington Regiment at the Somme, Arras and Ypres, recorded his concerns during the German retreat to the Hindenburg line:

> There was a rumour going round that the Germans were leaving booby traps as they retreated and we were warned to be on our guard. The rumour turned out to be fact. Once when occupying the ruins of a large farm just taken from the enemy we found that the well had been poisoned. Also in an outhouse of the farm, which had been the sleeping quarters for some German troops, was found a small home-made oil lamp, which when lit by one of our men exploded, turning his face and hands and uniform bright yellow, but otherwise not harming him. Also in an abandoned German trench running abutting the Arras–Cambrai road was a tripwire stretching knee height across the trench bottom, attached to a cluster of stick-bombs half concealed in a dug out entrance.[25]

The soldier that turned yellow was probably luckier than he realised. An explanation for him and his uniform becoming so coloured could be that the detonator in the device failed to set off the main high explosive charge. If the main charge was picric acid powder, and if just the detonator fired, then the explosive would have been blown out in all directions. As well as a high explosive, picric acid is also a well-known bright yellow dye commonly used in the textiles industry before the war. Had this explosive detonated it is most likely the soldier would have been severely wounded or killed.

As well as causing casualties, one of the principal purposes of deploying traps and mines is their psychological impact, because of their capacity to instil fear, foreboding and uncertainty in the troops that have to confront them. During the advance to the Hindenburg line, Captain Edwin

Campion Vaughan describes coming across a slightly wounded but jubilant soldier in the 4th Gloucesters who spoke of the German withdrawal. When asked how he was injured the soldier became serious and said:

> Ah sir we have lost a lot of good fellies. The trenches were left full of booby traps. All I did was pick up a Hun's helmet from the floor of a trench and a bomb went off underneath. Lucky for me sir it was buried and I only got it slightly. Ye'll perhaps know Mr Harcourt of the 6 Warricks, Sir? Well he's bought it. They went over on our right and he went down a dugout, but as soon as he put his hand on the handrail, the two bottom steps blew up, and took both his legs off. He died before they could get him away.[26]

Subsequently as the battalion advanced through the devastated countryside Vaughan described his extreme nervousness. The stories of booby traps causing him to be terrified by the sight of any old oil drum or coil of wire. At every crossroads he expected to be blown into the air by some delayed-action mine. On 18 March as night fell they found a house close by with a cellar, which was to be their accommodation for the night. The cellar had been partitioned off into cubicles and fitted with wire beds. Vaughan lay down, but tired as he was he could not sleep. He thought of his friend Harcourt who had survived so many trench raids, and yet had in an instant been killed by a booby trap. It was a terrible unforeseen death. As he lay there Vaughan described:

> An icy hand clutched my heart. Here was a perfect billet, dry, well furnished and comfortable. In the villages they had passed tiny hovels had been blown up, entrances to waterlogged dugouts had been smashed in, why had this been left? Obviously it was a trap and, fools that we were, we had walked into it. The sound of Kentish's light snoring maddened me. I strained my ears and above the dripping of the rain I fancied I could hear the tick tock of a fuze. This grew louder and louder until I could stand it no longer. And by coughing loudly and banging the bed I woke up Kentish.
>
> He sat up grumpily, rubbing his eyes, 'What was that blasted row?'
>
> 'Which one,' I said guiltily, 'there's a lot going on.'
>
> He listened for a moment and then lay down again growling. But I didn't intend to let him sleep. 'Did you hear about the booby traps in Boche lines?'
>
> 'Um.'
>
> 'You know Sullivan found several in Halle' – no answer.

'How long do they usually delay before exploding?' – silence. I paused for a bit and then asked timorously,

'I say, Billy, can you hear a curious ticking?'

He pulled his coat from off his head and said,

'You bloody fool' and snuggled down again.

I was hurt by that and felt that nobody cared if I was blown up, so I resolved myself to die like a martyr and then whenever we met in the after world I could say to Kentish 'I told you so'. The consideration of this possibility rather cheered me up and casting my fears aside I fell asleep.[27]

A nightmare followed:

I dreamt that I was lying there asleep, all being quiet except for the drip of water and the wind. Suddenly through the rain and darkness appeared a huge figure stealing across the courtyard to the grating above me. He was muffled up in a great grey great coat and spiked helmet. I tried to wake Kentish and shout, but I was powerless. I saw him take a smoking bomb from under his coat, and slip it into the chimney. With a frantic struggle I overcame my paralysis and sat up shouting as a metallic sliding sound came from the chimney. Waiting for the explosion, I sat staring into the darkness with an apathy that comes when fear had passed its bounds.

Nothing happened, but Vaughan now fully awake could stay not a minute longer and slipped on his mac and went out into the rain of the early dawn. Vaughan's fear was not at all irrational.

The retreating German army achieved a considerable success when the town hall at Bapaume blew up 8 days after it had been captured. An obvious mine had been removed from the cellars and the building had been regarded as safe. However on 25 March a new weapon added to the frightfulness of war when a second mine and probably the first acid-delayed-action device detonated, killing several Australian soldiers. Reports at the time indicated that this might have been a clockwork device. The fact that no purpose-built clockwork devices were subsequently recovered would indicate that it was not the case.

The charge was hidden in the tower of the Town Hall and blew out the walls and brought masonry crashing down everywhere. The soldiers sleeping above ground were killed, but those who had taken refuge in the cellars were buried alive. Fatigue parties were immediately formed and after digging furiously throughout the night and the next day managed to rescue six soldiers alive. In addition to the Australians, two Frenchmen were killed.

One was the Deputé for Bapaume. He had remained at his parliamentary post during the war up to this time, but was so excited at the capture of his native town that he rushed up from Paris to inspect the scene of the battle. This afforded some macabre amusement to the officers of the French Mission attached to Fifth Army. They pointed out that the Deputé had been keeping safely in the background in Paris for a long time until Bapaume was liberated, but he was, so to speak hoisted by his own petard on his return. For days the chief of the French mission, a Major Renondeau, kept coming round the staff with an air of earnest inquiry asking if the Deputé had been found.[28]

As the charge probably contained at least 100 pounds of explosive this was most unlikely. There had been some thought of transferring the HQ of the Fifth Army to Bapaume and had it gone there it would doubtless have occupied the town hall which was one of the few large buildings left undamaged. Shortly after this event a German wireless operator who had been captured told intelligence officers that he had been asked by some of his officers:

> Have any light effects suggesting explosions been seen from the direction of Bapaume during the last few hours? If not be on watch.[29]

He added that several other similar delayed-action mines had been laid elsewhere. Before this warning could be circulated, on 26 March at 12:37 pm a dugout system on the edge of Bapaume was destroyed by a similar explosion. This had been the HQ for the 7th Australian Brigade, but fortunately most of the staff had moved forward. Lieutenant N E W Waraker the bombing officer for the Brigade was blown from the dugout entrance unharmed. Unfortunately two signallers died at the scene. Digging parties that tried to rescue them were unsuccessful.

Other mines exploded over the following days. At Hermies a building on a small park in the centre of the town appeared suitable as a HQ, but was not used because a prisoner had warned of a hidden device. A few days later a massive explosion occurred turning the park into a huge crater. A diary captured later on 15 April indicated that the charge was 34 tons of explosives. Despite the warnings given to the troops about the dangers of delayed-action mines there were other casualties. The single cottage which the enemy had left standing in the village of Beaugnatre and which had been used successively as HQ for brigades and battalions was blown up on 29 March and an officer and three men killed. This was despite the warning order given on the 26th being reiterated that such places must be avoided.

Other mines exploded on 30 March: at Favrueuil two unoccupied dugouts blew up and at Vaulx-Vraucourt two wells were destroyed. Mines continued to explode throughout April. On the 18th a mine hidden under the station at Velu detonated killing one officer and eight soldiers and wounding nine others. It also destroyed the Australian 4th Battalion's mail.[30]

The Australians also encountered other booby traps left by the Germans. At Vaulx-Vraucourt soldiers billeted in a house were intent on the search for hidden valuables. One of them was poking a stick up the chimney of the house and dislodged a charge of explosive, which fell into the hearth. Had they lit a fire before this had been discovered, then there could have been casualties.

One solution adopted by some patrols as they advanced was to use captured German soldiers to locate traps and mines. Rather than being a nuisance to be escorted back to the rear areas, the prisoners were forced to lead the way where traps were suspected. They could be used to walk on duckboards and to enter dugouts. The theory was that if they knew of the presence of a trap they would disclose it, and if they didn't, well it was better for the prisoner to die than an Allied soldier.[31]

The official and staff view that the traps and delayed-action mines were ineffective in terms of operational efficiency and casualties during the German withdrawal is difficult to assess. The above accounts illustrate the value of these devices. They did kill and injure many soldiers, but it is impossible to determine accurately how many because there is no breakdown of the causes of the casualties. They clearly did instil fear, affect morale, and, in Vaughan's case, by depriving him of sleep, sapped energy and doubtless reduced efficiency. The traps also prevented soldiers from using captured dugouts and cellars until they were cleared, forcing them out into the open where they were exposed to the elements and were more susceptible to attack by other weapons, for example, enemy aircraft and artillery. The advancing HQ elements were also affected by the need to search and clear new accommodation before it could be occupied. Areas were sealed off and sentries had to be posted to prevent inquisitive soldiers from entering suspect areas where they might become casualties. A rifleman of the London Rifle Brigade described moving up towards Foncquervillers and being stopped by a sentry who refused to let them pass. When asked why he explained the whole area was being searched for booby traps and mines.[32]

The successful use of traps and mines by the Germans was not lost on the British when it was their turn to retire. Towards the end of the battle of Cambrai in December 1917 it became clear that there would need to be a limited withdrawal by 5th Corps of the Third Army from the

Marcoing–Bourlon salient. In the interests of secrecy, the Corps order to carry out the withdrawal was not issued until the last possible moment. This left little time for lower formations to make their preparations, but even so it specified a wide-ranging demolition plan covering the destruction of stores and ammunition. In addition it specified that 'if booby traps and other devices for inflicting loss or damage on the enemy plan it would be an advantage.'[33] The 47th Division, which was part of V Corps, accomplished a great deal in the way of destruction and laid some booby traps.

The Germans also suffered from the fear posed by booby traps. During the March 1918 offensive against the Third and Fifth Army Fronts the Germans forced the British back in a series of attacks. There is evidence that the Royal Engineers laid anti-tank mines on a part of these fronts just before the assault, and the design of these was such that they might function under the weight of a man. There is, conversely, no evidence in the war diaries that the retreating engineers laid booby traps. In forced retirements they were committed to demolitions, building hasty defensive positions and in many cases acting as infantry. This, however, did not stop some Germans being very wary. Fritz Nagel, a lieutenant in the artillery, was part of the offensive. An intelligent and perceptive officer he had observed that by then the German army was slowly but surely being starved of the necessary military resources to continue the war. There was not enough food for a substantial meal. Nagel dreamed of *Wiener Schnitzel* with fried eggs on top and loads of potatoes. All they had was fatless vegetable soups and black bread mixed with wood shavings. Their uniforms were no better; Nagel had a cap made of some sort of grass fibre, and his boots were in tatters.

In the advance, therefore, scavenging for abandoned stores was a necessity. As they moved forward through recently evacuated territory, he was scanning the ground around him when he saw a tidy-looking dugout some 50 yards away. This would offer excellent protection so Nagel went over for a look:

> It [the dugout] had a very small window in the rear, although the light was so dim I could hardly see. I was shocked when I saw two English officers at a table, one sleeping with his head on the table and the other sitting straight up. Both had their caps on. This sudden confrontation stupefied me. I stood there wondering if they would say 'Hello,' when I realised they were dead. To see these men in that dim light, motionless and so rigid made my heart pound. I quickly left. Once outside, I began to understand that something was wrong. Our infantry had not entered to look for food or good English shoes because the bodies were booby-trapped. How could a dead man sit

upright on a chair? I clearly remember the gruesome atmosphere of that episode. When I told my driver he, of course, was eager to go in there and get their shoes. He knew all about booby traps, he said. Nothing doing, I told him.[34]

After the failure of the German spring offensive and with the arrival of the Americans, the Germans were, by July, firmly on the defensive all along the Western Front. Whenever they made organised withdrawals they set about mining and booby-trapping in a planned and methodical way. The devices were viewed with indignation by the advancing Allied troops, particularly the delayed-action mines that erupted without warning. They did however have a legitimate effect of hampering the advance and impressing on all the need for caution. By then the need to allocate troops to deal with the devices was recognised and the staff had made plans for parties to search for, render safe and remove these traps and mines.

Using explosive traps to catch the unwary was not exclusively confined to the ground. For observation in flat country, extensive use was made of observation balloons. In November 1917 in Salonika, a noted German pilot was responsible for shooting down several observation balloons. In response to a request for help, a Lieutenant Finch of the Army Ordnance Corps was asked if it would be possible to load a charge of explosive into the balloon basket which could be detonated from the ground via an electrical cable. The ingenious Lieutenant arranged for some 5–600 pounds of explosive to be placed in a 60-gallon container, which was placed in the balloon basket. On 28 November the lure attracted the first plane which dived to shoot it down. When it was about 150 yards from the balloon the charge was fired. The massive explosion destroyed the aircraft and the wings folded, the tail flew off and the machine crashed to the ground killing the pilot, Oberleutnant von Eschwege.[35]

A similar ambush was tried on the western front when at Vis-en-Artois the harassed local Balloon Company Commander asked for assistance from the local Tunnelling Company RE. Although protected by anti-aircraft guns and machine-gun fire, his balloons were easy prey for a determined pilot willing to run the risk of a barrage of shells. In consequence the tunnellers prepared a charge of some 525 pounds of ammonal which was placed in the balloon's basket. It was floated off to 2,500 feet to wait for an attacker. A German plane approached and as it opened fire the charge was detonated. After a massive explosion the German plane could be seen rocking about in the air eddies. Dark smoke appeared from the plane for about 30 seconds. However the pilot managed to regain control and turned for home, no doubt having had the shock of his life and a lucky escape.[36]

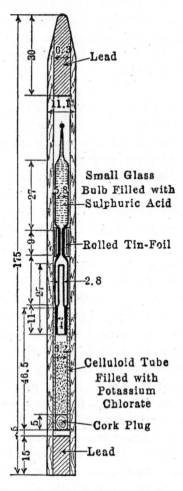

Diagram of an incendiary pencil

Finally, a brief note on sabotage. In the First World War there were many reports of subversive activities. For example, on 20 May 1916 information was received from the Italian secret police that two Germans were discovered trying to smuggle infernal machines into Italian ammunition factories.[37] Very few attacks however seem to have succeeded. The Germans did develop an incendiary pencil which was probably for sabotage. Similar in appearance to a common blue pencil and sharpened at one end, they could only be identified by a small almost imperceptible point placed on the outside, 11 mm from the unsharpened end. The interior of the pencil contained a glass bulb, with two compartments filled with sulphuric acid and celluloid tube filled with potassium chlorate. A small layer of clay separated these. The glass bulb ended with a slender point and when this was broken the acid spilt into the tube and on to the clay. After approximately 30 minutes the acid ate through the clay and initiated the potassium chlorate. To use the device the operator broke the point of the bulb and buried the pencil in some suitable flammable material, which half-an-hour later would catch fire.[38]

Notes

1 Dunn, Captain J C, *The War the Infantry Knew*, King, London, 1938.
2 Durrand Archive, Regimental History of 119th (Res) Regiment.
3 The Work of the Royal Engineers in the European War 1914–1919, Experimental Section, published in the *Royal Engineers' Journal*, 1924 and 1925.
4 Edmonds, C, *A Subaltern's War*, Cedric Chivers, Bath, 1966.
5 Hutchison, Lieutenant Colonel G Seton DSO MC, *Warrior*, Hutchinson, London, 1932.
6 Summary of Recent Information Regarding the German Army and its Methods – General Staff (Intelligence) HQ (SS 537) January 1917.
7 McBride, Captain Herbert W A, *Rifleman Went to War*, Small Arms Technical Publishing Company, North Carolina, 1935.
8 *op. cit.*, note 7.
9 Fairlie-Wood, Herbert, *Vimy*, Macdonald, London, 1967.
10 *op. cit.*, note 3.
11 PRO WO 95/405 181 Tunnelling Company RE, War Diary.
12 PRO WO 158/44 General Staff (Intelligence) Headquarters (SS 488) 23 October 1916: German Land Mines, Description of Mines and Firing Apparatus, etc., extracted from the '*Sprengvorschrift*', October 1915.
13 PRO WO 95/4298, 67 Field Company RE, War Diary.
14 PRO WO 95/4301, 72 Field Company RE, War Diary.
15 Croll, Mike, *The History of Land Mines*, Leo Cooper, Barnsley, 1998.
16 Linman von Sanders, General of Cavalry, *Five Years in Turkey*, Williams and Wilkins, Annapolis, 1928.
17 Pritchard, H L, Major General, *History of the Corps of Royal Engineers*, volume V, The Home Front, France, Flanders and Italy in the Great War, Longmans, London, 1952.
18 Jünger, Ernst, *Storm of Steel*, Chatto and Windus, London, 1929.
19 Grieve, Captain W Grant, and Bernhard Newman, *Tunnellers*, Herbert Jenkins, London, 1936.
20 Miles, Wilfred *Military Operations France and Belgium 1917: The Battle of Cambrai, etc.* [History of the Great War based on Official Documents], HMSO, 1949.
21 Gough, General Sir H GCMG, KCB, KCVO, *The Fifth Army*, Hodder and Stoughton, London, 1931.

22 Nash, TAM, *The Diary of an Unprofessional Soldier*, Picton Publishing, Chippenham, 1991.

23 Brown, Malcolm, *The Imperial War Museum Book of the Western Front,* The Imperial War Museum, with Sidgwick & Jackson, 2001.

24 Coppard, George, *With a Machine Gun to Cambrai*, Imperial War Museum, London, 1990.

25 Tucker, John F, *Johnny Get Your Gun*, William Kimber, London, 1978.

26 Vaughan, Captain Edwin Campion, *Desperate Glory*, Papermac, London, 1995.

27 *op. cit.*, note 26.

28 *op. cit.*, note 21.

29 RE Library, Chatham: Engineer-in Chief Field Work Notes Number 27, 22 May 1917.

30 Bean, C E W, *The Australian Imperial Force in France, 1917*, The Official History of Australia in the Great War of 1914–18, volume IV, Angus & Robertson, Sydney, Australia, 1933

31 *op. cit.*, note 19.

32 [Smith, A] *Four Years on the Western Front – By a Rifleman*, Oldhams Press, London, 1922.

33 *op. cit.*, note 20, Appendix 20, V Corps Operations Order G.S.306/1 dated 4 December 1917.

34 Nagel, Fritz, *Fritz -The WW1 Memoirs of a German Lieutenant,* Der Angriff, Huntington VA,1981.

35 Birchall, Peter, *The Longest Walk*, Arms and Armour, London, 1997.

36 *op. cit.*, note19.

37 PRO Mun 4/11642, Sabotage in Italy in World War I.

38 Fries, Amos A and Clarence J West, *Chemical Warfare*, McGraw Hill Book Company, New York, 1922.

CHAPTER TWO

The Devil's Own Game – Dealing with Booby Traps

We were flattered into becoming experts.   Tunneller, 1917

In the British Army the task of dealing with booby traps, mines and delay devices fell, in the main, to the Royal Engineers and in particular to the tunnelling companies. The first of these companies were formed in February 1915 in an urgent response to requests from the First and Second Armies after the Germans had fired small mines under the British front lines in December 1914. The underground war rapidly escalated and in the three years that followed British tunnellers alone fired over 2,000 underground mines.[1] Mining activity reached a peak in mid 1916 and then slowly declined. Even so, in early 1917 over 6,000 tunnellers and attached infantry were employed in the offensive mining scheme in support of the battle of Messines. This resulted in 19 deep mines being fired on 17 June with an aggregate charge of over 500 tons of ammonal.

During this time the tunnellers, many of them ex-miners or mining engineers, had become expert in the design and construction of subterranean works. More importantly, they had grown accustomed to danger, working in dark confined places and expert in handling and using explosives. As the networks of British and German tunnels spread below the front lines, a deadly cat-and-mouse game began, with each side trying to discover the location of the other tunnels. Listening posts were deployed, and if the enemy were heard approaching, a camouflet charge would be laid and fired to destroy their galleries. Should the listening posts fail to hear the approaching enemy, then the penalty could be that the sides of their own tunnels would be driven in with a devastating roar and the men in the tunnel blown to bits, asphyxiated or buried alive. On some occasions the miners broke into the enemy tunnels and in the pitch black fought deadly close-quarter battles underground. On the surface the tunnellers sometimes accompanied the infantry in trench raids to investigate and assist with the clearance and destruction of enemy tunnels and dugouts. Technically and tactically therefore, with their intimate knowledge of explosives and sound engineering skills, they had the best background for the job of dealing with traps and mines.

The main reason the tunnellers were selected for the task was that the fixed tunnelling systems below the front lines (so vital in static defensive systems) became largely redundant as mobile warfare returned towards the end of the conflict. Tactical changes also reduced the effectiveness of mining. The first occurred in 1917 when the Germans adopted a system of defence in depth. This meant the front lines were comparatively thinly manned and that undermining them and blowing them up was no longer an operationally effective use of troops. Secondly, after the Messines mines were fired, the Germans introduced a system of further reducing their front line garrisons wherever they suspected the tunnellers were at work. Having lost their primary role, the tunnelling companies were diverted to more general work. These tasks included the construction of dugouts, road repairs, pipe-laying and digging trenches, but where the enemy withdrew or was forced back, the tunnelling companies had the dangerous task of searching the vacated positions for mines and booby traps and rendering safe any explosive devices that might be found. This work began in earnest with the German withdrawal to the Hindenburg line in March 1917. After the first infantry casualties the tunnelling companies formed scouting or investigation parties whose task was to search and clear the abandoned areas.

As one tunneller described it at the time:

> After the first two or three 'accidents' no branch of the HM Forces showed any disposition to take chances if there was a 'Bloody Tunneller' available. We were flattered into becoming experts and called upon on each and every occasion – often we thought, without cause – 'fools step in, etc'.[2]

At the time nothing was known about the design, method of operation or setting of the various traps and it fell to the companies who were opposite the retreating enemy to take up the challenge. One of those involved from the start was 181 Tunnelling Company RE. The Germans retired on their front on 19 March 1917 and the following day three sections of the Company were in the Beaumetz area, opening dugouts and clearing booby traps. Several traps were disarmed but, from the outset, the potential dangers of the task were made clear when two men from one section were severely shaken by the explosion of a bomb in the entrance to a dugout.[3] Although the tunnellers were, without doubt, the best-qualified troops to deal with the devices left by the Germans, there was no time to give formal training on how they should be dealt with safely. From those early days Explosive

Ordnance Disposal (EOD) was a 'Black Art', practised by the few, of whom many became experts simply because they were in the wrong place at the wrong time when the need arose. Initially discovering and disarming the traps was very much a matter of 'suck it and see' and personal preferences. Early on, two enduring disposal principles were established: firstly, was the development of the art of observation, which enabled the searcher to pick out the odd, unusual or out of the ordinary from a seemingly normal scene (bearing in mind that 'normal' in this case might be a battle-scarred trench line or a village reduced to rubble); the second principle was the use of remote methods to deal with suspect items. In 1917 a key piece of equipment was a 'life line', today known as a hook and line. These were long ropes or cords, which could be attached to a suspicious object so that it could be pulled, moved or opened from a safe distance, normally from behind cover. In the worst case they could also be used to set off a trap deliberately from a safe distance. It was also established that the numbers involved in dealing with a suspect trap or mine should be kept to a minimum, although the principle of a one-man risk normally applied today was not then universally adopted.

An American, Captain H D Trounce, who served throughout the period with 181 Tunnelling Company RE, was involved from the beginning in the clearance work and succinctly described the task:

> The work involved the unearthing of mines left in dugouts and elsewhere and the removal of all bomb traps and devilish devices. This kept the companies involved very busy. Thousands of traps had been laid. All the railroads had been undermined and the first train going over the Achiet-le-Grand was destroyed. Contact mines were left under roads and especially crossroads, which would be fired when a heavy vehicle or gun crossed them. In other places delay action mines were used. Most of the dugout mines were placed halfway down the entrances and tamped with sandbags with detonators connected to leads which were fastened to the wooden steps. Any unwary soldier standing on the steps would be killed as the trap functioned. It required a careful eye to detect these traps. They could be seen by some slight change in the timber where the mines had been hidden. Moving the timber would reveal the sandbag tamping and behind it the high explosive and detonator. In some places where the Germans were running short of high explosive, bombs and trench mortars were thrown in to add to the chaos. Numerous bombs were found elsewhere which a touch would set off. In the barbed wire on top of the trenches there were German 'Hairbrush Bombs' tied by their fuzes to the wire, with the latter looped in a

half circle so that as a soldier walked along he would catch his foot in the loop and fire the bomb. In the trenches thousands of egg grenades had been connected to the underside of duckboards and laid in the trenches. These would be fired by anyone stepping on the duckboard, as there was no other place to step in the trench it was a case of Hobson's choice. It afforded us much amusement to fire these by throwing bricks at them from behind cover.

In dugouts that had not been destroyed there were attractive souvenirs to most of which a bomb had been attached. Some poor fellow would see a helmet hung up in a dugout, remove it and explode the bomb attached.

We decided to go very gingerly about this task and were lucky enough to get through it with only 10 casualties. After a few days it was not necessary to caution the troops about these little devices. They would hardly step on a twig for fear it was connected to a bomb.[4]

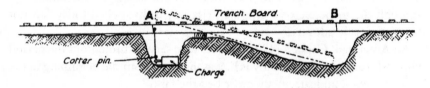

A trench-board trap

As well as disarming the devices it was vital that any information concerning their construction, deployment and method of operation was collected and collated. This would allow warnings to be issued to the advancing troops and prevent unnecessary casualties through ignorance. The details were also necessary so that proper training could be given to the Royal Engineers who were required to deal with whatever suspect items were discovered.

When the delayed-action mine hidden in the Town Hall at Bapaume exploded, nothing was known about its method of initiation. However, the device used was almost certainly what the allies were to call a German Automatic Detonating Device. The first of these recovered intact was by 181 Tunnelling Company RE.

Luck was certainly on the side of the miners as this account of its discovery reveals:

In one Company Headquarter location we had re-opened an extensive dugout system. We had been living there about a week when one of our enquiring youngsters discovered that certain old tele-

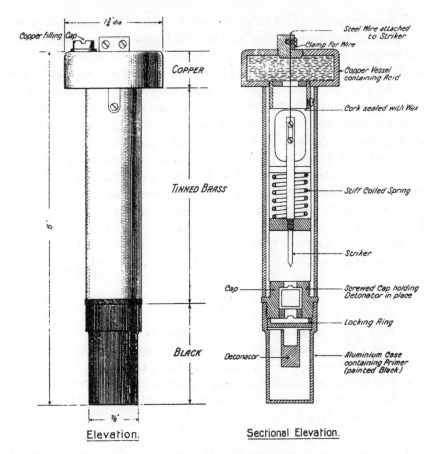

The German Automatic Detonating Device

phone wires disappeared into what was apparently a blank wall. Upon investigation, a central mine chamber containing not less than five tons of high explosive was discovered. It was during the removal of this mine that the first example of a chemically fired delay action detonator was unearthed.

We did not like the look of it, so having removed the bulk of the charge from its vicinity a long string was looped round it, the place cleared of men and the thing jerked out of its priming box; nothing untoward happened, so the detonator was recovered, placed in a bucket of water and a communication made to GHQ.[5]

Shortly after its discovery, General Harvey, the Controller of Mines, arrived to inspect the new device. He was most interested and when he left it was packed under the seat of his car to be taken back for further examination and exploitation. As a result the first Technical Intelligence Report on the device and was issued on 5 April 1917.[6] In principle, it was the forerunner of the modern time pencil. The switch utilised a spring-loaded striker, which was held under tension by a steel wire. This wire ran through a small copper vessel at the top of the switch. Prior to use, a filling cap was removed and the top container filled with acid. The acid ate slowly through the wire until it sheared, allowing the striker to fire a percussion cap and detonator. The time-delay could be adjusted by varying the concentration of the acid poured into the copper container. Trials carried out later by the Experimental Section RE showed that the time-delay was very erratic and was greatly affected by temperature. It was discovered that at the same temperature there could often be a 10 per cent variation in the time delays achieved. At 60°F the normal delay for the German fuze was 72 hours (±10%). At 100°F the delay would be halved to approximately 36 hours and at 45°F the delay could go up to 103 hours.

The original report concluded that:

> The device should be handled as little as possible after it has been removed from a charge, as it is liable to explode at any moment. It should be carried horizontally at arm's length holding it by the copper head, with the other end away from the body, and buried at least one foot deep or thrown into a well. [Not a disposal procedure that would be recommended today.]

The reason the mine found by 181 Tunnelling Company RE failed to fire, and thus caused no damage to the men, was due to the fact that the device was obviously new to the German who planted it because he had failed to remove a safety collar (not shown in the diagram here). This was placed between the striker and the percussion cap and had to be removed when the device was set. The failure to do so meant that when the wire corroded through, the striker was prevented from firing the percussion cap and thus failed to detonate the five tons of explosive in the dugout.

Three days later, on 8 April 1917, the General Staff issued a further intelligence report entitled German Ruses.[7] The concise one-page document was a compilation of descriptions of the traps that had been encountered as the troops followed up the retreating Germans. It pointed out that most devices took some time to prepare and they must therefore be looked for in places where there had been a planned and orderly withdrawal rather than where the enemy had been hustled or driven from his positions by a rapid advance.

It warned that the following should be regarded with special suspicion until experts had carried out investigations:

- Attractively furnished dugouts.
- Dugouts under roads.
- All new work or new trenches or other equipment, in the midst of weather-worn ground or articles. For example, recently disturbed soil, new metalling, new trench boards.
- Souvenirs such as helmets, shells, badges and bayonets left in conspicuous positions.
- Articles sticking in the ground, for example, stick grenades or shovels.

The method of firing the traps varied, but most were mechanical or electrical. The silent German Automatic Detonating Device already described initiated most of the delayed-action mines. The mechanical traps were set in action by treading or pressing on a board hidden under earth or by pressing against a railing. This would result in a safety pin being withdrawn from a spring-loaded striker or a striker being driven into a detonator. The electrical devices were dependent on a pull on a wire or pressure on some article completing a contact. There were reports of a grandfather clock being used which, when it ran down, completed an electrical circuit.

The advice given on wires was that, as a rule, they should be cut at once, but care must be taken not to cut taut wires or cords. It warned that these might be found mixed up with slack telephone wires and that cutting them could result in a weight being dropped on to an igniter. Wires, if cut, were not to be pulled, but the cut ends were to be turned away from each other and be carefully marked. Then when the experts arrived, they could trace the wires and remove the charge.

The report then went on to illustrate some typical examples of traps that had been encountered as a result of the German retreat. Many of these were located in dugouts where in the dark or dismal light they would be difficult to spot:

- A shovel stuck into the side of a dugout between the timbers; when the shovel is removed it pulls a wire that explodes a mine.
- A French stove with stovepipe dismantled, one wire attached to the leg of the stove and the other to a stovepipe nearby; when the stovepipe is picked up a charge is fired.
- A window-weight suspended by a fine cord stretched across the

entrance to a dugout; a man entering would break the cord and the weight fall on a detonator attached to a charge.

- Cap badges, artificial flowers, bits of evergreen, pieces of shell and other articles likely to be picked up as 'souvenirs' left behind in dugouts and attached to charges. (Clearly the Germans had very homely dugouts if they were adorned with artificial flowers.)
- Handrails on the steps of dugouts attached by a wire to a charge.
- In one instance, a timber on the side of a dugout projected slightly out at the top but was fixed at the bottom. A nail had been positioned inviting the new owner of the dugout to drive it home and secure the timber. Behind the nail was the cap of a cartridge and an explosive charge. Should the nail be driven home the charge would fire.
- In dugouts constructed with casing, mortice-and-tenon joints, the wedging of timber where the sides had been cut and removed could indicate the position of a charge.
- A dozen stick grenades, to be fired by means of a wire attached to a sandbag which has to be moved before the door of a dugout could be opened.
- A charge in a chimney with a length of fuse attached which would be ignited should a fire be lit.
- Detonators in lumps of coal.
- A book on a table with a wire running from it down a table leg to a charge hidden under the floor; this would be initiated if the book was picked up.
- Partially demolished dugouts with blown entrances were not always a sign of safety; charges were found in concealed portions of these, often using crude contact devices.
- A branch placed over an entrance to a dugout as if to conceal it. On moving the branch a short delay was initiated before an explosion was caused, which completely destroyed the dugout.

This last example of a dugout booby trap is a good illustration of cunning and ingenuity being applied to the setting of a trap. The German who configured it clearly expected the advancing troops to be wary and had taken this into account when laying the trap. He must have thought that the branch would be pulled away from the entrance using a line. When this failed to set off an explosive charge, the advancing troops would have gone back to examine the dugout only to be killed in the subsequent explosion.

The fact that the tunnellers took up the challenge of clearing the traps with such zeal and energy made them very popular with other units who needed assistance, and, equally important, reassurance that areas that they had occupied were safe. In the devastated land that was being occupied there were thousands of potentially suspicious items. If in any doubt the simple answer was to call for a tunneller as this entertaining account illustrates:

In the spring of 1917 the troops who followed the Germans had come to think that all Tunnellers were anarchists, experts in bombs and delay-action mines. As far as one–seventy fumph [*sic*] Company was concerned, none of us knew much about booby traps and concealed mines, except that like the weasel, they would go off POP if interfered with recklessly. However it is a trait in the British character that one is always willing to stick one's oar in if anyone appeals for help under the belief that he is appealing to an expert. Rather be blown up than shown up!

That night I was awakened, given a map location and told to take someone with me to investigate an infernal machine, which had been discovered by a nearby heavy gun battery. I was to unearth whatever it was that looked fishy and not come back asking for further advice, as there was none. In the streaky light of dawn my trusty corporal and I located the battery, two big guns rearing their snouts behind the banks of a gravel pit. At a respectful distance, ringed all round, was the battery detachment who had spent the night bivouacked in the open.

Sentries on the road were warning traffic to detour. Never had I felt more doctor-like and important. 'Pass Tunnellers' said the guard on the road. 'Hey' called the gunner OC, appearing from a blanket covered shell hole as we proceeded recklessly, 'Come back here a minute'.

He urged extreme caution, quite needlessly, for, whilst I had every sympathy for him not wanting his guns blown up, I had a much stronger bearing on the rein on my recklessness in my own desire to stay in one piece.

Apparently, in the dark the previous evening, just when every thing was nicely settled in, and a nice dry billet fixed up as the command post, some fossicking – that is perhaps a better word than the one used by the OC – bombardier had uncovered a steel box with dials and other gadgets sunk flush on the floor of the emplacement, between the guns. Some perisher had turned one of the handles before the OC arrived, and when he got there, there was awed silence in which the contraption was heard quite distinctly to be ticking. An alert soldier of masterly mind and quick design, he had at once led his men in a scattering movement, posted sentries and prohibited everybody from the dangerous area. Then getting in touch with his CRA [Commander Royal Artillery] whom he found more rude than helpful about the situation, he has sent to us for assistance.

The Gunner and a collection of his officers stood and watched as we went up the road. No longer buoyed up with that feeling of importance, my Corporal and I were shaking under a load of grief, in the awful idea that we were in for it.

There was no trouble in locating the tank. In the dreadful silence there was little doubt that it was ticking in its tummy. Slowly and solemnly, on it went seven ticks to a minute. In desperation I wrenched a handle and the ticking stopped. To say the least, we smiled and then I started cautiously unscrewing a plug, which looked as though it might contain a detonator. About four turns had been made when it started to fizz. Did we run, and how? A hundred feet back was a shell-hole into which we dropped, and the sloping back gave us a nice view of the erstwhile watchers still running.

We waited what seemed like an hour, but was in reality about fifteen minutes, but nothing happened. Meantime the OC and gunners had shouted themselves hoarse demanding details, which we could not give. Even if my mouth had not been so dry with the expectation of a sudden roar and cascade of earth, my voice could not have carried as far away as he was. Something had to be done so telling the Corporal to wait I crawled up again.

The fizzing had stopped and there was a faint smell of gas. So that was it, a gas tank! I could fix that easily. Cutting a short length of fuze, I stuck on a detonator and fixed it into a dry guncotton primer, all of which I was carrying in my haversack. Tamping the small charge on top of the tank I lit the fuze and again retired rapidly to the shell hole, this time getting some amusement once more from the retirement of the spectators. 'Only a gas tank' I told the Corporal 'it will pop open and do no harm.' Thinking to myself that if it was not the gunner major had lost his job until he got another set of guns. There was a little bang – only a little one. We waited a second or two, then with gas masks at the alert went forward to investigate the damage. There was no sign of gas – the top of the tank had burst in and showed the interior empty. A few minutes digging and we had the whole tank out of its hole. It was an acetylene gas generator and the ticking must have been from the water dripping into the empty carbide container.

Much shouting was going on in the distance, so I called back 'Keep clear it will be OK in a few minutes.' Between us we carried the empty tank ostentatiously and with exaggerated care to the shell hole in which we had sought cover. Here we dumped into it all the primers and detonators we had, stuck in another fuze and gave the multitude, which was now pressing in, another run for its money. It was a satisfying bang this time. The all-clear report was made and the troops swarmed back on duty.

In the gunner's mess a bottle of champagne which they had been hoarding for someone's birthday was produced although we modestly refused this, it was opened and finished. Our embarrassment was compete when the gunner major made a touching little speech to the effect that he would see that the saving of the guns was reported to the proper quarter. We dare not give the joke away then and our own mess kept the secret as tunnellers often did.'[8]

The incident, although amusing, is in retrospect another illustration of the value of the devices left by the Germans. On this occasion an innocuous acetylene gas generator was sufficient to halt the activities of a gun battery. There can also be no doubt that, despite the bravado, the sapper officer and his corporal would have been genuinely apprehensive the first time they approached the generator. When the cylinder started fizzing and they ran, adrenaline pumping through their veins, they would have been in fear of their lives.

The work dealing with traps and mines was not exclusively the tunnellers' and all sappers could expect to be called for assistance. For example 477 South Midlands Field Company RE recorded in their war diary on 31 March 1917 that they were required to assist with the search for mines, devilments, ruses, gins, traps, snares and other devices in the few houses left standing. A very ingenious electro-chemical detonating device was discovered with a 100-pound charge of high explosive in a cellar of a house occupied by 145th Infantry Brigade.[9]

On the Australian Front in May 1917 during the Arras Offensive the Germans pulled their line back across Hill 70. At about the same time 3 Australian Tunnelling Company formed an investigation detachment consisting of 3 Officers and 60 Other Ranks and they trained to deal with all manner of traps and delayed-action devices.

After their retreat, several enemy traps were found in dugouts, which were entered from Ahead Trench at Hill 70. In addition there, were delayed-action mines one of which exploded on 26 June 1917. The Germans had abandoned the trench on 24th and the first explosion took place 41 hours after they had left, completely wrecking the dugout entrance. Six more explosions occurred in dugout entrances afterwards, at intervals up to 10:30 am on the 28th, or 85 hours after the enemy had retreated. At 8:00 am on the 28th Lieutenant Russell with a party of sappers examined a dugout in this trench and found an explosive charge concealed in the entrance. Behind the timbers, half-way down the stairway, there was a charge of about 60 pounds of high explosive. It exploded within the hour and destroyed the dugout.[10]

The German deployment of traps and mines of all types made the British staff at divisional level and below reflect on how they could best deal with the new threat. Although it was generally accepted that devices would only be encountered after a deliberate withdrawal, there is some evidence that the Germans were able to set traps very quickly. In June 1917 the Engineer-in-Chief issued notes on the preparations and employment of Royal Engineers in offensive operations.[11] These provided details of recent enemy traps including the warning that these had been found not only in ground deliberately evacuated, but also in areas where the Germans had been compelled to retire hastily by force. Examples included traps hidden in cupboards, between mattresses on beds, in dugouts and cellars and in old trench lines. In one instance a brazier was located which was set ready for lighting with a fuze running down to a charge in the floor. Finally it warned that in some areas charges had been laid with electrical firing leads running back to rear enemy lines. These would be fired as advancing troops captured front line trenches or positions. These German observation mines could not be dealt with by the infantry and required expert knowledge to ensure they were safely disarmed. Clearly the best people to deal with these immediately after an assault on an enemy position were the tunnellers. In some attacks, therefore, where there was considered to be the threat of mines and traps, the Staff asked for the specific assistance of the tunnellers.

In the Third Army area in November 1917, the 3rd and 16th Divisions were required to assault part of the Hindenburg line in the Bullecourt area as part of the diversion for the tank attack at Cambrai. The area was known to contain a maze of tunnels and galleries. Prior to the attack on 19 November a German soldier from the 471st Infantry Regiment gave himself up. On being questioned he provided details of mines put in position in what he called the 'Siegfried Tunnel'. He said that he had attended a lecture and been shown the mines and their working arrangements. This valuable intelligence meant that the officers and men from 174 and 252 Tunnelling Companies RE were ordered to support the infantry to investigate any mines or booby traps that might be encountered. It was decided that the sappers should go over the top with the infantry rather than waiting to be called forward. This meant that they would not be subjected to the enemy barrage, which would be put down when the attack developed and would be able to provide immediate assistance to the infantry. The *quid pro quo* was that they would have to take their share of the fighting.

For 174 Tunnelling Company RE the assault began at 6:20 am on 20 November, with four parties of engineers each consisting of one officer and 10 soldiers going over the top and one party staying in reserve. In the assault the sappers were involved in some vicious underground fighting. The third party entered the Siegfried Tunnel ahead of the infantry, and encountered a German pioneer officer and a group of men who tried to resist. After a short fight, the officer and 43 men were forced to surrender. Twenty-seven mines were discovered which ran throughout the length of the tunnel and all these had their firing leads disconnected. The mines were discovered in recesses and generally consisted of two heavy trench mortar shells side by side with a primer box laid across the top into which detonators were inserted and connected to the main cables. There were four firing circuits leading to mines in a length of the tunnel between Fontaine and Bullecourt. The arrangements for detonating the mines were never discovered but it appeared that there was a firing position behind the German lines.

The fourth party encountered some resistance before entering the trenches and one of their mobile charges was unfortunately detonated and the sapper carrying it was blown to pieces and the officer in charge of the party slightly wounded. Despite this they continued and overcame resistance and using Mills bombs entered the tunnel by various entrances. At the opening entered by the officer and one of the corporals, a large party of enemy indicated they wished to surrender. Four German officers, seeing only a wounded officer and a corporal, evidently changed their minds and one of them, as he was moving up to leave the tunnel, struck the corporal hard in the face. The corporal responded to this assault by knocking out the officer, bayoneting the next and throwing the third down on top of a bomb. Getting the message, the rest surrendered without hesitation but after 57 men the count of prisoners became confused. The only remaining officer, believed to be a major, was forced to show the location of all the mines in that part of the tunnel and also the defensive mining galleries.

In the post-incident report, it was concluded that in cases of this kind severing the cables every few feet and disconnecting the detonators secured safety. Cutting the cables prevented the mines being easily re-connected by any enemy soldiers that might have been missed or who re-entered the tunnel. There were no booby traps and it was concluded that, contrary to the advice given in Field Work Notes 35, these were only likely to be found in areas where the positions had been voluntarily given up by the enemy, otherwise they would be too great a menace to their own troops. However the report on the raid noted:

> We have had several very silly scares [of booby traps] since but
> absolutely nothing has been discovered that any reasonably intelli-
> gent person could have investigated for himself.[12]

This seems a little harsh on the infantry when the final paragraph stated
that:

> One or two accidents have occurred in the trench itself owing to
> the buttons of the German stick grenades having become embed-
> ded in the mud and some careless person wrenching the bomb up
> with the result that it detonated. The head of any of these bombs
> can easily be unscrewed and removed, in which condition they are
> practically harmless.

For their part of the attack, 252 Tunnelling Company RE was tasked to
accompany the 9th Brigade of 3rd Division in the assault.[13] Six officers and
40 other ranks volunteered and were divided into two parties. One group
lay out in no-man's land and the others formed up in a support trench. At
zero hour, along with the infantry, the first party charged the enemy front
line trenches, cutting leads and putting ammonal charges in dugouts. Both
parties then examined dugouts for mines and traps and made them safe
before being occupied by the infantry. In the assault the tunnellers claimed
to have killed 42 Germans with small arms, 10 with ammonal charges in
dugouts and also to have taken 31 prisoners. There was, however, a price to
pay for such work and the tunnellers from both companies suffered casualties of one killed, six missing and 15 wounded.

Between the Cambrai battles and March 1918 there was very little significant fighting to record on the Western Front. The Russian Revolution
and the German diplomatic and military successes in the East effectively
removed any threat from that quarter. The German High Command therefore finished up with large reserves of manpower which they decided to use
in an all out assault on the West. The attack was to be on a scale unprecedented in the history of warfare and was to employ specially trained shock
troops to drive through the British lines.

The German offensive was launched against the Third and Fifth Armies
on 21 March 1918 and opened with a withering barrage. The tunnelling
companies, always close to the front, played their part in the defence and
found themselves involved in a war of movement. They were given a variety
of tasks and, in many cases, found themselves acting as infantry, digging in,
holding positions, beating off enemy attacks with machine-guns and
grenades and counter-attacking. In addition their explosive expertise was

called upon to carry out demolitions. The work included blowing craters in roads, demolishing bridges and the destruction of large dumps of stores, equipment and ammunition to prevent it from falling into German hands.

The Royal Engineers' Experimental Section had, by then, been looking at systems to replace the existing safety fuse delays for mobile charges. The fuze adopted was known as the McAlpine fuze. It provided delays of 12, 24 and 36 hours with intermediate six hours if required. Rather than relying on acids and wires the British fuze utilised acetone, which was used to dissolve celluloid discs. A striker under tension was held in place by a brass plug, which in turn was kept in place by a celluloid disc. Above the disc was a glass phial in which was a quantity of acetone. To start the delay running, the glass containing the acetone would be crushed allowing the liquid to drain on to the celluloid disc, which it would steadily dissolve. This would eventually release the brass bolt which would be forced back by its spring and so free the striker which would be propelled forward and fire a percussion cap. The whole fuze was designed to be fitted to the front of a 3-inch Stokes mortar bomb from which it could not easily be removed. Like the German chemical delay fuzes the biggest problem was that the delay was very erratic and could be affected significantly by the temperature. Despite this there is some evidence to suggest that the fuzes were used.

Repeated demands for an accurate delay fuze resulted in a commercial design being sent for trial. This was based on the Venner time-switch, an existing design which was used for turning lighting on and off in streets and factories.[14] It consisted simply of a clock and a cut-out mechanism that was connected to an electrical circuit. The fuze could be accurately set for anything up to seven days and when the cut-out reached the desired time, a switch would close and fire a detonator.

It was now clear that the Germans, having failed to make the decisive breakthrough and having exhausted their reserves, would be firmly on the defensive. It was realised that as they fell, or were forced back, they would make full use of the booby traps, mines and delayed-action devices to impede and deter the allies. It was decided that specially selected parties of tunnellers should be given formal instruction on the methods to be adopted in searching newly won ground and the removal, or rendering safe, of any explosive devices found. The Army Mining Schools set up courses to train the tunnellers. Specimen examples of all known types of enemy trap were arranged in dugouts and demonstrations given on their detection, their method of operation and removal. 'Booby-trapping' as the tunnellers named it, called for a quick eye, keen observation, caution and ready deduction.

Where it was impossible to get the soldiers on courses, training was

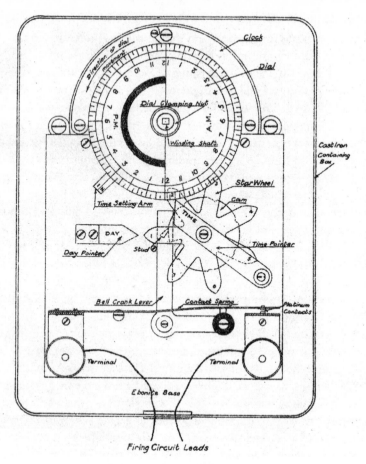

The Venner time-switch

carried out locally under the supervision of experienced officers. Captain
H W Graham MC, of 185 Tunnelling Company RE, set about training his
booby-trap men in September 1918:

> I felt things were going to happen soon and I wished to make every
> preparation in equipment and training of my booby trap men. With
> that end in view, Plummer allowed me to select men I knew well
> from his own section, and I did the utmost to train their minds for
> the detection of traps. The training was necessarily a difficult matter,
> in that one had to 'sense' the presence of traps as much as under-
> stand the types laid. Observation was the essential quality needed
> and after that some knowledge and fearlessness. At first I would take
> out three or four men for a walk and question them on what they

had observed, and later I would lay some hidden traps for them to detect without blundering into them. Finally I instructed them in the various types of 'traps', how to detect and to approach them without risk. Our equipment included a mingled array of implements. Saws, hatchets, knives, life-lines, wire cutters, etc were the chief items and they had to be divided in such a way that no man would be overloaded with his rations, rifle and equipment and to be able to march twelve miles a day.[15]

Some companies divided their investigation sections into scouting parties and working parties. The scouting parties would accompany the infantry and carry out a quick search of trenches and dugouts, signing anything considered suspicious. They would be followed by the working parties who would investigate anything marked as suspicious more closely and immediately remove any devices that were found. The investigation parties invariably worked independently from the Company HQ and were directly attached to brigades. The OC of 174 Tunnelling Company RE, Major Hutchinson MC, issued the following simple order to his men in September 1918:

You are to move forward on instructions of Brigade.
  Your duties are, in the first instance, to hunt for mines, booby traps, etc. To clearly mark the condition of each dugout and report the same to the nearest battalion or brigade HQ.[16]

All told, the tunnellers carried out their work with considerable success. They systematically searched the evacuated areas concentrating their efforts on dugouts, tunnels, observation posts, trenches, railways, cross- roads and anywhere else, which was suitable for trapping. Many contraptions of various complexities were discovered. Dugouts and tunnels were particularly difficult to clear because of their dark, dimly lit interiors and it was necessary to stand in the entrance for several minutes to allow the eyes to adapt to the low light levels. Electric torches, in short supply, were demanded and issued to the tunnellers to help clear such dark and dangerous places. In the early days of the advance, many of the officers insisted on dealing with all the traps as they were found. Once they had established how they operated, the details of their action or methods of operation were passed on to the men so that they became familiar with a large number of devices early on. To minimise the risk of casualties if a device was accidentally initiated, the men were organised to search and render safe traps in pairs. After a few days when they had gained in experience they were left to search and clear the traps on their own.

Information on new or unusual traps was reported for dissemination to other companies; however 'ordinary' or 'simple' traps were probably rendered safe without detailed analysis or records being kept. Typical of these would be improvised traps using stick or egg grenades that had friction igniters. The Canadian tunnellers noted, as a general observation, that these were used in ammo dumps, trenches and dugouts. In some cases a single stick grenade would have five or six other grenade bodies taped round it (less their sticks) to increase the size of the charge.[17] The central grenade would have had its safety cap removed and its friction igniter attached to a wire. If the wire were tripped then there would be a short delay before the trap functioned.

181 Tunnelling Company RE reported another example of a stick-grenade trap. This consisted of two boxes of stick grenades, placed side by side, with 25 bombs per box. The caps had been removed from the sticks of two bombs and a wire attached to the buttons. The wire was fixed to the top of a step of the dugout as a tripwire. When the strain came on the wire, the fuze would light in the bombs and detonate the charges. Dealing with these devices once they had been detected would be a simple matter of disconnecting the tripwire from the grenade.

Some Germans with no scruples even took to booby-trapping bodies. In one instance the body of a British soldier was found with a percussion device attached by wire to his wrist. Anyone recovering the body without checking would be killed or maimed by the subsequent explosion. Even worse, a dressing station was booby-trapped so that the removal of a dead body would result in a hidden charge being fired. Although not explosive traps, some obvious bathing areas were found with pointed stakes and barbed wire arranged under the surface.[18]

Many other devices made use of shell and trench mortar rounds. At a crossroads at Villers Outreaux the investigation party from 182 Tunnelling Company RE discovered four charges consisting of 8-inch shells which were arranged to fire by tripwire. Close by, in a dugout, another four 8-inch shells were discovered. These were located at the bottom of three entrances to the dugout with low tripwires connected at floor level to fuze-lighters and detonators in the tops of the shell. In another, an officer from the 29th Division had found a very nice-looking shanty to sleep in. He was just about to close the door when he noticed a cigar box with its lid open and ready to fall. Had it done so an electrical circuit would have been closed and a charge hidden under the floor detonated. Another trap, again using a grandfather clock, was also reported. This time shells had replaced the weights of the clock with modified fuzes pointing downwards. A metal bar was placed halfway down the clock, which would detonate the first shell to touch it.[19]

In the fog of war however things do not always go to plan. The clearance of booby traps was not always as easy as described above, particularly if the requirement was for the investigation parties to go forward with the infantry on ground which had not been thoroughly cleared of the enemy. Captain A Gowans of 181 Tunnelling Company RE wrote the following to his OC after a disastrous attempt to assist the infantry by searching for booby traps:

I beg to report that on the afternoon of the 11th (September 1918) I reported to 5th Infantry Brigade HQ at 3:30pm with 10 OR (other ranks) as instructed by CRE (Commander Royal Engineers).

We stood by until 10:15 pm when we were ordered to proceed to the front to hunt for booby traps in dugouts, etc.

We eventually arrived at the battalion HQ of the HLI at 12:30 am. After a great deal of trouble (no guide having been provided) and were informed we would not be required until 4:30 am when we had to proceed to the front line with a company of ROYAL FUSILIERS who were in support and to go over with them.

This we did but found it practically impossible to locate and investigate dugouts owing to the uncertainty of the situation.

We travelled several trenches and found isolated parties of enemy machine guns still holding on.

The infantry could not give me any information on the situation so I withdrew at 12:30 pm on the 12th instance after having examined trenches and dugouts which were at that time accessible.

I wish to state here most emphatically that I consider this method of working most unsatisfactory.

If it is necessary in future to do a similar stunt, I would suggest that the following procedure is the only one which can be adopted with any prospect of benefit accruing from tunnelling personnel co-operation:

i   Sufficient notice be given so as to allow Tunnelling Officers to get in touch with Company Commanders and get to know the ground he is going to operate on.

ii   Party to stay in the vicinity of Battalion HQ

iii Company commanders to notify officer i/c of party when ground has been consolidated and will provide guides (if possible) through the trenches he wishes examined.

iv   That the position must be definitely settled before Tunnelling party be called upon to make their investigation for booby traps. This is difficult enough at any time, but to do this work and pronounce dugouts safe under conditions such as those of this morning is impossible.

Casualties:-
No. 79312 Cpl Brown H – Killed G S W – head.
No. 151489 2nd Cpl Haley J P – Slightly wounded – G S W shoulder.[20]

Gowens signed the report on 12 September the same day that he withdrew his party and the tone of it reflects his tiredness and sense of frustration over the difficult and dangerous task he had been assigned.

At Albert, 181 Tunnelling Company RE did exceptional clearance work. The town had received special treatment from the Germans and when the sappers entered they were subject to machine-gun fire and a barrage of both high explosive and gas shells. They worked away undeterred amidst the gas-drenched ruins of the demolished town. The task was physically hard enough but the requirement to wear gas masks made it almost impossible. The masks in use then were of primitive design; the eyepieces of the goggles had a very limited field of view and were opaque at the best of times. In the heat after continuous use they would mist up, greatly reducing the wearer's vision so vital for the task in hand. For the men thus handicapped, the work of dealing with mines and booby traps became a very risky business indeed. For two days the company worked under such appalling conditions, during which time they removed 32 unexploded charges and over 100 landmines.

By this period of the war the Germans made extensive use of deep dugouts, subways and tunnels. One of the most elaborate of these was a tunnel which ran for about a mile between Bellenglise and Magny la Fosse. There were numerous entrances along its length and several vertical shafts supplied ventilation. Leading off it were 35 chambers, providing good and safe accommodation for the large numbers of troops. It also contained two magazines and an engine room with two lighting sets. The investigation party sent to clear it knew well from past experience that traps and demolition charges would have been secreted throughout its length. The easiest way to search the tunnel would be start up the engine and to illuminate it using the lighting sets. However, by now the sappers were sufficiently suspicious to consider that the light circuits themselves might be used to fire the demolition charges if they were switched on. This would not only destroy the tunnel, but also kill the man who threw the switch.

They decided to question the German engineers, who had been in charge of the plant and were now prisoners. They were returned to the tunnel and questioned about mines. Initially they denied the presence of any such charges connected to the switchboard. However, the tunnellers remained suspicious and elected to keep the prisoners with them while the engine was started and the circuits on the switchboard closed. This had the desired effect and the Germans soon indicated which circuits were connected to charges. The leads were cut and the detonators removed from the explosives. All troops were cleared from the tunnels and the lights switched on one by one. Once lit the task of clearing the tunnel was much simpler and enabled the search for booby traps to be carried out more quickly. In the event four tons of high explosive were removed, which would have been enough to destroy the whole subway. In addition numerous traps were discovered. These mostly consisted of stick grenades and 5.9-inch shells placed behind timbers in such a manner that they would easily be detonated by pressure on the timber.[21]

The Germans also made use of gas shells to deny troops the use of tunnels, dugouts and cellars and although not strictly traps they did cause casualties. They were discovered after several men from a dressing station were seriously gassed. They had been in a German dugout in which there was the faintest smell of mustard gas. This gas even in quite strong concentrations does cause immediate incapacitation so the faintest smell would not be enough to worry about. However, after a few hours' exposure the sheltering soldiers developed the symptoms of mustard gas poisoning: inflammation of the eyes, vomiting and burns on the skin which would form large liquid-filled blisters. Investigation by a tunneller revealed that the Germans had removed a plank from the dugout and behind it they had inserted a Yellow Cross (mustard) gas shell that had had its fuze removed. They had then replaced the plank and left the scene. The gas had slowly seeped out, poisoning the air. After this, dugouts with even the faintest smell of gas were placed out of bounds until a thorough examination had been carried out.

The most dangerous and therefore the most difficult and deadly devices to deal with were the delayed-action mines and they merit special mention. They were deployed in large numbers, and although 315 were rendered safe, many more exploded. They were often used in conjunction with large explosive charges; it will be recalled that the first delay fuze recovered by 181 Tunnelling Company RE was intended to detonate a 5-ton mine. Another, which functioned at Hermies, was reported to have had a charge of some 34 tons. If bulk explosives were not available then the charge would often consist of large trench mortar or artillery shells packed around a fuze with a small demolition charge. An investigation party from 184 Tunnelling Company RE discovered one such mine at Sweveghem railway station containing four heavy trench mortar shells.[22]

As well as large charges the mines were nearly always well concealed. At Sweveghem station, the only indication of the mine's presence was that there was slight subsidence, as the ground around it had sunk by about two inches. The signs of fresh clay from digging the mine in had been camouflaged by the use of ashes. The mine was eventually detected by the use of a probe, which sank down to its handle. In some cases in towns and villages, tunnels were dug under roads and a gallery built, into which a large charge would be placed and a delayed-action fuze set. The tunnels would then be back-filled or the entrance blown in. Finally a nearby building would be blown up throwing rubble all over the area and covering all traces of the work. Other delayed-action mines were hidden in or under the abutments of bridges even after the bridges themselves had been demolished. The aim here was to delay or deter the engineer repair parties or, if the mines were not found, to destroy the bridge again after it had been rebuilt. Finally the delayed-action mines were not always buried and some with comparatively smaller charges were placed in good observation posts such as church spires, clock towers, or factory chimneys.

An officer with considerable experience of dealing with such devices wrote:

> Charges under road junctions are often laid from cellars or dug outs. Without clearing every mound of bricks and other debris that might hide a dugout or cellar it is never certain that one [delayed-action mine] is overlooked. I suggest, therefore, that all said debris be cleared to a radius of 25 yards round all important road junctions or corners. This should be the first consideration in future and infantry should be detailed to help in the removal of over ground obstructions.[23]

Another ploy, which was first seen at Bapaume Town Hall, was the use of easily found or apparently failed charges designed to deceive the naïve into thinking that the area was safe. 3 Canadian Tunnelling Company recorded on 5 September 1918 that:

> The enemy had cleverly concealed charges in a number of cellars and dugouts to be detonated by delay-action acid fuses. As a blind he leaves easily discovered charges and when these have been removed the examining party naturally conclude they have rendered the location safe. The real demolition charges have been known to explode 104 hours after the enemy has retired. As the enemy concealed the charges at his leisure they are almost impossible to locate. Under these circumstances the OC has reported that he cannot pass any location 'safe', but only 'examined'.[24]

From the tunnellers' perspective nothing could be worse than clearing an area only to discover subsequently that someone was killed or injured. In cases where there was uncertainty about the safety of cellars, dugouts and pillboxes, provided they were not in locations vital to the prosecution of the war, it was quite common for the sectors to be simply put out-of-bounds for a period of a month. In the Second Army, buildings considered suspicious, but those in which no traps were found, were marked 'examined' but no occupation was allowed for six weeks. The exception to this rule was that they could be used as temporary shelter during actual shelling, although some considered this a classic example of 'out of the frying pan and into the fire'. The Third Army adopted the following system for marking buildings including dugouts and pill boxes: a green chalk circle with a unit name and date indicated the building had passed the first examination; a white sign lettered in black 'Considered Safe' indicated that a thorough search for delayed-action mines had been undertaken and none found; a red circle in chalk and/or a red tin sign lettered in black 'Mined Dangerous' with a unit and date indicated a building in which traps of some sort had been found. A similar system was adopted for roads: a red board with white letters 'Danger' indicated the road had not been inspected or was mined; white boards with green movable arrows and the word 'safe' was an indication they had been inspected and found safe.[25]

For the tunnellers, dealing with the delayed-action mines was a much more frightening proposition than the victim-operated booby traps. With the latter there was time to think. It was possible to observe, evaluate and plan and if necessary use 'life lines' or other remote methods of clearance. With the delayed-action mines the converse applied, the longer you waited the more likely it was that the mine would go off. Also the method of operation was such that if the acid had nearly eaten through the wire it was possible that the least vibration could set it off. If signs of a mine were discovered the first thing that had to be done was to uncover or dig it out to expose the acid delay fuze. Knowing full well that the longer they took, the closer the mine came to firing, the men that rendered them safe were very brave. Captain H W Graham MC gives some idea of the fear and bravery involved:

> We probed the ground and found no surface rupture until, as a last precaution I told a couple of men to turn over a pile of pavé stones at one side. There sure enough Sapper Ellis struck some loose ground, which I examined and thought to be a mine. I warned the traffic, and, as I had no previous experience of delay action mines, I took every precaution and kept only one man with me. I dug down warily and struck a box, which I opened and discovered the mine. I sent the other man away and gently unscrewed the time cap. My

nerves were fairly tingling, of course I had no idea of when it was due to go off. Anyhow I took the cap to pieces, removed the primer cartridge and detonator and all was as safe as houses. By this time I was sweating like a pig.[26]

Not all were so lucky. On 27 August 1918 Lieutenant Moore and Sergeant Carpenter of 183 Tunnelling Company RE were killed by an explosion of an enemy mine set with a delayed-action detonator. This went off as they were trying to remove it.[27]

The Germans developed a second pattern of delayed-action fuze known to the British as the '1917 Long Delay Action Fuze'.[28] This externally resembled a standard 1904-pattern German artillery-shell fuze. A shell fitted with one of these fuzes was an easy means of providing a delayed demolition charge. The delay fuze could only be distinguished from the real fuze in that the gaine (magazine) was painted red. Once screwed into a shell however it became almost indistinguishable from the normal artillery fuze. As well as delayed demolitions, it could be used to destroy guns and ammunition and was fitted to shells with calibres from 10 cm to 21 cm. Its method of operation was exactly the same as the German Automatic Detonating Device. However, it was issued with tubes containing different-strength acids which allowed the time to functioning to be set for approximately 1, 2, 24 or 72 hours.

But it was possible by close and detailed observation to identify the new delayed-action fuze. All German shells with a calibre of 10 cm and above were issued with fuzes fitted, so the lower edge of the fuze was stabbed with a centre punch to prevent them working loose. Usually there were four to six stabs in high-explosive shell, and in gas shell the fuze was sealed in position with cement. The absence therefore of punch marks or cement could indicate that the fuze was the long-delay pattern. The fuze would normally be screwed in by hand, and therefore could be removed in the same manner. Failing that, an adjustable spanner easily removed the fuzes. Another possible clue that the long-delay fuzes might be fitted to shell was the presence of packaging. The fuzes were issued in pairs in special wooden boxes. These had a red label on which was written 'Lgz. Z. 17. Nicht verfeurn, nur für besondere Zwecke' which meant that the fuzes were not to be fired but were for special purposes only. If on abandoned gun positions or in ammunition dumps there was evidence of the boxes, then it was a fair assumption that some shell had been fitted with the delays.

Locating the delayed-action mines hidden in dugouts, roads and pillboxes was a major problem. Lieutenant R G J Ashcroft of 3 Australian Tunnelling Company carried out trials using a service compass to detect the heavy shell and large trench mortar rounds.[29] After a number of tests and under varying conditions the Lieutenant discovered that it was possible to locate shell hidden behind a wall. He noted while walking along the wall using a compass that if there were hidden shell the compass needle would deflect, in some cases up to 30–40°. It was impossible to test for shells hidden under floors or ground because a 'vertical' needle would be required. However, the tendency of the needle to dip as it passed over a buried metal object was noticeable. The OC of the Company, Major Alex Sanderson, tested the method and also found it reliable and practical. In the test, a shell was concealed behind a 4-inch close-timbered wall. Without any other indications whatsoever and with no knowledge of where the shell was, he located the position exactly with a geophone compass. Several tests were made and in each case the results were perfectly satisfactory. As a result he ordered the testing of the sides of all the HQ in enemy dugouts recently occupied by the 15th Division. He concluded that a small and simple instrument with a powerful magnetic needle, which could swing, both horizontally and vertically could be easily obtained and would be invaluable in investigation work searching for delayed-action mines. The report was submitted to the Controller of Mines, but the war ended before such an instrument could be devised. The French also developed a primitive mine detector which was issued to 256 Tunnelling Company RE at the end of the war for trials. Unfortunately it proved cumbersome and not particularly effective.[30]

In the last three months of the war there was plenty of booby-trap and mine work for the tunnelling companies' investigation parties. Although, as already noted, the task was not exclusively theirs, and the field companies attached to the various divisions undertook such duties where necessary. By then some of the sappers engaged in booby-trap and mine work were sporting broad red stripes down their sleeves. Clearly identified for the task they undertook, they were welcomed wherever they went. The official summary for this period (8 September–11 November 1918) reveals that the tunnellers removed 6,714 enemy land mines, 315 delayed-action mines, 536 traps and 24,725 demolition charges, involving a total weight of 2,641,660 pounds of explosive.[31] The figure for booby traps seems very low and personal accounts and award citations would indicate that many more were actually encountered. For example, Captain Graham stated that:

> We found so many booby traps that every member of my party soon became an expert, and, after the third day I was able to divide my party into groups to work individually.[32]

And later:

My party alone on 29th October discovered 95 booby traps. They included tripwires, head wires, loose steps on stairways, telephone wires attached to charges, many demolition charges and a field of 44 anti-tank traps.

Another indication of the number of traps dealt with comes from the citations submitted by the Australian Tunnelling Companies. The two selected are from a sample of six made to two officers for Military Crosses and four sappers for Military Medals. The investigation parties they controlled were responsible for dealing with over 900 traps. Sapper Sheridan's citation is included to reinforce the point that the task was not exclusively for the Officers and senior NCOs:

Lieut Ashcroft MC commanded an investigation party during the advance from Hulluch and Hill 70 (near Lens) on 1st to 16th October 1918. He set a fine example of bravery to his men by personally removing the detonators from a large number of ingenious traps, which had been laid by the enemy. His party removed over 600 dangerous traps and rendered the area safe for the advancing troops.

Sapper Michael Joseph Sheridan MM showed the greatest bravery and devotion to duty in removing delay action traps and mines laid in the area through which the troops were advancing from Hulluch and Hill 70 (near Lens) on 1st to 16th October, 1918. He personally rendered safe at great risk over 100 dangerous enemy traps.[33]

On 30 November 1918, 185 Tunnelling Company RE noted in their War Diary that 23 Military Medals were issued to members of the investigation parties for their gallantry in removing booby traps. They were supporting the advance of 8th Division and the official history recorded that:

Fresh ruses were discovered every day and as each came to light appropriate warnings were issued to all ranks. The extent of the danger can be gauged by the fact that by the 27th October the 185th Tunnelling Company, of which a party under Capt G Howatson was attached to the division, had removed no less than 1350 mines and booby traps in the divisional area.[34]

An accurate tally of the actual number of booby traps laid and dealt with will never be made. The investigation parties as we have seen were often attached to brigades and worked for short periods independently from their

Company HQ. When operating under these conditions it is quite possible that many of traps dealt with went unrecorded, especially those which were hastily laid, easy to locate and simple to render safe.

Considering the number of victim-operated booby traps that were dealt with it is remarkable that the numbers of casualties among the sappers was so low. The skill, courage and dedication of those involved in the task were clearly major factors in this. However, with the victim-operated traps deployed there are other factors which may account for the low numbers of casualties.

Firstly, many of the traps were of an improvised nature and as such were prone to failure. The reason for this is that constructing and laying booby traps can be a hazardous and nerve-racking business. Often, the more complex and cunning the trap, the more dangerous it is for the layer to set and the more reasons it may fail. Most of the victim-operated traps deployed previously used safety fuse igniters or the friction igniters from grenades. Unlike the switches developed subsequently, these igniters were not specifically designed to work on a clearly defined stimulus. The friction igniters from grenades needed a deliberate, firm and sustained pull to initiate them. When cautiously searching, it would be quite possible to feel resistance from a wire without actually setting off the trap.

Another factor was the delay of a few seconds built into the grenade igniters. Sometimes there was just sufficient time to take cover, or make a quick exit from a dugout, between the trap being sprung and the explosive charge functioning. Evidence to support this comes from 185 Tunnelling Company RE's Captain Graham:

> On one occasion I entered a dugout and, finding some detonators scattered on the floor, I made my way out to place our signals of warning at each entrance. Having searched it to my satisfaction I went on my way and had gone about 200 yards when a loud explosion came from the entrance I had just left. All manner of objects were blown up into the air, stoves, stove-pipes, planks and even a chair. I hurried to the spot to find LCpl Luce and Sapper Singleton crouching in the trench, both very white and shaken. I revived them with a mouthful of rum and they told me what had happened. It seems they were curious as to the nature of the trap I had discovered, so went down to investigate. They had only got a little way down when they saw a suspicious-looking fuse to which they attached a life line and in doing so they suddenly heard a fizz. They dashed out, and were just in time to fling themselves to the side of the entrance when the explosion occurred.[35]

77

The dangerous work of the tunnelling company investigation parties did not cease when the guns fell silent on 11 November 1918. When details of the armistice were drawn up between the Associated Powers and Germany, specific clauses relating to the Western Front were included. The German Command were to be responsible for revealing, within 48 hours of the signing of the armistice, details of all mines or delayed-action devices located in territory evacuated by German troops. They also had to assist with the discovery and disposal of these. The Germans complied with this directive providing the relevant information. One of the delayed-action mines described was timed to detonate on Christmas Day 1918 with others scheduled to explode up to 2 January 1919.

Not everything, however, was disclosed, although this may well be because, as they fell back, detailed records of the devices laid were not kept. On 13 November 1918 a party from 182 Tunnelling Company RE came across three ammunition trains consisting of 67 trucks with an estimated 20–40,000 shells of all calibres in Felleries station.[36] Nearby they discovered several boxes containing '1917 Pattern German Long Delay Action Fuzes' of a new type. These were *No L.W.M.Z.dr2** (*Leichter Warf Minen Zünder 2**) complete with acids which were designed to fit on smaller shell than the original 1917 Pattern. It became apparent that some of these fuzes were fitted to munitions in the trains and the task of checking each individual shell and trench mortar began. In the end two such fuzes were discovered in trench mortar shells in different trucks.

Sadly, the deaths continued and tragically 2nd Lieutenant P Barclay RE and seven other ranks were killed four days after the armistice while trying to defuse a delayed-action mine. They had been searching the railway line from Epéhy south of St Emilie when they discovered two such mines. Immediately work started to remove the first mine and after a short while the tamping had been removed and the charge exposed. Suddenly without warning there was a tremendous explosion that killed them all. German prisoners were coerced by force to remove the second charge.

With the end of the war the miners from the tunnelling companies were urgently needed back in the British coal mines to help the country recover economically, so many of the units were rapidly disbanded.

Field Marshall Douglas Haig paid the highest accolade to the tunnellers when on 4 December 1918 he penned a special message to thank them for all the work they had undertaken. With regard to booby traps he wrote:

> Their work in the very dangerous task of removing enemy traps and delay action charges on subways, dugouts, bridging, roads and the

variety of the other services on which they have been engaged has been on a level with their work on mines.

They have earned the thanks of the whole army for their contribution to the defeat of the enemy. Their fighting spirit and technical efficiency has enhanced the reputation of the whole Corps of Royal Engineers, and of the Engineers of the Overseas Forces.[37]

Notes

1 Register of Tunnelling Company Officers, Roll of Honour 1915–18.
2 Barrie Papers Imperial War Museum: Tunnellers Old Comrades Association Bulletin 5,1930.
3 PRO WO 95/405, 181 Tunnelling Company RE, War Diary.
4 Trounce, H D, Fighting the Boche Underground, Charles Scribner's, New York, 1918.
5 op. cit., note 2.
6 General Staff (Intelligence) Report 1a/31532 dated 5th April 1917.
7 General Staff (Intelligence) Report 1a/31737 dated 8th April 1917.
8 op. cit., note 2.
9 PRO WO 95/2751, 477 South Midlands Field Company RE, War Diary
10 Barrie Papers Imperial War Museum: Notes from 3 Australian Tunnelling Company 1915–1919.
11 Engineer-in-Chief Field Work Notes No. 35.
12 PRO WO 158/165, 174 Tunnelling Company RE, Report to Controller of Mines Third Army 5 December 1917.
13 PRO WO 95/406, 252 Tunnelling Company RE, War Diary 19–20 November 1917.
14 Military Engineering (Vol IV) Demolitions and Mining 1923, War Office, May 1923, WO code 8616, HMSO, London, 1923.
15 Graham, Captain H W MC, The Life of a Tunnelling Company, J Catherall & Sons, Hexham, 1927.
16 PRO WO 95/404, 174 Tunnelling Company RE, War Diary.
17 PRO WO 95/336, 3 Canadian Tunnelling Company, War Diary.
18 Engineer-in-Chief Field Work Notes No. 59: German Traps and Mines, revised to 29 September 1918.
19 Guillan, Captain Stair, The Story of 29 Division, Thomas Nelson, London, 1925.
20 PRO WO 95/405, 181 Tunnelling Company RE, War Diary.
21 Grant-Grieve, Captain W and Bernard Newman, Tunnellers, Herbert Jenkins, London, 1936.
22 PRO WO 95/356 184 Tunnelling Company RE, October 1915–June 1919.

23 Engineer-in-Chief Field Work Notes No. 20.

24 PRO WO 95/336, 3 Canadian Tunnelling Company, War Diary.

25 PRO WO 158/178 Proceedings of Third Army Conference RE, 18 September 1918.

26 *op. cit.*, note 15.

27 PRO WO 95/406, 183 Tunnelling Company RE, War Diary.

28 PRO WO 158/144, SS 734 1a54195 German Traps and Mines General Staff (Intelligence) HQ 24 August 1918.

29 PRO WO 95/489, 3 Australian Tunnelling Company, War Diary, Note re Booby Traps.

30 PRO WO 95/488, 256 Tunnelling Company RE, War Diary.

31 *The Work of the Royal Engineers in the European War 1914-19 Military Mining*, Institution of Royal Engineers, Chatham, 1922.

32 *op. cit.*, note 15.

33 *op. cit.*, note 10.

34 Boraston, Lieutenant Colonel J H and Bax, Captain CEO, *The 8th Division in War 1914–18*, Medici Society Ltd, London, 1926.

35 *op. cit.*, note 15.

36 *op. cit.*, note 30.

37 Letter, D Haig FM, Commander-in-Chief British Armies in France, General Headquarters 4 December 1918.

PART TWO

World War Two

CHAPTER THREE

Designers and Devices

The toys we produced were rather dangerous ones.
Colonel R Stuart Macrae

If the First World War was characterised by the static trench systems along the Western Front, the Second was, in contrast, a war of manoeuvre. With the exception of the 'Phoney War' and the impasse caused by the English Channel, the movement of the forces engaged was a major feature in all of the individual campaigns. This was because of the mechanisation of the forces involved, especially those engaged at the very forefront of the fight and the development of the combined arms battle. The result, amply demonstrated by the Germans in 1940, was *Blitzkrieg*. The use of concentrated forces employed *en masse* to overwhelm the opposition by punching holes through their lines was the key to success. As a consequence in all theatres (North Africa, Italy, north-west Europe, Russia and to a lesser degree the Pacific) the tide of battle ebbed and flowed. Denial of freedom of movement was vital for effective defence and mines were used more and more extensively as the war progressed. The use of these devices, which had largely been ignored by some armies in the interwar years, expanded rapidly. In the British Army, for example, the Royal Engineers, who were responsible for mine warfare, had little true idea of its value. As late as 1937 it proved impossible for a Commander Royal Engineers of a Division to obtain one mine, even unfilled, for demonstration purposes.[1] By the end of the war anti-tank mines, anti-personnel mines and booby traps were being deployed in their millions. In 1944 the Germans were producing a copy of a simple Russian pull and pressure igniter known as the *Zugzünder 42 (ZZ 42)* for use in mines and booby traps. Forty factories were making these with output running at 7,000,000 switches a month.[2]

In contrast to the First World War where the majority of the victim-operated traps were made using improvised switches, in the Second all the combatants developed firing devices which were mass-produced and, most importantly, designed to operate under predictable and repeatable stimuli. The standard switches used pull, pressure, release of pressure and release of

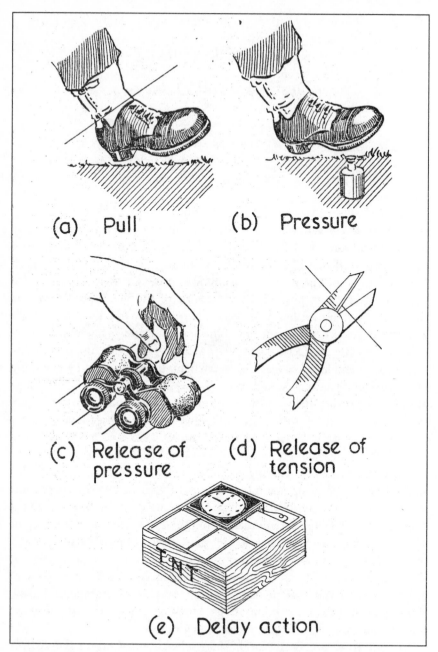

(a) Pull

(b) Pressure

(c) Release of pressure

(d) Release of tension

(e) Delay action

Methods of setting booby traps: pull, pressure, release of pressure, release of tension and delayed-action tension to cause them to function. In addition there was a wide range of both chemical and clockwork delays.

The Germans entered the Second World War with a much clearer understanding of the need for mines and their tactical deployment than they had had in the First. When they began the process of re-arming, anti-tank, anti-personnel mines and booby-trap switches were all included in their programme. In 1935 they developed the *Tellermine 35*, which was to remain in service throughout the war. It was well designed, a very effective tank-stopper and was adapted for use in many ways. From a booby-trap point of view it was also fitted with two sockets to take anti-handling switches, one in the side and the other beneath the mine.

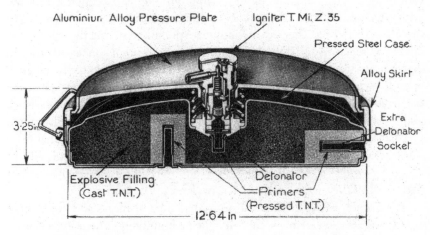

Tellermine 35 anti-tank mine with built-in booby-trap sockets

The anti-personnel *S* mine was one of the German's new, iniquitous and innovative contributions to the complexity of the modern battlefield. Also designed in 1935, the early models could be operated by pressure or pull igniters and from a technical point of view it was a superb piece of engineering. The mine was really a small mortar, 5 inches in height and 4 inches in diameter, which fired a double-walled container holding about 350 steel balls and a bursting charge. A pyrotechnic delay exploded this container, sending it some 3 to 5 feet in the air, according to the nature of the ground, where the fragments would prove most lethal. The range of the shrapnel and case fragments was up to 200 yards and they were lethal up to 100 yards. It was ideally suited for use as a booby trap and throughout the war many were used in this manner. Rather than being deployed as part of a defensive barrier they would be sown at random in every conceivable place where some unfortunate soldier would initiate them by the three-pronged igniter or a tripwire.

In the same year the Germans produced two booby-trap switches, the first a simple pull igniter, the *Zugzünder 35 (ZZ 35),* designed to meet the requirements for all types of mines, demolitions and to fire hidden charges. It was a well-made, easy-to-use igniter, which remained in service throughout the war. A pull of 4 kilograms was sufficient to fire it once it had been armed. It was the standard S mine tripwire fuze as well as being used as the anti-handling booby trap with Tellermines and any other booby traps requiring a trip or pull system to operate.

The second igniter, a more dangerous affair, was a combination switch working on the principle of both pull and tension release, designated the *Zug und Zerschneidezünder (Zu ZZ 35).* This was designed for limited applications by specially trained engineer battalions only. It was intended for use with prepared charges in roadblocks, timber barricades or other heavy obstacles. In 1939 further instructions were published stating that the igniter could be used as an anti-removal switch for mines, and in concealed charges. Apparently subsequent operational use called for a reversion to the original role on account of the extreme sensitivity and high accident rate that occurred when setting the igniter. By 1942 it was withdrawn from service and modified to act as a pull igniter only. A combination of well-trained German soldiers and suitably adaptable mines and switches meant that from the outbreak of the war the *Wehrmacht* was well equipped and able to produce a wide variety of booby traps, although full use of them was not needed until they were on the defensive later in the war.

The French Army in 1939 introduced a range of mines and booby-trap switches. Like the Germans, they designed a bounding mine using a 60 mm mortar shell that was propelled into the air to mid body height and then detonated. They also produced a range of igniters suitable for initiating booby traps. A pull igniter, the *Modèle 1939,* was used to initiate their bounding mine, but could also be used with demolition charges, grenades and in improvised mines and traps. A rupture igniter known as the *Olivier* igniter was developed for use with booby traps and improvised mines. This was designed to fire when it was bent or pushed. It was used with pickets in wire obstacles or hidden in thick undergrowth or bushes. For this purpose the base of the igniter was threaded so as to fit on to the nose of obsolete 12 or 15 cm shell and its head was in the form of a boss over which a hollow picket could be fitted. Once fixed to a buried shell it made an effective improvised trap or mine. Finally, a dual-purpose push-pull igniter was designed for use with their bounding mine. After the collapse of France large quantities of all these devices were pressed into service with the German Army and used in North Africa, Italy and later in France itself.

In the British Army, tactical doctrine in the mid 1930s reflected the First

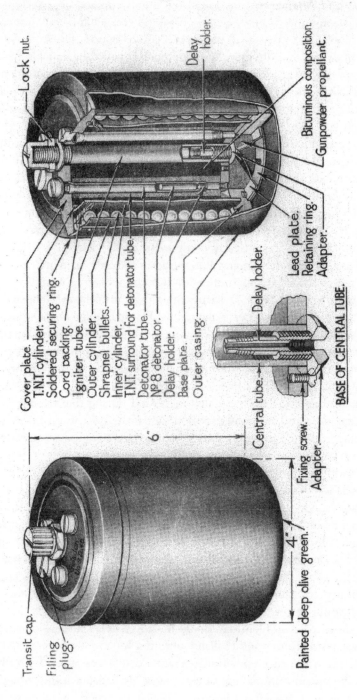

Transit cap.

Filling
plug.

Painted deep olive green.

Fixing screw.
Adapter.

6"

4"

Cover plate.
T.N.T. cylinder.
Soldered securing ring.
Cord packing.
Igniter tube.
Outer cylinder.
Shrapnel bullets.
Inner cylinder.
T.N.T. surround for detonator tube.
Detonator tube.
Nº8 detonator.
Delay holder.
Base plate.
Outer casing.

Lock nut.

Delay
holder.

Bituminous composition.
Gunpowder propellant.

Central tube.

Delay holder.

Lead plate.
Retaining ring.
Adapter.

BASE OF CENTRAL TUBE.

The German S mine, a bounding anti-personnel mine often used with tripwires in booby traps

World War experience and advocated the use of contact, observation and delayed-action mines.[3] Only one purpose-built contact anti-tank mine was available and that only in small numbers. Delayed-action mines employing charges of several hundred pounds were considered to be suitable for the destruction of railway lines and bridge abutments. But no details of the necessary delayed-action fuzes were given. The doctrine of the time advocated the use of booby traps of an improvised nature which were to be set whenever possible.

As the war clouds gathered in the late 1930s it was recognised that there might be a need for some form of irregular and clandestine warfare. To fulfil this requirement the Secret Intelligence Service set up a secret department known as Section D under a Royal Engineer officer, Major Lawrence Grand. Its purpose was to investigate every possibility of attacking potential enemies by means other than the use of operations by military forces. A devices 'division' was an early component of the section and the first recruit was Commander Langley RN who was to be the principle architect of the time pencil, of which more later. Before the war Section D worked closely with a War Office Department known initially as General Staff (Research) (GSR) but later renamed Military Intelligence (Research) (MIR), which was also set up to look at unconventional warfare techniques. Another sapper, Lieutenant Colonel Joe Holland, ran this. His own experience of warfare had been far from ordinary: he had fought during the First World War, won a DFC as a pilot, served with T E Lawrence in the Middle East and after the war was wounded in Ireland during the 'troubles'. His experience in Ireland, combined with studies of the Boer war, in which the British had been tied down by forces a tenth their size, and more recently the fighting by irregulars in Spain and China, convinced him there was a need to investigate further the problems of the mobility, weapons and tactics of guerrilla forces. With Holland in MIR was another officer, Major Colin Gubbins RA, who had also served with distinction in the First World War and later had observed the fighting during the civil war in Russia around Archangel. One of his first tasks was to write two pamphlets on irregular operations, *The Partisan Leader's Handbook* and *The Art of Guerrilla Warfare*. Gubbins was later to head the Special Operations Executive (SOE) for which much specialist weapons and equipment including booby-trap switches would be needed.

One immediate problem that could be solved was the development of special weapons. To this end Holland recruited yet another sapper, a Major Mills Jefferis, who had a reputation as a rather dangerous officer with a bent towards the unconventional use of explosives. He was the author of a third pamphlet, *How to Use High Explosives*. He was an expert on sabotage and,

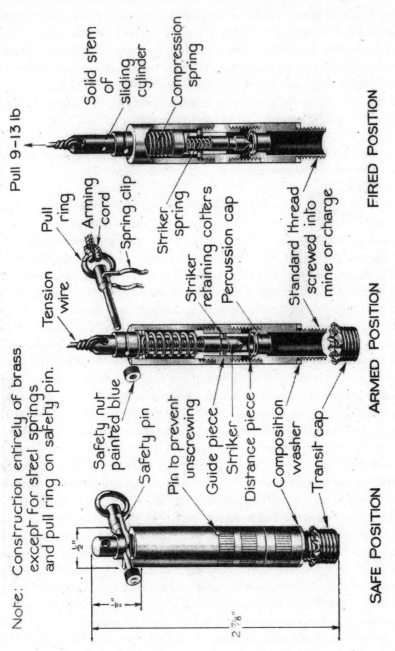

Note: Construction entirely of brass except for steel springs and pull ring on safety pin.

Pull 9–13 lb

Solid stem of sliding cylinder

Compression spring

Pull ring

Arming cord

Tension wire

Spring clip

Striker spring

Striker retaining cotters

Percussion cap

Standard thread screwed into mine or charge

Safety nut painted blue

Safety pin

Pin to prevent unscrewing

Guide piece

Striker

Distance piece

Composition washer

Transit cap

FIRED POSITION

ARMED POSITION

SAFE POSITION

½"

½"

2⅞"

German pull igniter, the Zugzünder 35

given a problem that required death and destruction as an outcome, would devise a solution that could be developed, engineered and put into production quickly and cheaply. One of Jefferis' first tasks was to design a magnetic mine for attacking enemy shipping in ports. For this he needed powerful magnets so he contacted a civilian, Stuart Macrae, who before the war edited a magazine called *Armchair Science*. In early 1939 the magazine had run an article on new and exceptionally powerful magnets such as Jefferis needed. They arranged to meet, and as Macrae said later:

> After lunch, brandy and deep thought I offered to design such a mine for him free of charge.[4]

And so began a long and fruitful relationship. Macrae was commissioned into the General Service Corps and he and Jefferis established an organisation initially known as MIR(C), which was later to become known as Ministry of Defence 1 (MD1), outside the control of the orthodox design and development procurement system. To all intents and purposes they were under the direct control of Churchill, who himself had a magnificent and far-ranging imagination. It was not surprising therefore that, to the staff, MIR(C) became known as Winston Churchill's 'Toy Shop' or 'Toy Factory'. From small beginnings, it rapidly grew into an organisation that was able to design and develop a wide range of novel weapons. In general they were simple devices when compared with developing an armoured fighting vehicle or aircraft. Given the limited range of the weapons they produced, and the fact that they were unhindered by many of the normal bureaucratic restraints, MIR(C) was able to produce rapidly a number of simple but effective weapons. Among these were sabotage and booby-trap devices that were issued first to Special Forces and later to the regular army.

Jefferis and Macrae were both full of enthusiasm and set about their task with a vengeance. In 1939 resources and production facilities were in short supply and much work had to be subcontracted to small engineering firms. Macrae delivered as promised the limpet mine to be used by swimmers to attack shipping. It was an interesting example of the improvisation necessary to get such weapons into service. The mine was designed from scratch using locally available items and powerful ring magnets. The initial casing was made from tin bowls bought from Woolworth's and was fashioned by a local tinsmith. The magnets were emplaced using plaster of Paris. The idea was to stuff the bowl full of explosives and then screw a lid in place. The main problem with the mine was finding a safe and reliable method of initiating it at the right time, normally anything between half an hour and two hours after it had been positioned. Initially trials were carried out using a spring-loaded striker that was held in place by a pellet which was soluble in water. When the pellet dissolved, the striker would be released to hit a percussion cap and hence initiate a detonator, which would set off the main charge. The principle was sound, but great difficulty was found in finding a pellet that would dissolve at a repeatable and reliable rate. This depended on all sorts of factors including the pellet's composition, its density and water temperature and flow. A pellet that dissolved too quickly would not permit the laying of several mines and allow the saboteur time to escape. A pellet that dissolved too slowly would allow the enemy to search for and remove mines. According to Macrae, some children who had dropped some aniseed balls provided the solution. He discovered that these dissolved in a predictable and dependable way. By drilling a hole in them and fitting them in the igniter, a safe and suitable delay fuze was designed. Two of these were issued with each limpet mine. They did, of course, have to be protected from damp and this was achieved by sealing them in a rubber sleeve. A readily available rubber product that was suitable was used and purchased from the local chemists.

One switch inherited by MIR(C) was known as a TV switch. It is uncertain what TV actually stands for although it has been suggested that it is Time Vibration. As a result of the experiences of the allied armies in the advance in 1918, great emphasis had been placed on the importance of the demolition of railway lines, preferably as the trains were passing. To this end a 'Light Camouflet Set' was developed. The term 'light' was relative, as the total weight was nearly 80 kilograms. It consisted of a long steel tube which was driven into the ground using a hammer. The tube would then be removed using an extractor. A small charge would be dropped into the hole and fired to make a chamber for the main charge of some 40 pounds of ammonal. The mine was then fired using the TV switch. This was a delicate mechanism, which once armed would close an electrical contact when subject to the vibration of a passing train. With such a delicate vibration switch the main problem was arming the device safely. This was achieved by a spring-loaded safety pin inserted between two electrical contacts, which was in turn held in place by a salt pellet. Once the charge was laid and the switch inserted, water was added to a container above the pellet. This slowly dissolved the salt, which eventually allowed the safety pin to be withdrawn from between the contacts. The problem was that, as with the limpet, the soluble element (here a salt pellet) did not dissolve at a predictable rate and it was not uncommon in cold weather for it not to dissolve at all. Clearly this was an unsatisfactory solution for an operational piece of equipment. Worse still, once the charge was armed, if the decision to fire it was changed, approaching it to disarm the system was extremely dangerous. There are some indications that

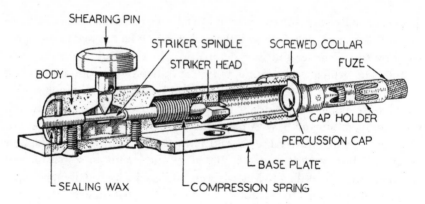

SHEARING PIN

STRIKER SPINDLE   SCREWED COLLAR

STRIKER HEAD   FUZE

BODY

CAP HOLDER

PERCUSSION CAP

BASE PLATE

SEALING WAX   COMPRESSION SPRING

British Switch No. 2, Pressure Mk I

some of these switches might have been taken to Norway by Gubbins, but afterwards the TV switch appears to have faded into obscurity.

Much of MIR(C)'s early work consisted of designing booby traps. The pressure switch was designed to replace the TV switch, intended for use in blowing up railway lines. But some device was required which could be placed under a railway line, was simple to adjust and which would fire an explosive charge as a train passed over it. This sounds easy, but there was a problem, that railway lines, unless badly laid, do not deflect very much when a train runs over them.

Making a switch that would operate reliably yet be safe to use was not going to be achieved with conventional designs. Jefferis solved the problem. The eventual pattern used a conventional spring-loaded striker in a barrel, which was maintained in the cocked position by a steel rod hardened to the point of brittleness. A shearing pin with a flat mushroom head and V-shaped chisel was positioned above the hardened steel rod in such a way that when pressure was applied the brittle metal would shatter, releasing the striker. The top shearing pin was designed to sit comfortably under a railway line. A safety pin through the centre of the shearing pin was designed so that if the trap was emplaced, but the load on it was too high, it would be almost impossible to withdraw the pin. This ensured that there was no risk of the trap being fired when the pin was withdrawn.

Once laid, a deflection in the rail of a few thousands of an inch would be sufficient to cause the trap to fire. The eventual design was only 6 ounces in weight. It worked on a pressure of approximately 50 pounds and would therefore be set off by the weight of a man. The switch entered service in October 1939 and eventually a total of 2,250,000 were made and issued.

Macrae also designed a pull switch, which was made to operate with a tripwire. The inspiration for this was the front stud of a detachable collar, which was in regular use at the time. Macrae describes this:

> The front stud I was using I always considered to be a clever little gadget. It had a detachable head, which was as firm as a rock when in place. But pull out a little centre pin and the head would be pulled out. Having a thin split tube attached to the head, the end of which was bulged out a little, the body of the stud consisted of a kind of hollow button from which projected a stem in the form of another little tube. To assemble the stud, one had to pull out the centre pin in the head as far as it would go, push the split tube right home, and then return the centre pin to the home position. The end of the split tube would have passed through the other tube, and pushing in the centre pin would expand it and make quite sure that it could not pass back again. In reverse this was just the action we wanted.[5]

The pull switch was designed to fire under a pull of 4 pounds, although provision was made to vary the strength of the springs, thereby increasing or decreasing the pull required. It consisted of a hollow tube into which a

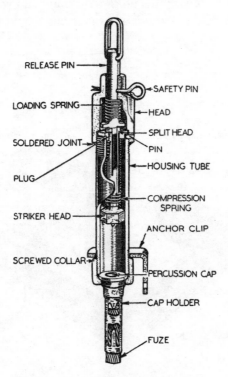

British Switch No. 1, Pull Mk I

93

striker was held under compression. The rear of the striker was a split hollow tube which, when compressed, had a reduced diameter. A spring-loaded release pin plugged into the housing and forced the split head apart and held the striker in position despite being under the influence of the compression string. When tension was applied to the release pin, the striker was pulled back and the split end of the tube opened and allowed the release pin to pull free. When this happened the striker was forced forward under the influence of the compression spring and the striker head impacted and fired a cap attached to the switch.

To prevent accidents, when setting a trap a safety pin was fitted which was almost impossible to remove if there was too much tension on the release pin. When correctly set the pin would almost fall out on its own accord. This was the second switch in production, with deliveries starting in November 1939.

To complete the anti-movement series MIR(C) developed a release switch. This was a flat rectangular box 3 × 2 × ¾ inches with a hinged lid and open ends. A strong leaf spring with a striker at one end was arranged internally so that with the lid closed it was prevented from flying forward and striking a cap. To keep the lid closed a minimum weight of 1½ pounds was required. Any less than this and the spring would force the lid of the

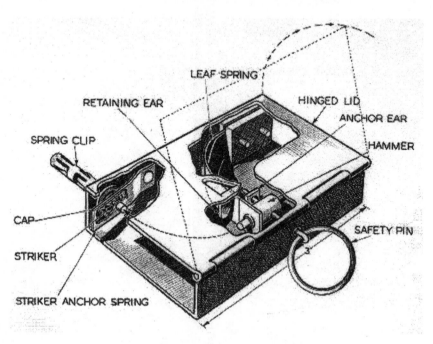

British Switch No. 3, Release Mk I

box to open and then the leaf spring would impact on the attached igniter.

Finally, two time-delay switches were produced. The first, the time pencil, was a product of the devices division of Section D. This was a chemical delay, which in principle used the same method of operation as the German acid delays from the First World War, the design being improved and refined to make it more useable. The work was undertaken by Commander Langley RN and was in experimental production in May 1939. Some have argued that the time pencils were Polish designs because between 14–16 August 1939, Gubbins had visited Poland and was thought to have been shown such devices. It seems likely, however, that the British delegation took models of the Section D design and that the Polish General Staff ordered quantities of these which were to be modified to fit their own demolition stores. The German invasion halted all such liaison. The eventual design of the time pencil utilised a crushable glass ampoule containing cupric chloride to eat through a fine wire, which held a striker under tension. These ampoules were enclosed in a small copper container, which could be crushed, but would not allow the cupric chloride to leak out. Coloured bands on the pencils indicated different time delays. Like the original German device from the First World War these suffered from considerable variations in the time delay owing to temperature variation. The timings were so variable that they were given in no more accurate terms than a few hours, a fair number of hours or a lot of hours. Another problem with the time pencil was that if for any reason the glass ampoule broke in transport the cupric chloride would corrode the wire. For this reason a safety pin was added which interrupted the path of the striker. Operators were taught to pull this out first before setting a charge so that if the striker were released only the cap would fire.

The second, the time-delay device, was a product of MIR(C) and was known as the L delay, which was intended to provide a more predictable performance. This was similar in usage to the standard time pencil. However, instead of using a corrosive chemical, the striker, which was under tension, was held back by a soft metal element made of lead. A safety pin through the switch prevented any tension being put on the metal but when this was removed the spring would exert a stress on the lead. This would slowly stretch to a point where it failed, releasing the striker and allowing it to fire a percussion cap.

By November 1939 MIR(C) had eleven devices in production and a further five in the development stage. By then, Poland had been conquered and the British Expeditionary Force (BEF) had been deployed in France. A return to static trench warfare seemed inevitable. With the French safely ensconced in the Maginot line and the British preparing defensive positions along the Belgian frontier, an unhealthy siege mentality developed. During the Phoney War, the BEF were situated about 100 miles from the enemy. Stationed in the middle of the countryside with the local population going about their business they were in no position to lay mines, let alone consider the use of booby traps. Nevertheless the Royal Engineers did set up a mine and booby-trap school to train soldiers in the basic techniques.

The illusion of security was shattered on 10 May 1940 when German tanks struck through the Ardennes. During the first few days, as the spearhead of the German divisions sliced through the allied lines, rumours were rife and all the news uncertain. By the time new allied plans had been made and orders issued, the pace of the advance had already made them irrelevant. Invariably the allied defence unravelled. There was much hard fighting, and the Royal Engineers managed to carry out numerous demolitions including many bridges, some under the very noses of the Germans, but there was no time for mining or booby-trapping. By the end of May it was obvious that France would be lost and it was only the miracle of Dunkirk, which saved the majority of the BEF less their equipment, which gave some cause for hope.

In mid 1940 with much of Europe under Nazi domination and all previous plans redundant, British priorities were forced to change. It was clear that there was much duplication between Section D and MIR and there was a need to amalgamate the two departments. After an apparently acrimonious dispute both were swept into the newly formed SOE. However, the technical branch of MIR, MIR(C), later MD1 as noted earlier, was left out of the new organisation although it would remain a major supplier of devices. The new amalgamated section grew through the course of the war and was given a number of names and worked at various SOE stations. One cover name that was often, but not exclusively, encountered was the Inter Services Research Bureau (ISRB), which will be used throughout the remainder of the book.

On the home front in the dark days of 1940, the defence of the mainland took top priority. During this time plans had been made by Lawrance Grand of Section D to organise stay-behind parties which would set up resistance movements in the rear of the German lines should they invade. Unfortunately apart from scattering dumps of explosive around the countryside, Grand had no time to produce an effective organisation. This was left to Gubbins, who was given the task when he returned from Norway where he had been leading a force of Independent Companies that were later to be absorbed by the Commandos. His new mission was to create an underground army whose purpose was to harry any invading German troops and in the worst case set up a resistance movement in the event that part or all of the United Kingdom was occupied.

96

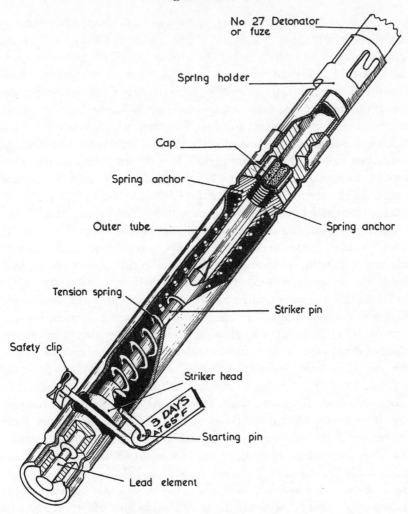

No 27 Detonator or fuze

Spring holder

Cap

Spring anchor

Outer tube

Spring anchor

Tension spring

Striker pin

Safety clip

Striker head

3 DAYS AT 65°F

Starting pin

Lead element

British Switch No. 9, L Delay Mk I

Gubbins went to the Commander-in-Chief, Home Forces Field Marshal Ironside, and agreed in principle how the units would be established. The new secret organisation would be given the inconspicuous cover name of the 'Auxiliary Units'. They were to be given modern weapons, plastic explosives, incendiaries, booby traps and delay devices. It was decided to concentrate the units in a 30-mile strip around the south and east coasts where the German invasion was most likely. To start with Gubbins selected twelve intelligence officers and gave them areas of responsibility. Where possible they were sent to locations where they had lived so that they could immediately recruit known and trusted people. Where this was not possible recruiting was a difficult and slower process. The main source of recruits was from the Local Defence Volunteers (LDV), later to become the Home Guard. Contrary to popular belief the Home Guard was not completely made up of old soldiers and enthusiastic youths. There were those who were in reserved occupations and others who were clear-thinking and capable soldiers. It was from among these that Gubbins' intelligence officers recruited. They were local men: farmers and farm labourers, gamekeepers, poachers, tin miners, publicans and local officials. All had superb local knowledge, were sworn to secrecy and were prepared to die for their country. They formed patrols, established well-stocked and meticulously hidden hides and began training to resist the enemy. By late 1941 there was a total of 576 separate patrols manned by over 3,500 men with 534 completed hides.[6]

Much of the training was done at Coleshill House, about 8 miles north east of Swindon. Here the Auxiliary Units personnel were taught sabotage techniques. This included the use of delayed-action devices using time pencils and the setting of booby traps using the switches produced by MD1 and ISRB. On returning to their patrols some began preparing improvised mines and charges to attack bridges and also houses that might become German HQ in the event of an invasion. Excluding the costal defences, this setting of explosives was done nowhere else in Britain and lasted for a short time only. One patrol under Captain Michael Phillips and his sergeant did set about Brighton, Worthing and Eastbourne piers, blowing out their centre sections. At Brighton, before blowing the centre section of the pier, they placed booby traps at the far end to deter unwelcome visitors. After they had set all the tripwires and were leaving, they heard a sudden explosion. They turned round in time to see a second detonation. A seagull had set off one of the traps and fragments of splintered planks had been thrown into the air which, when they came down, landed on other tripwires setting off more explosions.[7] The remaining traps would claim another victim later in the war.

This highlighted the dangers of using booby traps even when the enemy were not around, and many other accidents occurred. In the West Sussex Clapham Patrol one of the members recalled helping build a hide-out and acting as a lookout during its construction. He recalled

> Some local people wandered too close for comfort, prompting Lieutenant Fazan to lay many booby traps in an attempt to deter this and also giving his men advanced warning of their approach. The booby traps were made up of a small amount of explosive attached to a pull switch, with a tripwire to set it off. Lieutenant Fazan was assembling one of these traps when it accidentally went off, pep-

pering his face and chest with soil. He spent two weeks recovering in Worthing Hospital.[8]

To assist the Auxiliary Units with their work, two publications were prepared which were disguised as a calendar and a diary. The first was a simple document, which gave the outward appearance of an old 1937 calendar. It contained basic information on demolitions. The other document, which was written by another sapper, Captain Phillip Tallent, and produced in 1942, was called the 'Countryman's Diary of 1939'.

This contained a wealth of information on demolitions and sabotage, including details of how the pull and pressure switches should be used and how to work with L delays and time pencils.

It also gave advice on making improvised munitions such as filling cocoa tins with gelignite and then placing that in a biscuit tin filled with scrap metal or flints. An equally good device could be made using an old motorcycle cylinder filled with explosive; it noted that the fins flew very well. Tallent concluded that the essential point about booby traps used out doors was that you must aim to kill with splinters and not with blast. Both the documents were designed to look like ordinary everyday items, which could be left in country houses or farms. It was hoped that they could be left in full view because their innocuous exterior would deceive the casual observation of a German soldier. Fortunately this was never put to the test, and neither were the Auxiliary Units, which were finally disbanded in late 1944. They did, however, provide an excellent opportunity to try and test methods for unconventional warfare. They were able to study and prove the techniques of resistance using the basic and most modern weapons of the time including mines, delay devices and booby traps. Furthermore some of the original recruits moved on when it was apparent that a successful German invasion was unlikely. They went on to serve with distinction in the Special Air Service, Long Range Desert Group, the Commandos and with the Special Operations Executive where they put to good use the techniques they had learnt.

In 1940 there were many accidents involving soldiers and civilians straying into coastal areas where mines had been laid. Royal Engineers were invariably called to assist with such cases and the initial procedures learned for the drills required to set about minefield clearance and breaching.

Booby traps were also laid in coastal areas; at Lydd, for example, a house was set up with a booby trap. On 21 September 1940 Private H R Perriam of the Somerset Light Infantry was killed when investigating the house. He was not on a specific duty but was 'nosing around' in an area in which a number of houses had been prepared with booby traps. These were marked with a red X and a personal warning had been given to Private Perriam. Ignoring the warning he had entered a house and one of the traps exploded severely damaging the house and killing the unfortunate Perriam whose body was found in the wreckage. If that was not bad enough, the enquiry into the incident concluded that his death was due to his own negligence and the subsequent claim for a widow's pension was rejected.[9]

With the threat of invasion over in 1943, the slow and deadly task of clearing some of the mines and traps from around the British coastline began. It was to be a long and lethal process. In September Captain Ken Revis Royal Engineers, later awarded an MBE, was given the job of clearing the West Pier at Brighton that had been sown with a number of booby traps. While undertaking this work he set off device that severely wounded and blinded him.

Notes

1 Pakenham-Walsh, Major General R P, *History of the Corps of Royal Engineers,* volume VIII, 1938–1948, Institution of Royal Engineers, Chatham, 1958.

2 Illustrated Record of German Army Equipment 1939–1945, volume V, Mine, Mine Detectors and Demolition Equipment, MI 10, The War Office, London, 1947.

3 Manual of Field Engineering, volume 11 (RE) 1936, HMSO, London, 1936.

4 Macrae, R Stuart, *Winston Churchill's Toyshop,* The Roundwood Press, Kineton, 1971.

5 *op. cit.,* note 6.

6 Lampe, David, *The Last Ditch,* Cassell, London, 1968.

7 *op. cit.,* note 6.

8 Angell, Stewart, *The Secret Sussex Resistance,* Middleton Press, Midhurst, 1996.

9 PRO PIN 15/3055 Details of accidents involving mines and booby traps in the UK.

CHAPTER FOUR

The North African Campaign

Ponder the path of thy feet, and let all thy ways be established. Turn not to the right hand or the left: remove thy foot from evil.

Proverbs 4.26–27

War came to North Africa in June1940 and swung back and forth like a pendulum across Libya, Cyrenaica and Egypt. An initial Italian assault in September 1940 was repulsed and a British counter-stroke gained momentum all of its own and pushed the Italians back some 500 miles into Libya. In the face of the defeat of their Allies, the Germans came to the Italians' aid and in February 1941 the Africa Korps, commanded by Rommel, landed at Tripoli. After stabilising the defence in March 1941 he launched an offensive, the speed of which was bewildering and drove the Allies back towards Egypt.

British counter-attacks in May and June failed and both sides stopped to regroup and recover. The British struck first again in November in Operation Crusader and initial successes were once more reversed. In January 1942, the Germans drove the allies back to the Gazala Line. Rommel tried to break through this at the end of August 1942 at the battle of Alam Halfa, but failed. After another short period of comparative calm, Montgomery launched his El Alamein offensive in October and began to force Rommel back through Egypt and Libya. The Axis forces' fate was sealed in November 1942 when a combined Anglo-American force landed in French northwest Africa and advanced into Tunisia. Here, in a sharp counter-attack the Axis forces briefly repelled them, but thereafter the combination of Allied forces squeezed the German and Italian forces into submission in early May 1943.

The ground over which the combatants fought was confined to a narrow coastal strip of land 1,000 miles long, bounded by the sea on one side and the Libyan Sand Sea and the Qattara Depression on the other. The Qattara Depression was a vast area of salt marsh reaching 400 feet below sea level and walled by steep cliffs. It was effectively impassable and, along with the Sand Sea, formed a flank that could not be turned. Further south there were

routes but only specially trained and equipped forces such as the Long
Range Desert Group (LRDG) and Special Air Service (SAS) could use
these. The majority of soldiers fought on hard sand or stony ground dotted
with hills and ridges. It was a vast empty area, almost completely devoid of
obstacles to armoured vehicles and not unlike the sea as a theatre of war.
Capturing and holding land meant nothing. The opposing forces had to
seek out and destroy their enemies. Naturally a quickly constructed anti-
tank obstacle was vital and mines became a key weapon, denying movement, channelling forces into killing grounds and delaying or checking
advances. Initially very few mines were available, but as the campaign progressed they were deployed in ever-increasing numbers and in the lead up
to the battle of El Alamein the Germans and Italians laid 500,000 mines. At
first the anti-tank mine prevailed but later both anti-personnel mines and
booby traps were deployed, as increased production and consequently supplies of the various mines and switches were made available for operations.
North Africa was a key testing-ground and all the armies involved had to
learn by experience, often bought with blood, and develop strategies to
overcome these new hazards.

With respect to booby-trapping, it was established by the conclusion of
the campaign that in principle there were four areas in which they could be
employed. These were structures, terrain, objects and finally mines themselves. This latter category will be examined first because it introduces the
vital, courageous and dangerous work mainly undertaken by the combat
engineers on both sides.

A significant feature in the desert mine-warfare campaign was the protection of anti-tank mines with anti-personnel mines and booby traps. The
entry of the Germans into the conflict with their modern Tellermines and
limited quantities of S mines was to have a major impact on the fighting. In
their defensive positions the Germans and Italians deployed large numbers
of mines. After taking many casualties, the forward Allied troops had to
spend considerable time detecting, marking and lifting these. This was done
by the most elementary means and was carried out by troops employing
detailed observation of the ground and prodding using bayonets or feeling
with the fingers. Any mines found were removed by hand. Even without
booby traps, this was a dangerous and demanding task that called for a calm
and cool nerve and a steady hand. No formal instruction on how this should
be done was available. The Germans booby-trapped their Tellermines using
the built-in igniter sockets and ZZ 35 pull switches. This simple technique
was used repeatedly and effectively throughout the campaign. It was easily
countered by using a line at least 50 metres long to pull mines out of the
ground while the combat engineer took cover or lay down.

A simple variation on this type of trap, designed to catch out the over-confident soldier who had pulled a mine from the ground at a safe distance was to use a short-delay fuze, often from a grenade, between the mine and the trap. When the soldier initially pulled the mine from the ground nothing would appear to happen. However, a few seconds later, as he approached it, it would suddenly detonate.

In a German minefield near Bir Temrad in Libya in mid 1942 it was recorded in a technical report that a skull and cross-bones always indicated the presence of booby traps in minefields.[1] In this particular field the area around it was marked with pickets linked by barbed wire. Fine binding-wire was attached to some of the pickets or the barbed wire, which was in turn connected to pull igniters and explosive charges buried nearby. In addition some tripwires were placed 6 inches above the ground. It was noted that by careful observation booby-trapped pickets with charges underneath could be detected because, not surprisingly, they had always been dug in, whereas the others had been hammered into the ground. Other German traps discovered around this time included pull igniters attached to captured British mines and ambush charges consisting of tar barrels filled with 6-inch shell fitted with electrical initiation systems and fired by command wires. At one point where a road cut through a small hillside, grenades were suspended by wires and were arranged to fire when tripwires across the road were pulled.

In the British Army the responsibility for the task of both laying and removing mines and associated traps belonged to the Royal Engineers, but they had insufficient resources to work on the scale that was required. It was therefore established that while the laying of formal minefields and breaching the enemy's lines would be the Engineers' task, all troops must understand the basic principles behind mines and booby traps. This would enable them to lay minefields for local defence and as a delaying action during a retreat. More importantly, they had to be able to extricate themselves without too many casualties if they suddenly discovered they had entered an unmarked minefield. In practice, however, wherever possible it was the sappers who carried out most of these tasks. Although best qualified because of their basic explosives skills, the sappers still needed specialist instruction, and much time was spent in early 1942 recovering and rendering inert enemy ammunition, particularly mines, so that they could be used for training purposes. Internal courses were also run which had the object of teaching sappers how to lay, detect and clear booby traps. This included the methods of operation of the various switches and how they could be safely neutralised. The courses included practical exercises where sections would lay and clear traps. Once qualified, engineer officers and NCOs would go out and train other teeth arms. Later a mine training school was established by Major Peter Moore RE to formalise the training process.

Clearly the sappers put this training to good use and the trapping of mines was not the exclusive preserve of the Germans; Rommel made the following statement about the British minefields after the battle of Alam Halfa in 1942:

> Shortly after passing our eastern boundary our troops came up against an extremely strong and hitherto unsuspected British minefield which was stubbornly defended. Under intense heavy artillery fire, the sappers and infantry eventually succeeded in clearing lanes through the British barrier. Although at a cost of very heavy casualties and a great deal of time, in some cases it took three attempts. (According to our estimate, there were 150,000 mines in the sector where we attacked.) They were of great depth and protected by numerous booby traps.

Field Marshal Rommel was a great advocate of mines. When in September 1942 the Germans had been fought to a standstill at El Alamein, they set about preparing an impregnable defensive position. Rommel, by then a sick man, relayed his ideas at a commanding officers' conference at the desert HQ of the 443rd Panzer Grenadier Regiment. Rommel eagerly propounded his idea of protecting his positions not only with normal minefields, but also by huge fields of great defensive depth that he called 'Devils' Gardens'. His defensive system was designed to withstand the enemy's superiority in artillery and air power. Present at the conference were a Leutnant Pfanzagel and his company commander, Leutnant Junkersdorf, from the 220th Engineer Battalion. When he had finished outlining his plans Rommel asked for their views:

> 'What do the sappers think of the idea?' asked Rommel. He had already discussed the matter with their commander, Hecker, and worked out the plans. Pfanzagel and Junkersdorf replied that: 'To lay special minefields should entail no difficulties for the sappers, but where are we to get the material and the mines, Herr General Feldmarshall?'
>
> 'I will attend to that,' replied Rommel 'The main thing is that the sappers have to build efficient "Devils' Gardens" through which no British soldier can pass and which no mine sweeping squads can clear.'
>
> 'Don't worry sir' chuckled Junkersdorf, mentioning a few tricks he had learned with the 220th and which he had used with some success.

If, for example, a few telegraph poles were laid with the wires down on a road, the British scout car drivers would get out to remove the obstacles. If the harmless-looking wires were attached to a charge of high explosive built into the road detonated when the wire was moved, not only the men but also their car would be blown sky high.

Such booby traps made an opponent nervous and unsure of himself. This effect was perhaps more valuable than the actual losses. Hecker's sappers thought out new stunts daily for this infernal psychological war.'[2]

Rommel's plan for the 'Devils' Gardens' involved building four huge box minefields to protect the northern front. The base of the box was between 2 and 3 miles long and the sides about 2½ to 4 miles. Each box was naturally open to the front to allow the enemy to enter the trap. The German sappers understood the need to confront mine clearers with new and difficult clearance problems to slow down any advance. Many novel techniques were employed. Tellermines were used, sometimes laid in tiers two or three deep. If the enemy mine-sweeping squad forced its way through the field and removed the top mine, the second exploded, and on very careful sweeping which might have revealed the second mine, the third would prove fatal.

Many booby traps were improvised: for example, Italian hand grenades were used to trap Tellermines. As a special feature, 50 and 250 kilogram Luftwaffe bombs were added. These were laid in chessboard fashion and covered with debris of demolished trucks surrounded by tripwires. These wires lay like a web round a spider, and the slightest touch detonated a bomb. Additionally vast numbers of captured British aircraft bombs and artillery shells might be built into the defence, some designed for electrical initiation.

In one case, bundles of hand grenades and artillery ammunition (again) were equipped with detonators in a precision-tool workshop, and secured together with small explosive charges. Harmless-looking poles were coupled to pull switches and huge charges of explosives so that an enemy tank which drove past would move one of these, touching off the well-camouflaged charge and being blown sky-high.

All this work was carried out in the broiling sun of the late African summer. In all, the German engineers laid half a million mines and improvised charges in the sands before El Alamein. They worked not only by day, which was tolerable, but also at night, which was far more dangerous. Everything had to be organised down to the last detail to prevent accidents. The laying of thousands of mines in a night was not unusual. One sergeant who liked scaring the infantry used to walk over freshly laid captured French anti-tank mines, which required a pressure of several hundred pounds to make them operate. As always familiarity breeds contempt and the sergeant forgot that S mines had been laid as traps around the French mines. He was buried quite near them.

On the Allied side prior to the opening of the battle of El Alamein, much work was done by joint infantry and engineer patrols to establish the types of obstacle that they would face when the battle commenced. The Green Howards, for example, sent out many reconnaissance patrols. The aim of these was to find the front of the enemy's positions, and locate obstacles, such as wire entanglements, booby traps on the wire and anti-personnel mines and anti-tank mines.

For the Allies the battle of El Alamein was truly a combined arms operation. One of the key factors was the clearance of lanes through the 'Devils' Gardens' so that the enemy could be engaged. In the event the Royal Engineers had developed the necessary skills and drills needed to breach the minefields and to deal with any booby traps that might be encountered. Unfortunately there was a scanty supply of mine detectors, and many of those that were issued became unserviceable. All this threw an enormous physical and mental strain on the sappers who undertook this dangerous and exhausting task. The deliberate, continuous sweeping with detectors involved men going forward slowly and carefully with eyes glued to the ground and earphones on the head while the noise of battle crashed around them, and it required intense concentration. Then when the alarm sounded there was the cold blooded task of investigation of the contact and lifting the mines never knowing if some new and fiendish booby trap would blow the clearer to eternity. This induced a terrific strain. A British report on the incidence of battle-related psychiatric casualties in North Africa commented that, after El Alamein the incidence of severe battlefield shock cases fell most heavily on the RE whose task was to clear passages through minefields. These men had a very dangerous and arduous job, not only clearing mines, but also being subjected to artillery and mortar fire.

The staff recognised these problems and the Chief Engineer of the Eighth Army fought for, and obtained as far as possible, 'rest' periods for those heavily involved in mine clearance. Even so many sapper units continued lifting mines and clearing booby traps for weeks on end suffering a constant drip of casualties.

From the Eighth Army experience at El Alamein there is conflicting evidence about the effectiveness of the mines and booby traps laid by the Germans and Italians. As always, as you go further down the chain of command, the perception of the problem changes.

The Australian 9th Division recorded that:

> The defences were wired, mined and booby-trapped, but these
> obstacles were easily overcome.

Conversely the 7th Argylls of the 51st Highland Division reported:

> The enemies in the advance were not so much the Germans and
> Italians as anti-personnel mines and booby traps.

Colonel J L Finnegan of the 40th Royal Tank Regiment fought in
Valentine tanks and was in action at Thompson's Post at El Alamein. The
Post was protected by part of Rommel's 'Devils' Garden'. During the assault
in heavy fighting on 30 October, Colonel Finnegan's command tank was
hit and he and his adjutant and driver were forced to abandon the vehicle
and escape under machine-gun fire. On 1 November they returned to the
tank to recover some of their personal equipment. They discovered that the
tank and their kit had gone up in flames. Worse still, the three survivors
noticed that in their dash to escape in the dust and confusion they had run
across a number of tripwires attached to aerial bombs. Fortunately these had
not functioned.[3]

Not all were so lucky. The Australian 2/34th Battalion (part of 9th
Division who considered that the mines and traps were not a problem)
passed through a minefield of aerial bombs, two of which detonated. There
were 28 casualties, 12 fatalities and 16 injured, including the commanding
officer who was badly wounded.

As the Afrika Korps fell back they left numerous mines and booby-
trapped mines. Improvised wooden box mines were booby-trapped using
ZZ 35 pull igniters. In some cases a wire was attached to the bottom of the
lid of the box-mine, passing down through the charge and through a hole
in the bottom of the box, to a pull igniter screwed into a demolition charge
so that anyone lifting the lid would fire the charge. Sometimes the wire
would be attached to the bottom of the box so that lifting it would have the
same effect.

In one case a mine was found on the surface with the igniter set to '*sicher*'
(safe). It looked as if it had been simply abandoned in the haste of the
retreat. However, woe betide the unwary individual who picked it up
because it had been set with an anti-lift device attached to the bottom of
the mine.

In the final stages of the campaign well-trained German troops refined
the mining and booby-trapping of a road to a fine art and were able to

deploy the devices speedily and effectively. Equally the Allied sappers lifted the mines as quickly and safely as they could. On 24 February 1943 one subsection of 229 Field Company RE cleared 100 Tellermines and a number of booby traps of various kinds from 2½ miles of road in 6½ hours. As the advance proceeded, the work was taken over by two troops of 8 Field Squadron RE who picked up 350 Tellermines in 10 miles, of which 75 per cent had been booby-trapped with pull mechanisms.

Rommel made the following comment:

> Throughout our retreat, we called on all our resources of imagina-
> tion to provide the enemy with ever more novel booby traps to
> induce the maximum caution in his advance guard. Our engineer
> commander General Buelowiuson one of the best engineers in the
> German army did a splendid job.

Even though the procedures for dealing with booby-trapped mines were by now well known, as always, the theory taught in a classroom needed rein-forcing by experience in the field. When 59 Field Company RE arrived in Africa in early 1943 they were soon deployed on mine clearance.

On 11 April they recorded:

> The first incident was in the morning, when a booby-trapped mine
> exploded wounding a number of men. The Tellermine had been
> located, uncovered by hand, and a cord fixed to the handle in the
> usual way; but unfortunately due to familiarity and over-confidence
> the party stayed standing when it was pulled. As the mine came out
> of the ground it was exploded by a booby trap switch fixed under-
> neath it. It was the first booby-trapped mine we had found; many
> others were to follow later, but we had learned our lesson: always lay
> flat on the ground when a mine is lifted.[4]

The Germans had other successes too. 78th Division, part of the First Army in western Tunisia, had in ten days' bitter fighting captured most of the enemy's main positions facing Medjez. In these operations most of the engineering effort was centralised in the hands of the Chief Engineer of V Corps, the sapper's main duties being clearing mines, booby traps and demolition charges, and making and maintaining roads. At the crossing of the Qed Hamar, an officer of 7 Field Company RE withdrew the demoli-tion charges from two bridges under heavy fire. A party from 225 Field Company RE then went to remove the roadblocks on the first bridge, but these must have been booby-trapped, for during the work the bridge blew up killing the whole party. The second bridge was subsequently thoroughly searched and the roadblocks were successfully removed from it, though 37 booby traps were found connected to them. The work on this bridge took 8 hours.[5]

One of the main methods of booby-trapping was by setting devices in installations, especially those at key ports and airfields, which were of vital importance for resupply and maintaining effective air support. During the Eighth Army advance from El Alamein, the enemy obstruction of airfields became a very important factor in determining the rate of advance of the supporting air forces. The clearance of airfields was a high-priority task and made very heavy demands on the Field Engineers at a time when they were already very fully employed. Consequently specialist Bomb Disposal Companies from the Royal Engineers and Royal Air Force Bomb Disposal teams undertook the work. In the ports there was often a Navy presence for underwater clearance tasks.

The Germans used every available resource to deny the airfields. Both anti-tank and anti-personnel mines were thickly sown. Empty S mine boxes were used as tyre bursters and booby traps. The tops of the boxes were cut with hacksaws to make sharp upturned teeth, which would penetrate any tyre that ran over them. These boxes were then buried with the teeth extending 2 inches above the ground. Before being buried, however, a wire was fixed to the bottom of the box and attached a pull igniter and a charge of explosive. Any attempt to lift the box without disconnecting the igniter would cause an explosion.

In some areas 44-gallon oil drums were encountered buried down to the first ring and then connected to hidden charges or Tellermines with pull igniters. Use was also made of surplus bombs and these were buried with anti-personnel pressure igniters under floorboards. Where time permitted the airfields were ploughed up using a large grader, which left a furrow 2 to 6 feet wide and 6 inches deep. These furrows were sown with S mines, which were very difficult to find and clear. Finally any abandoned enemy aircraft invariably were booby-trapped.

Getting such airfields operational could be a long and dangerous task. Merduma West landing ground was cleared from 18–20 December 1942. The Germans had methodically mined and booby-trapped it, a task that must have taken several days to complete. There was every indication that the personnel who had carried out the work were highly trained. Little trace was found of the telltale mine and igniter boxes, nearly all of which had been removed or buried apart from those used as booby traps. This also applied to Tellermine claw wires, S mine dust caps and detonator boxes. These were often buried with the mine as it was laid. The large 44-gallon drums were all pulled from the ground using long lengths of cable and this more often than not resulted in a huge explosion often the equivalent of several Tellermines in magnitude.

Two dummy minefields were initially suspected. One employed rows of smoke candles that were buried about 4 inches below the surface and which caused mine detectors to alarm. The other consisted of two rows of dug earth that gave the appearance of mines having been laid. Much to the nasal discomfort of those sappers clearing these areas they turned out to be filled-in latrines.

On occasions even senior ranking officers had to get their hands dirty clearing traps. At Tobruk the Commander Engineers of the Eighth Army himself was involved in this work. He discovered what he described as the 'mother and father of all booby traps'[6] in which the shifting of a petrol drum would have set off a large stock of 200-pound RAF bombs stacked in a passage of the main underground petrol store.

Buildings are particularly suitable for booby-trapping. They invariably offer a degree of protection and comfort from the elements, something that is always important to the front line soldier. In harsh conditions soldiers will often take additional risks to secure buildings and make them habitable. Equally importantly buildings are often used by headquarters and by second line units to establish support services, for example, dressing stations and workshops. They are often focal points for communications and transport and, as such, are ideally suited for leaving devices. Often the method of trapping the building would be by using its contents, especially those items which are of interest to soldiers: for example, food, stoves, beds and other loot. Buildings often give the layer the opportunity to use a large concealed explosive charge, which, if placed carefully, will cause the structure to collapse. It is possible therefore that one trap, initiated by an inquisitive, greedy or unwary soldier, may kill many more. The area surrounding the structure can also be trapped.

When an occupying force enters an urban area once it has been secured, steps will need to be taken to repair and restore all the basic utilities, water and power supplies, communication systems and the transport infrastructure. All these can be booby-trapped. In addition to victim-operated traps, these facilities may be suitable places to leave hidden delayed-action charges.

The Germans suffered at the hands of the retreating British as they retreated in 1942. Sergeant Sid Leader, who served with 43 Section of 18 Bomb Disposal Company RE, recalled that as they fell back they sowed likely enemy laager areas, and the ground outside a NAAFI which was likely to be used by the Germans, with switches they knew as 'Ground Pistol Spikes'. These were designed by MD1 and officially known as Switch Number 8, Anti-Personnel. The switch consisted of a hollow spike which

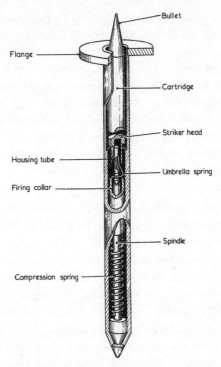

Bullet

Flange

Cartridge

Striker head

Housing tube

Umbrella spring

Firing collar

Spindle

Compression spring

British Switch No. 8, Anti-Personnel

was driven into the ground and which housed a striker system designed to fire a round of ammunition. The action of stepping on the bullet would be sufficient to release striker, which would fire the bullet up into the unfortunate victim. Sixty years on Sid explained that they took little pride in the sowing of these switches, but pointed out that it was simply their job to slow down the advancing Germans.[7]

Later the Germans retaliated in kind, apparently with some justification, as described in the following account from an NCO in the 220th Engineer Battalion:

> Karl, a corporal from one of the engineer combat groups, produced the most diabolical ideas. Since Mersa Matruh he had been consumed by hatred. In the summer of 1942 the British had left cunning booby traps in the hotels and officers' quarters. In the toilets, for example, the plug was attached to detonators so that when it was pulled a mine exploded. Mines were even built into drawers. There were many casualties. Amongst them was Karl's best friend, the battalion commander's orderly. Since then Karl had concentrated his ingenuity on these instruments of mutilation.

111

'You must approach the matter psychologically,' was his eternal cry. He could not stand for a long time in front of a house. 'Attach a mine to a door handle? That's for kids! The British did it until they got bored. It no longer takes anyone in and it does not affect the adversary's morale'. On the wall of a room a picture hung crooked. 'Tommy wouldn't bother at all about a crooked picture' Karl declared. 'But it would annoy the British officer that saw it. He would go over and put it straight. But that would be his last action on earth. Therefore, attach a fine wire to the picture leading to a charge in the plaster wall, put it breast high.[8]

Another victim was injured at Mersa Matruh when it was the Germans' turn to retreat, but this time on the Allied side. When the 30th Section of 18 Bomb Disposal Company RE arrived in December 1942 they found much of the area booby-trapped. On the 8th they suffered a casualty when Driver Towle was injured in an explosion. As a result the whole area had to be checked for booby traps and this work continued on and off until 31 December 1942. In these areas there were huge ammunition and bomb dumps, which had changed hands many times and these had to be cleared.

Sergeant Sid Leader was involved in such a clearance, in his case an ammunition depot outside Benghazi, which had been trapped with S mines, particularly around the entrance. Tripwires had been attached to the front gates and other mines sown at random in various places. In all, some 20–30 mines were cleared before the site could be declared safe. Sadly, his friend, driver Kenneth Arthur King, aged 27, was killed by an S mine while working nearby. What happened was never fully established and he was the first fatality for the 43rd Section of 18 Bomb Disposal Company RE in the desert. Sid and his colleagues arranged for the unfortunate King to be buried nearby in a local cemetery, although after the end of the hostilities his body was moved by the Commonwealth War Graves' Commission to the Benghazi War Cemetery.[9]

During the advance from Benghazi to Tripoli many other facilities were found to be booby-trapped.[10] These included large a charge of gun-cotton cleverly hidden in a generating plant with the detonator wired into the start-ing circuit.

Terrain can also be effectively booby-trapped and this can be done using firing switches and hidden charges or mines. A nuisance or harassing mine-field is one laid to disrupt, delay and disorganise the enemy and to hinder his use of an area or route. This type of mining can be used in defence or withdrawal, but also by raiders behind enemy lines. Because any mines or traps left in this way will not be covered by fire, good concealment and cunning are vital if they are to be effective. They are not used *en masse* as a barrier, but laid with a specific target in mind. Rommel made the following comment on the problems caused by this type of warfare:

> British raiding parties from the area south of Bir Hachem were continually harrying our supply traffic, to our great discomfort. Mines were laid on the desert tracks and attacks made against our supply columns.[11]

The reality of 'nuisance,' 'harassing' or 'great discomfort' should not be misunderstood. On the ground in the desert a driver might pull off the road at some convenient point for a rest. Suddenly there would be an ear-splitting explosion, an eruption of sand and black smoke, and the front of the vehicle would disintegrate. Other soldiers would rush to assist, and the driver, if not killed, would be pulled from the smashed remains of his cab deaf and dazed and with his legs and life shattered.

In war, the heaviest burden always falls on the foot soldier. It is he who endures the most hardship and suffers the most casualties. Within that small band of men there are those officers and soldiers who are imbued with an aggressive spirit and who seem to relish every chance to take offensive action and the opportunity to harass and kill the enemy. While many are content to do what is required and no more, these men will take the battle to the enemy on every possible occasion. Patrolling often gives them the chance to do this.

Captain Peter Beall was one of these aggressive soldiers. He served with the 6th Battalion of The Queen's Own Royal West Kents and was involved in the latter stages of the campaign in Tunisia. He organised and led several fighting patrols against the Germans positions on the road to Bizerta over the Christmas period of 1942. On one he made use of 36 grenades as booby traps:

> We went as before, but this time the assault group went via Bald Hill. Before leaving I had got the artillery registered on the railway cutting, and up to this post, and was to ask for gunfire support with a 'red over white'. We cut an OP cable and then trying to be clever and get round the back of the post, went too far and missed it. I was right behind the lines.
>
> The first place I came to was the station yard with drums etc, we booby-trapped these with grenades with the pins out and I spread leaflets around. Just then the fun began and we hit a Boche position.[12]

For those soldiers with even more initiative and aggression there was the SAS and the LRDG. In the North African campaign the combination of the two was to prove highly successful, with the LRDG being the experts in the desert, and the SAS being the specialists with firearms and explosives. Their actions forced Rommel to divert precious troops and aircraft to counter the attacks on his airfields, logistic units and lines of communication. The exploits of both units have been widely recorded and rightly much attention has focused on the bold and aggressive actions of the SAS leaders, men like David Stirling and Paddy Mayne, who, with groups of heavily armed jeeps, stormed airfields at night relying on their considerable firepower to overcome the defences and destroy aircraft and ground facilities.

However, equally effective were the stealthy raids where delayed-action bombs and mines were left to confuse and confound the enemy. The fledgling SAS in particular needed to be able to prove their worth, destroying enemy facilities, transport and aircraft if they were going to survive as a unit. One of the difficulties was that the bomb that the Middle East HQ offered the SAS was unsuitable for their needs. It came in two parts, did not produce the desired combined explosive and incendiary effect, it weighed at least 5 pounds and finally it took 10 minutes to assemble. To attack an airfield with say 50 aircraft even with 10 men there would be an unacceptable delay because of the time involved in laying the bombs. To resolve this problem Jock Lewes, the co-founder of the SAS, set about designing a bomb that was light, quick and easy to use and had the required explosive and incendiary effect. After much experimenting in the desert, Lewes through sheer persistence developed a lightweight bomb with the requisite characteristics. This involved using new plastic explosives that were rolled into a mixture of oil and thermite. The resultant bomb proved capable not only of destroying the aircraft structure by blast, but also of setting it on fire, thus ensuring that the aircraft was totally written off. The initiation was by time pencils developed by ISRB, and a short length of safety fuse.

The explosive mixture remained malleable and it was suggested that it could be packed into the tubular seat of an aircraft with a long-delay time pencil so that it would explode days after a raid. Better still it might detonate while the aircraft was flying, which, it was thought, would really put the fear of God into the enemy.[13]

The bombs were very effective in providing the dual explosive incendiary effect that was required; they also proved to be dangerous to the users. In one raid against Benghazi Stirling, Mayne and four others used a Ford staff car that had been made to look like a German vehicle. Both sides used captured equipment, and with German recognition markings it was not completely out of place. After the raid the occupants were *en route* to meet the LRDG when Sergeant Cooper in the back heard a sharp crack and immediately realised that one of the time pencils in one of the reserve bombs had gone off. These had a safety fuse time delay of about 30 seconds, and Cooper shouted a warning to the others. They all bailed out running as fast as they could. A few seconds later the car disintegrated in a massive explosion; it was a narrow escape for the nucleus of the SAS.[14]

The SAS attacked the coastal railway between Tobruk and Dorba on many occasions and successfully put it out of action for 13 of the 20 days immediately preceding the Alamein battle. In addition they carried out scores of attacks against smaller installations and on the lines of communication. Everything stationary would be blown up and then mines and traps sown to greet new arrivals.

The raiders did not, however, get it all their own way. As well as being attacked from the air the Germans and Italians mined likely routes and booby-trapped abandoned vehicles. In particular they used Italian air-dropped 'thermos' bombs (see illustration overleaf). These ingenious devices were the forerunner of the modern scatterable sub-munitions. The bombs were the invention of the Italian Commandatore Manzolini; each consisted of a 4 kilogram aluminium and steel body, which resembled a thermos flask. The bomb contained half a kilogram of TNT and produced lethal fragments out to 100 feet. They were not designed to function on impact, but simply to arm. They had an extremely sensitive vibration fuze, which would detonate it at the slightest movement. These bombs injured both LRDG and SAS personnel. In *Born of the Desert*, Malcolm James, a doctor with the SAS, describes how he was summoned to assist with injuries caused by them:

> The casualties, it appeared, were a gunner officer new to the unit and his corporal driver: they had driven up to inspect a derelict truck and in doing so their jeep had run over a thermos-bomb. It was not an uncommon accident, for the enemy delighted in surrounding any abandoned vehicles with such anti-personnel devices. In the explosion that followed the jeep was set on fire and the officer badly burned. Cox, the driver, jumped out and ran round to pull the officer out, but as he did so he stepped on another bomb which exploded and shattered his leg. By this time others had realised what was happening and a few of them dashed over and dragged the wounded men away to safety.[15]

The LRDG also suffered casualties with derelict vehicles that proved too much for the inquisitive. In this instance G Patrol of the LRDG had been

The thermos bomb

operating miles behind enemy lines and were monitoring how much traffic was about. On 24 June 1942 the patrol stopped for a few minutes near some derelict vehicles. Guardsman Hopton opened the door to one of the vehicles and touched off a booby trap and was killed instantly. He was buried on the spot.[16]

The final booby-trapping technique turns common objects into lethal devices. Some were specially manufactured items and others improvised designs, using the issued firing switches and explosives. These devices can be very effective although, like all booby traps, they are indiscriminate, and if not well controlled will kill not only the enemy, but also civilians and possibly other friendly forces. Made up to imitate a useful object, when picked up, opened or operated they function, killing or maiming the unsuspecting victim. Typical examples include everyday items such as torches, books and ration packs. Some military pamphlets claim that most of these types of trap were purposely manufactured, but there is little evidence to indicate that these were issued to troops in the Middle East. If they *were* manufactured, no pictures or examples seem to have survived to go into record books or museums. There are some reports of their use, but these are hard to corroborate.

Lieutenant Michael Halstead was a tank commander who served in the Queen's Bays and took part in the advance towards Libya in late 1941. He recorded in his diary for 21 December that they had a day's breather and that they spent time looking for loot. This was tempered however by news that there had been two accidents in the 10th Hussars. An Italian 'Red Devil' grenade had injured one trooper and another was wounded by a water bottle that exploded when the cork was pulled out.[17]

Although the precise nature of the trap will never be known, subsequently warnings were issued about such deadly objects left on the battlefield. A diagram of similar 'canteen traps' was included in a US manual.[18] It consisted of a water bottle, into the bottom of which an explosive charge had been fitted. A pull igniter that had a wire attached to the screw top set this off. Cunningly water was also poured into the bottle, so, if found by a soldier and shaken, it would appear to contain nothing but liquid. In the desert where water was so scarce, a full or partially full water bottle would be treasure indeed. Unscrewing and removing the top would, in theory, prove fatal. This trap is interesting in that it in reality it would be difficult to build and set. If produced locally, how was the pull igniter locked in position and how was the pull wire connected to the cap so that it was reasonably taut? Tensioning the wire to the pull switch in such a device would need to be done very carefully indeed.

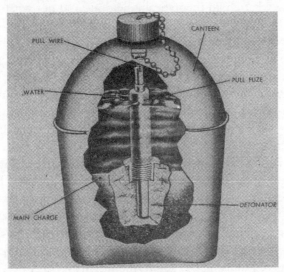

Water bottle

As the campaign progressed, the laying of object-type traps increased in sophistication, ingenuity and wickedness. In Bardia in mid 1942 a booby-trapped headset for a radio was found. This was detailed in a technical intelligence summary in June 1942 and was later attributed to the Italians. A single earphone headset had been found and while being examined it exploded. The charge was sufficient to blow the hand almost completely off the soldier holding it. It could not be reconstructed, but it may well have been designed to operate when a current was applied as in normal use, in which case, with the charge pressed up against the side of the victim's head, it would have undoubtedly been lethal.[19]

Another report described a whistle of the dark brown Bakelite plastic kind which when examined was found to contain a charge fitted with a cap and a striker.[20] This has never been independently verified. An American pamphlet detailed a similar whistle, but this reported that the device consisted of a friction-sensitive charge, which would be activated by the rubbing of the ball which was coated in a rough material. When the whistle was blown the vibrating ball would initiate the charge, causing an explosion. No photographs or actual examples of this device appear to have survived for subsequent examination. An exploding bar of chocolate was another extraordinary device reported. It must be questioned whether such booby traps really existed or whether they were the result of rumours, or the figment of the imagination of the writers of the subsequent reports. Some of these authors, perhaps with the best intentions in mind, seem to be describing what could theoretically be done and not what had actually been done.

What cannot be denied is that all forms of booby-trapping went on throughout the campaign. They also illustrate the point that a cunningly contrived trap, properly set, can be a lethal device. Whereas hundreds of mines might have to be laid or tons of ammunition fired to cause a casualty, a booby trap springs suddenly on the unwary victim. For the price of a firing switch and a small charge of explosive plus some time and imagination, an efficient and cost-effective casualty rate can be achieved.

The American forces involved in the North African campaign were able to benefit from some of the British experience of mines and booby traps. Some of their engineer units, which were routed through the United Kingdom in mid 1942, were given additional training. For example, the 16th Armored Engineer Battalion stationed in Northern Ireland received some specialist training in mines, booby traps and demolitions. It was not enough, however, and after the Torch landings in North Africa, hard lessons had to be learned. At Kasserine American troops encountered mines and booby-trapped mines on a large scale. One combat engineer company commander at the battle had never seen a German mine, even in a picture or as a model, before entering combat, and had to rely on an NCO who had attended a British mine school. There was just time to train a few key men before encountering their first live devices.

During the retreat into Tunisia the Germans scattered mines indiscriminately. The Americans had to learn the tricks the Germans used to slow down clearance teams. Some mines were booby-trapped, others were laid 2 or 3 feet deep. Around some they scattered scrap metal that Allied mine-detectors would locate and require further investigation. One of the most effective tricks was to bury the mines too deep to be detected. In this way scores of trucks would pass safely over the mine and then when a rut became deep enough the mine would explode.

Elsewhere, the Germans observed Americans laying their own defensive minefield using stocks of British Mark V Mines. Realising that the Americans would have to lift their own mines before they could continue the advance, the Germans crept out at night and booby-trapped the mines on the edge nearest to them with anti-lift devices. Such methods had a heavy psychological effect on the advancing troops.[21]

The concluding report on the US Forces' combat experience in North Africa noted that the most effective enemy mining was the sporadic mining of long stretches of road, road shoulders and craters, and areas upon their withdrawal. Heavily mined, soft, sandy fords strewn with metal fragments were also effective in causing delays. The US 9th Infantry Division recorded at the conclusion of the desert campaign that:

> The failure to recognise the fact that the enemy is a master in the art
> of mining and booby-trapping will cost lives.[22]

Training to deal with mines and booby traps became a key issue before the landings in Sicily and Italy. One of the prime difficulties was obtaining deactivated stores to train with. Although thousands of mines were deactivated in the combat zones, they were scarce in the rear areas. The situation was so critical that Lieutenant General Mark Clark's private plane was used to ferry mines back to the Fifth Army Training School. Most, but not all, training was done without enemy mines because of the dangers involved. Besides the risks of handling unfamiliar mines, some of the explosive fillings used became dangerous with age, particularly after being subject to the desert's extremes of temperature. In one case a 109th Engineer Combat Battalion truck carrying some 450 neutralised, but live, mines exploded, killing an entire 12-man squad instantly.

The Americans set up mine training schools staffed by instructors who had attended courses at the British Eighth Army. The courses provided a week's training, which covered the basic handling of explosives, demolitions, anti-tank and anti-personnel mines, booby traps and tactics to deal with them. A course attended by men of 31st Coastal Artillery

Brigade was particularly realistic. S mines were demonstrated as follows: firstly, a live mine was taken apart in front of the class and then the bursting charge removed. The mine was then taken and placed in the ground and fired. The mine pot popped up out of the ground rising to some 40 feet in the air. A second mine was then dismantled and all the steel ball bearings removed. Sensibly the men moved a little further away and the mine was fired and clearly seen to explode at head height.[23] Following this graphic demonstration, the men would be given a lecture on all the known booby trap switches. Then they were sent through a small house, which had been booby-trapped. As an incentive they were told that if they could discover and disarm a trap they could they could keep it. A total of 45 traps of all types had been placed in the house. After the men had been through, the instructors would show how the traps had been planted and set.

This training and preparation went on throughout all the Allied armies that were waiting in North Africa for the next phase of the campaign in the Mediterranean. In the desert, mine- and booby-trap warfare had come of age. It had grown from almost nothing to a point where in any operational planning, at any level, it was a fundamental factor that had to be considered if the enemy was to be overcome. What was not known was what new types of device would be encountered, and what new and cunning methods would be deployed to catch out Allied soldiers.

Notes

1 PRO WO 208/3578, Technical Intelligence Summary No. 76, 13 June 1942.

2 Carell, Paul, *The Foxes of the Desert*, Bantam Books, New York, 1960.

3 Perrett, Bryan, *The Valentine in North Africa 1942–43*, Ian Allan Books, London, 1972.

4 Daniell, A P de T OBE, MC TD, *Mediterranean Safari March 1943–October 1944*, Buckland Publications, London, *c.* 1990.

5 Pakenham-Walsh, Major General R P, *History of the Corps of Royal Engineers,* volume VIII, 1938–1948, Institution of Royal Engineers, Chatham, 1958.

6 Pakenham-Walsh, Major General R P, *The Second World War, 1939–1945, Army, Military Engineering (Field)*, The War Office, London, 1952.

7 Interview with Mr Sid Leader, London, 6 March 2002.

8 *op. cit.*, note 2.

9 *op. cit.*, note 7.

10 PRO WO 204/5992, Air Ministry Instruction 306, Instructions to RAF Bomb Disposal Units.

11 Landmine and Countermine Warfare, US Report 1972 – North Africa.

12 Riches, Paul, *The Spirit Lives On*, privately published, [UK], 1992.

13 Lewes, John, *Jock Lewes Co-Founder of the SAS*, Leo Cooper, Barnsley, 2000.

14 James, Malcolm, *Born of the Desert*, Greenhill Books, London, 1991.

15 *op. cit*, note 14.

16 Crichton Stuart, Michael, *G Patrol*, William Kimber, London, 1976.

17 Halsted, Michael, *Shots in the Sand*, Gooday Publishers, East Wittering, 1990.

18 FM 5-31, Use and Installation of Booby Traps.

19 *op. cit.,* note 1.

20 *op. cit.,* note 1.

21 Jamison, Captain Wallace H, 'Achtung Mines', *Infantry Journal,* November 1943.

22 Landmine and Countermine Warfare, US Report 1972 – North Africa.

23 PRO 204/5332, Mine Warfare Courses.

CHAPTER FIVE

The Italian Campaign

Look before you leap, afterwards you might not be able to.
Achtung! Minen, US Mine Training Pamphlet

By mid 1943, with victory in North Africa and air and naval supremacy in the Mediterranean, the Allies were free to begin the assault on southern Europe. Operation Husky was launched on 10 July 1943 with an airborne and amphibious assault on Sicily. The Axis forces were compelled to undertake a slow systematic withdrawal, delaying the Allies as long as possible, but knowing that evacuation to the Italian mainland would be the final outcome. Sicily was no pushover and was bitterly contested by the Germans. As a foretaste of what was to come the Germans made good use of both mines and booby traps.

A major undertaking, which was to continue right up to the end of the war, was bridge-building. The German engineers demolished most bridges and more often than not mined and trapped the approaches and exits which then had to be cleared before reconstruction could take place. Soon after its arrival in Sicily, 501 Company RE was involved such work. They suffered their first casualty on 12 August when a sapper was killed by mortar fire while clearing mines at Macchia. Three days later a mine at Giardini killed another.

The Americans had similar problems with German bridge demolitions, but were particularly successful with their use of armoured bulldozers, which were able to clear areas rapidly or cut new by-passes. The Germans, impressed by the speed at which these bulldozers operated, resorted to heavily mining all the obvious by-pass routes. As the Germans fell back the mining and trapping became more deliberate and prolific. Some of their pioneers planted mines in pot holes and then poured hot asphalt over them to make them look like repair patches.

In one incident the Germans left behind a number of grenades, which had been booby-trapped.[1] These were egg grenades which had been doctored. The grenades used a blue-coloured *Brennzünder (BZE)* pull friction igniter with a 4.5-second pyrotechnic delay pellet. Specimens of these blue

BZE igniters were recovered in Sicily that were fitted to egg grenades with the normal delay pellets removed. Any Allied troops using such grenades would discover to their cost that they exploded immediately the friction igniter was pulled. Before using captured stock it was recommended that the fuze was removed from one grenade and it was pulled, to see how long the delay was. If it was all right, the other grenades would be checked for the presence of a similar undamaged pellet and, provided it was in place, the grenades could be used.[2]

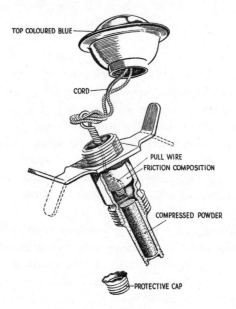

TOP COLOURED BLUE

CORD

PULL WIRE
FRICTION COMPOSITION

COMPRESSED POWDER

PROTECTIVE CAP

The Brennzünder igniter

The Germans fought a successful delaying battle in Sicily. In this the geography assisted them, because the island tapers down towards the port of Messina closest to the Italian mainland. As they fell back the width of their front line naturally shortened and it could be held by fewer and fewer troops, and in this controlled environment there was ample time to set and carry out a planned denial programme. The 2nd Battalion of the Northamptonshire Regiment recorded in early August that while advancing across the Catania Plain that they were hindered by both mines and booby traps and their pioneer platoon, assisted by a section of 38 Field Company RE, did valuable work in clearing the booby-trapped mines and making diversions around craters. In his book *Heaven and Hell, the War Diary of a German Paratrooper*, Martin Pöppel makes a passing reference to the sowing of these devices:

There are engineers everywhere, mining roads, preparing bridges for demolition and installing all kinds of 'Joke' articles. But it's certain that Tommy won't be laughing himself to death over them.[3]

Reference has already been made to the pioneer platoons in infantry battalions assisting with mine and booby trap clearance. This merits further investigation because by mid 1943 these soldiers were assuming important new tasks. The 'pioneer' within the army goes back to well before the 'Standing Army' of 1660. In medieval times, muster rolls of the British garrison in Calais record the presence of pioneers whose tasks included building and fortification. In more recent times, the pioneers consisted of a senior NCO and a number of soldiers who were normally tradesmen, such as carpenters, bricklayers, smiths and stonemasons. It was recognised that the senior NCO needed to be skilled in field engineering and as such should attend courses at the School of Military Engineering in Chatham. In the First World War this role continued and the importance of constructing field fortifications ensured that the pioneers were retained with their infantry battalion. However, the nature of the war was such that all infantry were expected to be capable of this role and often the pioneers were grouped at brigade where their tradesmen skills enabled them to produce stocks of structures like barbed wire knife-rests, loop-holes, trench-board signs and countless other items needed in the trenches. As the Second World War progressed, so mine and booby-trap warfare became of increasing importance, notably, as we have seen, in North Africa.

In 1943 the infantry battalion's establishment was revised to reflect recent experience and the pioneer platoon was now located with support company. A junior officer now commanded it rather than an NCO and its name changed to 'Assault Pioneer Platoon' to reflect its greater combat role. In the subsequent fighting in Italy the importance of the assault pioneers with both infantry fighting skills and explosive- and mine-clearing skills meant that as well as supporting the assault of enemy positions they were also required on most patrols. It was noted in training that the offensive role of the assault pioneer platoon must never be overlooked. It will be seen that the assault pioneers took great pride in their work with mines and booby traps and were always at the fore when their own battalion encountered these devices.

The last of the Germans escaped from Sicily on 17 August and their departure heralded the start of a new and deadly contest. The port of Messina, which was vital for future operations on the Italian mainland, had been thoroughly trapped. The Navy took responsibility for clearing the harbour and Royal Navy Port Clearance Party No. 1500 was given the task. It had two

Bomb Safety Officers (BSOs), Lieutenant A R J Firminger GM RNVR and Lieutenant Bridge GM and Bar RNVR, both of whom were experienced divers and had dealt with many enemy sea-mines and aircraft bombs.[4]

Lieutenant Firminger and a small party of men were despatched by the officer in charge to the harbour at Messina to carry out an initial reconnaissance of the port. The Germans had carried out some demolitions and had left many booby traps. There were large numbers of depth-charges lying around with a variety of fuzing systems. In the harbour were more depth-charges and many other unidentified objects. The Mediterranean water was crystal clear and at the end of one jetty it was possible to see a group of depth-charges wired together with another unidentified cylinder. Lieutenant Firminger arranged for a hook and line to be placed through the wire rope holding the depth-charges together and for the other end of the line to be passed back over the jetty and fixed to the back of a vehicle. Under Lieutenant Firminger's direction the vehicle moved very slowly off the pier pulling the depth-charges clear of the water. Lieutenant Firminger, Warrant Officer Bratley and three able seamen stayed at the end of the pier and watched the charges and the additional cylinder being lifted. Unfortunately one of the depth-charges hit the underside of the pier and a huge explosion instantly killed all those standing watching. Some distance away on the shore one able seaman was so badly injured that he spent some months in hospital. The luckiest man was the driver of the vehicle who escaped with relatively minor injuries and he was released from hospital after only three weeks.

In war death does not change the military situation and the need to clear the port remained paramount. Lieutenant Bridge RN was therefore despatched with another clearance party, to establish what had happened and to complete the dangerous clearance task. He arrived on 26 August and after three days had completed his preliminary reconnaissance and prepared a clearance plan. The situation was dangerous enough, but to make matters worse the Germans in Italy were sporadically shelling the port.

With Sicily secure, the next step was the invasion and liberation of the Italian mainland, which was to be one of the most gruelling military operations of the Second World War. Two factors made Italy ideal for mine and booby-trap warfare. Firstly, at a strategic level, the Germans had suffered major defeats in Russia and Africa and were now firmly on the defensive. During the Italian campaign there were only two serious attempts to dislodge the Allies, firstly during the landings at Salerno and later at Anzio. Other than that the Germans were restricted to vicious, short, sharp counter-attacks with limited objectives. The German High Command recognised that with the limited resources at their disposal the only option would be to fight a series of defensive delaying battles as they retired up the length of the country. As they would be unlikely to recover areas that had been lost to the Allies, especially after the Italians had capitulated, they implemented a scorched-earth policy. This was complemented by the liberal use of mines, delay demolitions and randomly set booby traps. The second factor was the geography of Italy itself. The massive Apennine Mountains run like a spine down the centre of the country, and from them spring fast-flowing rivers. These had, over the centuries, cut deep valleys and ravines, running out like ribs from the spine. Along the coast there were flat plains, but these were divided up into isolated areas by the mountains that, in many places, run right down to the sea. Nature could have provided no better basic defensive system. The Germans, by use of the Todt Organisation and local labour, fortified these natural defences at certain points. Observation posts, gun emplacements, minefields, machine-gun nests and logistic supplies were all skilfully sited, protected and camouflaged. In addition a host of minor ploys were woven into the defence to cause disruption and death, ranging from tripwires and booby traps to almost invisible individual snipers' positions. The defence lines were given names; the Winter Line, Gustav Line, Hitler Line and the Gothic Line. These lines were the setting for major set-piece battles, some of which lasted for weeks or months at a time. Between these lines the Germans fell back in a series of controlled withdrawals.

The campaign on the Italian mainland started on 3 September 1943 when troops from the British Eighth Army were ferried across the straits of Messina to Calabria. Six days later amphibious landings were made at Salerno. The Germans, who had just taken over from the Italians, reacted strongly and in the first week the beachhead was fiercely contested with the Allies just managing to hang on. Booby traps and mines were encountered from the start. The American 111th Engineer Combat Battalion landed at Salerno and between 12–17 September spent many hours both clearing mines and booby traps and then mine-laying to block enemy approaches. Booby traps caused casualties from the outset and on 13 September the Battalion recorded that:

> Late in the afternoon Lt Morton and the first platoon of 'B' company removed an enemy roadblock Northwest of Albanella and whilst so engaged PFC Robert N Jobs received light wounds in the abdominal region and legs from a booby trap whilst cutting a tree.[5]

And later on 17 September:

> The three operating platoons of 'A' company under the direction of the company commander Lt Ausland, moved to the vicinity of

Albanella on the mission of removing road blocks. And anti-tank mines two kilometres west of the town. In this vicinity it was noted that the blocks had been heavily booby trapped by the enemy.

British Sappers were also involved in the clearance of booby-trapped mines. There was a minefield on one of the main beach exits, which the Germans had laid the day before the landings and it had to be quickly cleared. Sergeant Forder of 503 Field Company RE with a section of men cleared the minefield which consisted of 900 mines of which over 40 had been trapped. This was done quickly and efficiently and without casualties. For this outstanding work Sergeant Forder was awarded the Military Medal, although his platoon awarded him the soubriquet of 'Fearless Fred'

After violent assaults on the Allied troops failed, the Germans had to concede that the Salerno bridgehead could not be dislodged and began a general withdrawal. By 5 October 1943 Naples was in Allied hands, but like Messina had been sown with a variety of mines and traps. Teams of British and US Engineers set about the task of making the area safe. The navy dealt with the port, but a section of 17 Bomb Disposal Company RE carried out much work clearing the town of other explosive devices. The section, commanded by Lieutenant J G Allen, during the period from 9–15 October cleared 85 booby-trapped and mined buildings and searched many more. At Prince Piedmont Barracks, which had been previously declared safe by other troops, a delayed-action device functioned with a massive explosion that killed 22 American soldiers. Lieutenant Allen and his section were then asked to clear the two other barracks and in doing so discovered and rendered safe a German firing mechanism connected to a charge of 725 kilograms of explosive.[6] The task was not only extremely dangerous but time- and manpower-intensive. The Americans cleared many items and the 345th Engineers spent 22,405 man-hours, over 18 days, clearing an area for the 49th Quartermaster Group. The same unit at a hospital site north of Naples recovered 230 Tellermines and 47 other mines and booby traps.

After Naples the Italian topography began to impinge on the fighting. A pattern was set for both the Allied forces pressing forward and the retreating Germans as they fell back to the Winter Line. The terrain through which the Germans moved allowed them ample opportunity to slow the Allies. Along the costal highways a popular tactic was to fell lines of big trees so that they interlocked across the road, usually in places were alternative routes were impractical. The trees would be booby-trapped and mined, and artillery and mortars would be registered on the area. It would take time, a crucial commodity in war, and a steady flow of casualties to remove the obstacle. Once cleared a short advance would reveal another and then

Soldiers standing outside Baupame Town Hall, unaware that a delayed–action mine hidden in the tower was about to explode, March 1917. (IWM E 393)

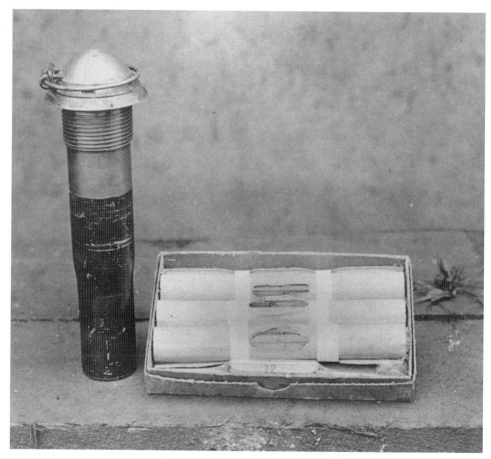

A German 1917 Pattern Long Delay Action Fuze (Lgz Z 17) used in traps and delay
mines, at the American Chemical Warfare School at Chaumont Hte, Marne, October 1918.
(IWM Am Off 29465)

A mantrap set in the German wire at Perousse, found by the Americans on 21 July 1918.
(IWM Am Off 21835)

A mine crater in the middle of the village of Athies, 9 April 1917. This gives some indication of the force of the explosion when a large charge is used. Some of the bigger delayed-action mines could have produced craters this size. (IWM Q 1941)

A German Automatic Detonating Device, an acid delay system first seen in 1917 when the Germans fell back to the Hindenburgh line. (IWM)

Driver Kenneth Arthur King was killed by an S mine in Benghazi on 19 February 1943. He was buried locally by Sid Leader and his colleagues but later moved to the Benghazi War Cemetery. (Sid Leader)

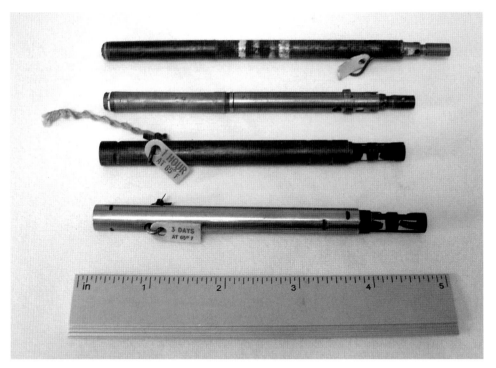

British time-delays, front to back: Switch No 9, L Delay Mk I; 3 day, 1 hour, Switch No 10; time pencils, Mk I and Mk II. These switches were produced in significant quantities and distributed widely all over the world

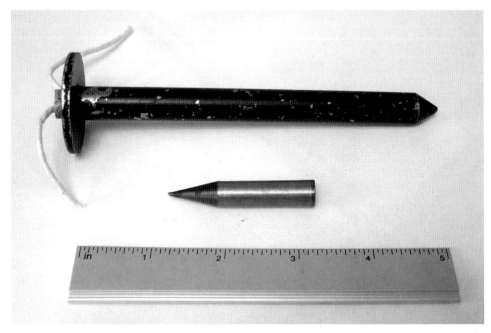

British Switch No 8, Anti-Personnel Mk I – the 'de-bollocker', or Ground Pistol Spike – with its cartridge. These were sown by Sergeant Sid Leader, RE, in North Africa and used against the Allies in Italy

A booby trap in a pear tree, consisting of an egg grenade with a pull friction fuze with the delay pellet removed and connected to a trip wire. (IWM NA 1800)

A booby-trapped wine bottle with a pull wire and 1 kilogram demolition charge, left in the ruins of the village of Faella, 21 August 1944. (IWM NA 18011)

A booby-trapped doll in the same village. (IWM NA 18007)

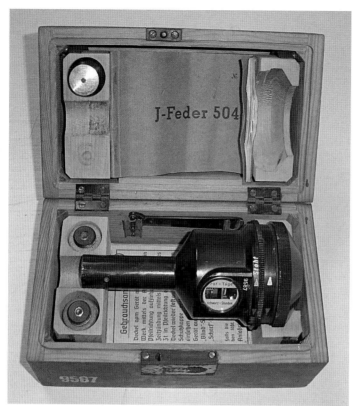

A J Feder 504 long-delay igniter in its transit pack with logbook and spare initiator sets. They were designed for sabotage or long-delay demolitions in territory to be ceded to the enemy. When deployed in this manner they were often used in conjunction with large explosive charges. (Author's collection)

A McAlpine fuze

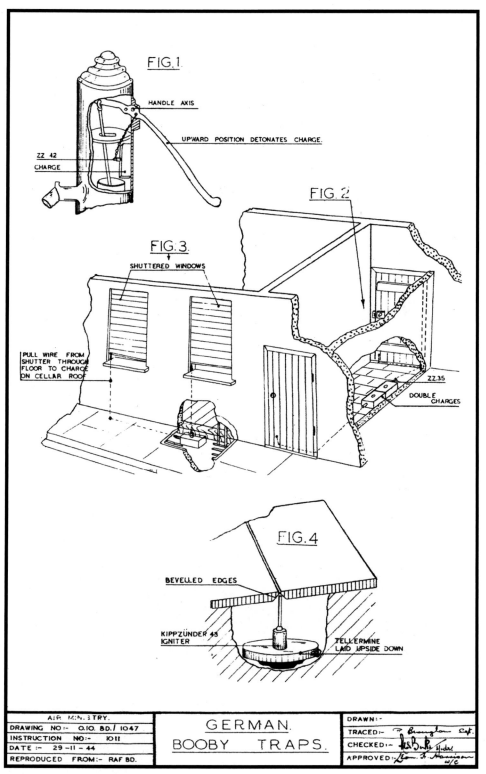

FIG. 1.

HANDLE AXIS

UPWARD POSITION DETONATES CHARGE.

ZZ 42

CHARGE

FIG. 2.

FIG. 3.

SHUTTERED WINDOWS

PULL WIRE FROM
SHUTTER THROUGH
FLOOR TO CHARGE
ON CELLAR ROOF

ZZ.35

DOUBLE
CHARGES

FIG. 4.

BEVELLED EDGES

KIPPZÜNDER 43
IGNITER

TELLERMINE
LAID UPSIDE DOWN

AIR MINISTRY.	GERMAN.	DRAWN:-
DRAWING NO :- O.IO. BD./ 1047		TRACED:- P. Bringdon Sgt.
INSTRUCTION NO:- 1011	BOOBY TRAPS.	CHECKED:-
DATE :- 29-11-44		APPROVED:-
REPRODUCED FROM:- RAF BD.		

Air Ministry bomb-disposal instructions showing a schematic of a booby-trapped house.
(PRO WO 204 5998)

The German EZ 44 anti-lift igniter, used with anti-tank mines. It was almost impossible to render safe once laid and was invariably destroyed in situ

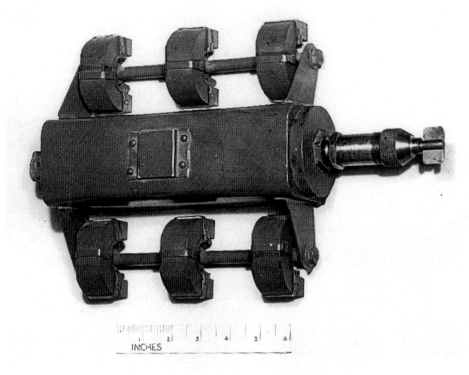

The Type 6 Limpet Mk II with a booby-trap anti-disturbance device

A booby-trapped Junker 88 night fighter, abandoned by the Germans in 1944. The examination of the radar equipment would be a high priority for allied intelligence officers and therefore a good target for a booby trap

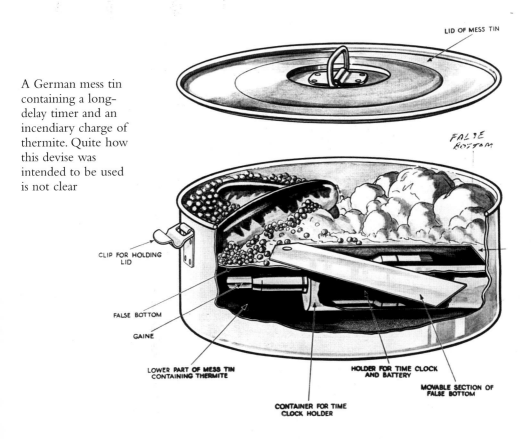

A German mess tin containing a long-delay timer and an incendiary charge of thermite. Quite how this devise was intended to be used is not clear

LID OF MESS TIN

FALSE BOTTOM

CLIP FOR HOLDING LID

FALSE BOTTOM

GAINE

LOWER PART OF MESS TIN CONTAINING THERMITE

HOLDER FOR TIME CLOCK AND BATTERY

MOVABLE SECTION OF FALSE BOTTOM

CONTAINER FOR TIME CLOCK HOLDER

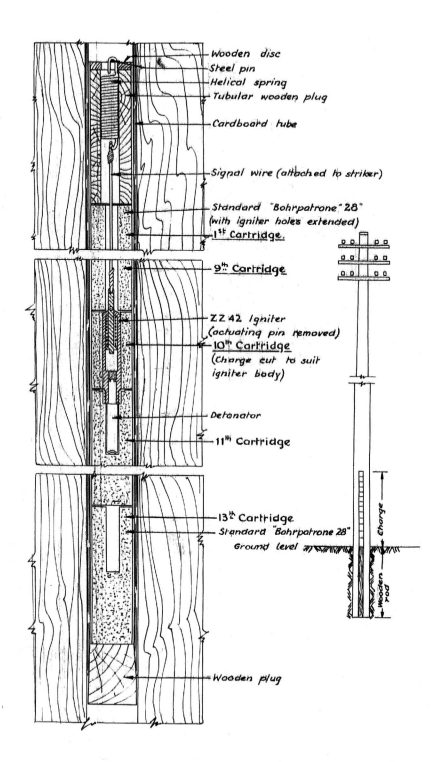

Wooden disc
Steel pin
Helical spring
Tubular wooden plug

Cardboard tube

Signal wire (attached to striker)

Standard "Bohrpatrone" 28"
(with igniter holes extended)
1ˢᵗ Cartridge.

9ᵗʰ Cartridge

ZZ 42 Igniter
(actuating pin removed)
10ᵗʰ Cartridge
(Charge cut to suit
igniter body)

Detonator

11ᵗʰ Cartridge

13ᵗʰ Cartridge
Standard "Bohrpatrone 28"
Ground level

11ᵗʰ Cartridge

Charge

Wooden rod

Wooden plug

In Greece the Germans got fed up with their communications being disrupted by saboteurs constantly cutting down telegraph poles. To stop it they booby-trapped one in four poles on one main line.

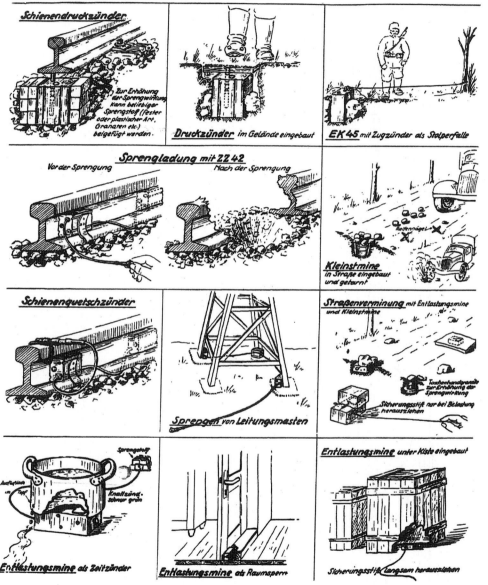

Diagrams from the German sabotage school showing methods of booby-trapping and sabotage. (PRO WO 204 12362)

A booby trap found on Tarawa: a high-explosive projectile (partly submerged in the water) connected to a pressure-firing device (shown by arrow), which was placed under the boards of the pier. (US Navy)

Palestine: A building demolished in the David Quarter of Jerusalem on 9 November 1946. A booby-trap device killed four policemen investigating an alleged arms cache

Korea: Cartoons designed to get the booby trap message through. (US Army)

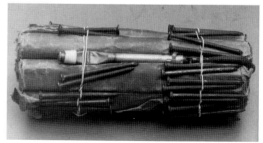

Aden: A nail bomb incorporating a British time pencil. Note that the safety strip is still in place, which would have caused the device to fail

Booby-trapped pipe bomb in Cyprus, showing the use of a German Second World War ZZ 42 igniter

Aden: The results of an explosion of a booby trap on a motorcycle

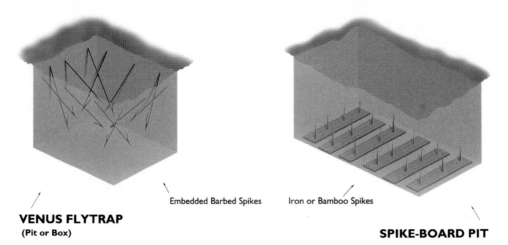

VENUS FLYTRAP
(Pit or Box)

Embedded Barbed Spikes

Iron or Bamboo Spikes

SPIKE-BOARD PIT

(Pits covered / camouflaged with bamboo stakes and leaves etc)

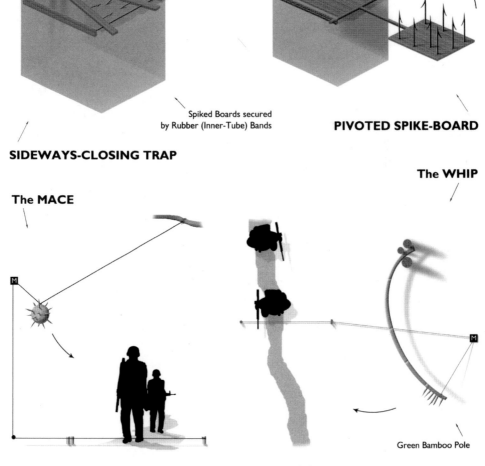

Spiked Boards secured
by Rubber (Inner-Tube) Bands

PIVOTED SPIKE-BOARD

SIDEWAYS-CLOSING TRAP

The **WHIP**

The **MACE**

Green Bamboo Pole

A selection of non-explosive traps in Vietnam. (Tony Debski)

Vietnam: A Viet Cong tunnel complex located during operation Cedar Falls in 1967. In the centre with the field phone is tunnel rat Sergeant James Lindsey, who was killed, two days after this picture was taken, by a booby trap in a tunnel

another roadblock. The Germans laid down detailed procedures for such actions. Off the roads, in the mountains, perilous trails were of vital importance, and mules had to be used to move essential stores and ammunition. Along these all the culverts and bridges would be blown. These trails were then mined and the areas around the demolitions sown with booby traps which were a constant threat to the pack trains.

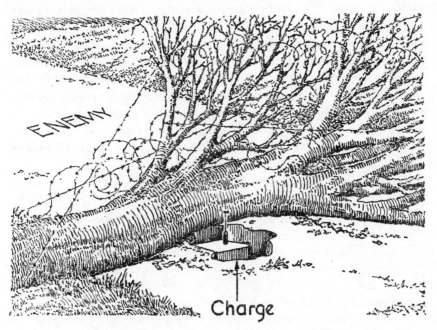

Schematic of a roadblock using felled trees and a booby trap

In the picturesque towns and villages, explosives would be used to blow out the fronts of buildings filling the narrow streets with rubble. This would invariably be mined or booby-trapped. The only way forward would be to clear the traps and then move the rubble.

As the days grew shorter, the winter came early in 1943. Rain fell incessantly, day after day, turning streams into raging torrents and the flat lands into quagmires. The engineers on both sides became invaluable. Each German infantry division had its own engineer battalion manned by some of the most skilful and versatile troops. They were expert practitioners in penetrating and laying minefields, breaching obstacles, constructing obstacles and laying booby traps and delayed-action devices. On the Allied side the engineers were equally first-class troops, and cleared the German obstacles and built new roads and bridges in the most appalling conditions. Such men were in constant employment, regularly at the front with the infantry and always a prime target for the German mortars and artillery, which as already noted were invariably registered on the sites of demolished bridges and other obstacles.

Brian Harpur was commissioned in the 1st Battalion of the Princess Louise's Kensington Regiment, The Middlesex Regiment, and fought up the length of Italy; he was decorated at Monte Cassino and later awarded a Military Cross in 1945. During the battle of the river Sangro in November 1943 he briefly met an old school friend in the Royal Engineers, identified simply as Terence. He was involved in a night crossing of the river to clear mines from the enemy side. They had to advance through the rain and ford the river crawling on to the bank through the freezing mud. Only then could they begin edging forward sweeping or probing for mines, knowing that at any moment machine-gun fire, mortars or artillery might descend upon them. The task required complete concentration as any lapse might result in an explosion. If a mine was located it had to be checked for booby traps before it could be neutralised and removed.

According to Brian Harpur, Terence died in such a task:

> The next day I learnt that the shattered body of Terence had been found in a trench. He had been in the process of lifting a mine in open ground when he was caught by some mortar fire which the enemy had a habit of putting down at irregular intervals just to harass our own positions. He had jumped into a slit trench, which appeared, miraculously at hand for his protection. What he did not know was that it had been recently vacated by the enemy who had booby trapped it by placing a mine at the bottom.[7]

In a similar incident it was reported in *Achtung! Mines*, an American training pamphlet, that a British NCO was killed in a booby-trapped trench in the following manner. Allegedly a German Luger, a prize possession, was found lying in a street. The NCO being wary of a trap explained to his men that the safest way to deal with such a weapon was to put a line on it and pull it from a safe location. He approached the pistol and tied the end of a length of line round the trigger guard and then carried the other end over to a convenient foxhole, his intention being to pull the pistol to activate any traps from a safe location. However when the NCO jumped into the foxhole he was caught by a double bluff because the Germans anticipating this reaction had mined the trench with S mines, which functioned, killing the NCO.[8]

It has proved impossible to obtain first-hand or corroborative accounts of the incident, nor that recounted in the introduction, and it may well be that they are apocryphal. However, it is probable that they reflect the sorts of traps that had been encountered. One of the difficulties with this type of incident is that there was no formal system of investigation into what had happened. Therefore when a booby trap of this nature functioned, killing or maiming soldiers, quite often, other than dealing with the casualties and perhaps a quick look at the scene, there was simply no time for a detailed investigation into the events leading up to the tragedy. The fact that many booby traps used large charges meant that often there would be nothing left to investigate anyway.

Back on the ground in Italy this difficult and dangerous work continued. The American 111th Engineer Combat Battalion, part of the 36th US Infantry Division, reported on operations in November 1943 as they approached and attacked Mount Lungo. This account provides an insight into what was involved. The clearance of mines and traps both before an assault and after areas had been seized was of vital importance, the unit diary records some of the items dealt with:

> 16th November – During the progress of the attack on Mt LUNGO twenty-four S mines and 12 booby traps were found. The charges on the booby traps were of wide variation ranging from hand grenades to Tellermines.
>
> 18th November – All mines and booby traps encountered by the infantry during the attack on Mt LUNGO were removed.
>
> 22nd November – The second platoon worked on a road by pass three miles east of MIGANO and began checking the road leading to LECAVE for mines and booby traps. Four wooden German box mines were found in this area. It was during this search on the road leading to LECAVE that an explosion of a booby trap, which had been placed in a dug-out beside a road, killed Technician Grade V Stanley Dardginski.[9]

On the Adriatic coast the Gustav line was anchored at Ortona, which could not be easily by-passed. The town was defended by a battalion of the elite German 1st Parachute Division and was to be attacked and seized by the Canadians. It was a classic example of defensive tactics at their very best and showed how determined, well-motivated soldiers could, in built-up areas, ensnarl the attacking troops in a bitter, stubborn and vicious battle. Each sturdy Italian house they elected to defend was turned into a strong point, others they blew down to open fields of fire and mined the rubble. Buildings left intact were turned into death traps by booby traps, or by large hidden delayed-action charges. The clash commenced two days before Christmas 1943, with the Canadians advancing into the town, house-by-house and street-by-street, in fighting that continued with unabated fury.

On 27 December, a house with an officer and 23 men from the Edmonton Regiment was blown up by a large delayed-action charge. Only four men were dug out alive from the ruins. Retaliation was swift. Two buildings occupied by the paratroops were reconnoitred under cover of smoke, and the infantry pioneers laid heavy charges of captured explosives during the night. When these were blown simultaneously, it was estimated that two German platoons were destroyed.[10]

On the west coast, the Germans used the time gained by delaying tactics in the Winter Line to prepare one of their strongest natural defensive positions south of Rome. Based on a series of fortified positions on the hills and mountains, including Monte Cassino, which overlooked the Rapido and Garigalono rivers, the Germans had a formidable line of defence. The strong points included belts of deep dugouts and machine-gun positions, slit trenches and concrete bunkers. Double wire fences, booby traps and trip-wire mines protected these with other devices concealed amongst the reeds and the brush of the riverbanks. A cunning German trap was encountered during the crossing of the Garigalono river by the 2nd Battalion of the Northamptonshire Regiment. During bitter fighting A Company had managed to cross the river but found themselves isolated and running short of ammunition. The sappers despite their best efforts were unable to bridge the river. The only practical method of supplying the beleaguered infantry was by boat. This was achieved by using two RAF Wellington bomber life rafts that were discovered close by. Both, however, had been booby-trapped and had to be cleared before they could be used. The Germans had clearly anticipated that the British would be short of boats to cross the river and realising this had trapped the two they left behind. The Northamptonshire Regiment history also records the outstanding work undertaken by Captain A J Roberts and the men of the pioneer platoon who did sterling work lifting anti-personnel mines from the supply routes during this period.

About this time a German officer with an armoured pioneer battalion spoke of the importance of mining and booby-trapping.

> A Tellermine should be laid every 50 to 100m or 100 to 200m. Very many dummy mines (metal, pieces of every kind) should be laid between the two real mines. If an enemy motor vehicle strikes a mine then they will naturally look for other mines. He will then look for other mines and find only dummy mines which will tend to irritate him, but eventually he will become careless after searching for mines along a stretch of 100m without finding anything but iron fragments. After he has become tired of searching and drives

148

on, several other vehicles may pass over a live mine before one comes along which causes it to explode. In this way almost every mine becomes effective and the enemy has corresponding losses. In addition, the enemy becomes very uncertain in his movements, he is greatly influenced psychologically, and ceases to have confidence in the safety of the highway even when it has been travelled by several vehicles.

If he wants to be absolutely sure, he has to examine each highway for a distance of several kilometres. He has to remove every rusty nail and loses so much time that this proves advantageous to our own troops.

In addition, all turning places on roads and all widening should be planted with two or three mines. It is not necessary for the first vehicle to cause the mine to explode. The main thing is that the mine should detonate at some time or another. Some vehicle will want to park at this point or try pass other vehicle, and that will prove fatal. Another advantage of this erratic mining is that trained combat engineers must be at hand to deal with the problem.

Parking places should also be mined, not only with anti-tank mines, but also with anti-personnel S mines. These should be employed in a thoroughly erratic manner and no system should be used. The mines should be laid along the edge of these places, on footpaths leading to them and points where troops are likely to erect their tents and deposit their weapons.

When so employed, the mine is a very effective weapon of the combat engineer. It will not only cause losses to the enemy but it will also serve to disintegrate his morale. He will soon be unable to get rid of a feeling of insecurity, and he will be afraid of striking a mine at every step and on every trip.

Greater use than before must be made of the so-called engineering deviltries [*sic*: German *Pionierschweinerrefen*]. Every piano, every accordion, old tin cans lying around, house doors, windows, chairs everything imaginable before our own lines must be planted with explosives. Whenever the enemy touches any thing, he must always have casualties. The charges must be so powerful that they do not serve merely as frightening charges, but always inflict losses on the enemy.[11]

There is evidence to support the view that a well-laid trap needs only to wait for a victim. In August 1944 2 Platoon of 7 Field Company RE went on detachment to Lake Piedilucio, the place chosen for a permanent divisional rest camp. The platoon camped on the edge of lake and began erecting German sectional timber huts and general plumbing work. In the course of this construction work Sapper T Lawson and H Footitt had a lucky escape when they were held up for some reason one morning. As a result, they were not in the boiler room when an undetected German booby trap in the heating boiler blew up and killed two men from the 2nd/4th Hampshire Regiment.[12]

On the fourth attempt and after a massive bombardment, and some of the bitterest fighting, Monte Cassino fell to the Allies in May. The advance to Rome began, but any thoughts that it would be a rapid advance to the city were quickly dispelled. The Germans continued to fight a skilful and controlled withdrawal falling back on a series of pre-prepared defence lines. J M Lee-Harvey who fought with the Eighth Army wrote:

> One had to be so careful because there were booby traps every-where. It was obvious that Jerry in retreat was determined to cause as much havoc as he could and it was so easy to be careless in the exhilaration of a victorious advance. It was never certain that the dead bodies and equipment left behind would not be booby-trapped and it was advisable to keep to the roads and not venture on any mission of exploration, tempting as it might be.[13]

He went on to explain how he and a friend ignored this advice:

> I did, however, with Jim, a Scot from Stirling, go into a large house by the side of the road. We entered through the back door very care-fully and found the room was full of Italian red devils and other anti-personnel mines. The floor was strewn with them and it was vital to pick your way very carefully across the room ensuring that these instruments of death were not disturbed in any way. There were many of what the British soldier called de-bollockers. This was a particularly fiendish device shaped like a pencil and placed in the ground at a certain angle. When trod on, a spring would be pressed down and as the foot rose so the spring would release a catch expelling explosive at the required angle to shoot off the soldier's penis and testicles. As can be imagined, this was a particularly fright-ening prospect and after the first casualty had been reported every-body was very wary.

Harvey would probably been even more disgruntled had he known that the most probably origin of these devices was SOE. The US authorities also recorded finding SOE sabotage equipment in Italy and not knowing what it was. It is clear that the 'pencil-shaped de-bollockers' which were so feared by Harvey were in fact stocks of captured British Switches, No. 8 Anti-personnel Mark I. These as we have seen were made by MD1 and were designed to fire a cartridge vertically propelling the bullet into the victim.

Other sabotage devices, both Allied and enemy came to light during the Italian campaign. On 24 December 1943 the Allied Force HQ issued a warning about the possible use of Speedwell oil tin sabotage bombs by the Germans. It said

> Info from a source recently in contact with the enemy, which has proved reliable in the past and which is of paramount importance to safeguard indicates that this device is likely to be used behind Allied lines in Italy.[14]

That Speedwell oil tin bombs existed is not in doubt as the diagram below shows. A more difficult question to answer is who made them. They are recorded as enemy equipment but it has proved impossible to verify this. They may have been made for SOE, the security services or another covert agency. These were really camouflaged charges which required a detonator, battery and some form of timer to make a device.

A Speedwell tin

Another report was received that a child had been injured at Arezzo on 14 August 1944 by a device camouflaged to look like hair dye. Surprisingly even in wartime it seemed people wanted to disguise their grey hair. The trap was in the form of a tube 3¼ inches long and half an inch in diameter, made of metal with a hexagonal milled edge cap. Round the narrow end of the tube was a band of purple. The remainder of the tube was black with decorative printed material in white.

Further investigation into the incident, however, indicated that the pencil was not a device. It was confirmed by a Lieutenant Colonel Gibson RE that one specimen of the 'pencil' was dissected by bomb disposal officers and no trace of explosive or mechanism found therein. Furthermore, no other specimens of this device were found, and no fragments of the one, which was reported to have exploded, were recovered.[15]

There was a report, which described the booby-trapping of German wireless sets. These were used by German Secret Service wireless operators, and were hidden by being buried in the earth. In the event that Allied authorities unearthed them they would explode if incorrectly opened. The sets were placed in a special box, the lid of which had two knobs. These appeared to be for the purpose of lifting the lid of the box. However, they were actually connected to two small bombs about the size of a hand grenade, which were concealed in the lid of the box lid itself. When the knobs were pulled the bombs were set off. In order to open the box safely the lid had to be opened by the two edges, thereby not setting off the bombs. After opening the lid the two bombs could have been disposed of intact.[16]

At the front, the Allies continued their advance and the Germans continued to lay traps for the unwary. The weather was still a major factor; it was bitterly cold with strong winds and snowfalls making surviving a problem, let alone fighting. Young soldiers lived for days in the open on hills or mountainsides pushed to the extremes of fatigue by constant cold, sleepless nights and the ever present fear of death or injury from a shell, mortar or mine. The Germans destroyed the scenic villages by attaching Tellermines to the houses and farms and detonating them as they left. To add insult, they would leave scrawled messages: 'Hope you like your winter billets Tommy.' If any buildings were left then it was a brave or foolish man who ventured inside without thoroughly checking for traps first.

One night a small enemy patrol infiltrated their way through the American lines and cut an artillery telephone wire leaving the ends some ten yards apart. They then buried two S mines so that about an inch of a pull igniter was showing above ground. Each of the loose ends of the wire was attached to the S mines with a length of fine cord. The result was that in the dark when a linesman picked up the loose end of the telephone wire and pulled it to mend the break, the fine line attached to one of the S mines caused it to explode.

In another incident, a box of Tellermines in their original packing case was discovered apparently abandoned. However the mines had had pull igniters attached to them so that anyone deciding to use the mines and extracting them from their packaging would be killed.[17]

In many cases the Germans would use a combination of various mines and booby traps thickly sown to deny the Allies access to particular locations. A typical example of a booby-trapped villa was reported in Air Ministry Instructions to RAF Bomb Disposal Units in December 1944. An Italian villa, presumably well suited for use as an HQ was trapped in the following manner. The gates at the entrance had been wired with ZZ 42 igniters linked to buried demolition charges so that anyone opening the gates would detonate the hidden explosive. The avenue leading up to the villa was mined with Schu mines buried at least 2 inches deep. These were small wooden box-mines that were very difficult to detect. In addition S mines were hidden in bushes with tripwires across avenues and others buried in a bank with tripwires at chest height.

Inside the villa itself a variety of traps had been laid, again making use of an assortment of munitions. A stick grenade with several loose grenade heads was found buried in the springs of a chair. This was fired by a pull igniter attached by a tripwire to a door which would function if the door was opened, the chair was moved or, finally, if the wire between the chair and the door was tripped. In other furniture, Schu mines were wedged into position so that anyone sitting on the chair would cause the mine to function. Finally a mattress was found with a 3-kilogram charge hidden in it and arranged to fire if anyone sat or laid on it.[18]

The same report also detailed the use of large hidden delayed-action charges linked to the German Long-Delay Timer, the *J Feder 504*. This was one of the most elaborate pieces of demolition equipment available to the Germans and gained its name from the time-delay of 21 days or 504 hours. It was a precision-engineered clockwork timer designed for sabotage or long-delay demolitions in territory to be ceded to the enemy 'according to plan'. It could only be employed on the authority of an army commander. The timers were all serial numbered and were packed in special wooden boxes. They were regularly tested and the results of the tests recorded in a logbook. The allowable inaccuracy of the clock was +10 to −15 minutes in 24 hours and + or −5 hours in 21 days. Generally they were much more accurate that, but the figures took into account the extremes of temperature from the desert to the frozen wastes of Russia. The minimum official time for the mechanism was 15 hours, although in practice it could be set for just a few minutes. The reason for this was that it was the intention to limit the employment of this expensive store for tasks that could not be as efficiently accomplished by other timers.

One example of these systems used in Italy was a charge of 350 pounds of explosive, set with a J Feder 504 with the maximum 21 days' delay, hidden in the basement of a vegetable store in a farm house. The timer had been laid on its side and inserted into the explosive and the charge covered with boards and dirt. The local population had no knowledge of the charge. In a second case, a delay of 14 days was used in a device hidden behind a stone wall and beneath the floor of a schoolhouse sub-basement. The charge was 500 hundred pounds of explosive. This had also been booby-trapped with another 10-pound charge attached to a tripwire, so arranged that, if activated, the smaller charge would set off the main charge. In a third case, a layer of approximately 350 pounds of dynamite had been concealed in the 2-inch airspace between the floor and concrete subfloor of a post office. The timer was set for 14 days. When the charge was found and examined it was discovered that the J Feder 504 had functioned but for some inexplicable reason the main charge had failed to detonate.

The town of Colle Ferro had a large explosives factory with storage areas in the surrounding hills. Before departing the Germans left delayed-action demolitions in ammunition storage bins timed to go off three days later. In addition charges consisting of 500-pound bombs were left under all the bridges that had not already been blown. Fortunately for the Americans, among the prisoners taken was a German sergeant who had helped place the explosives. He was temporarily liberated from a prisoner of war camp and assisted the Engineers in locating and disarming the charges.[19]

The intensity of the mine and booby-trap warfare continued increasing right up to the end of the war in Italy. The Germans, unable to fight a decisive battle, continued their withdrawals, but never gave up ground without causing maximum delays and casualties. The ingenuity and thoroughness in using demolitions mines and traps never ceased. In particular elite troops seemed to make good use of them. In the *History of the British First Division* from 28 August to 12 September 1944, when describing the enemy it noted:

> 4 Parachute Division were our principal opponents during this stage. They were good troops and particularly nasty users of mines and booby traps.[20]

In some towns the problem of clearing these cunningly set traps was made even more complicated by small pockets of enemy machine-gunners or snipers. It can be imagined that the sappers or pioneers in the vanguard of the advance became very anxious about clearing such areas. There could be nothing worse than attempting to neutralise a mine or trap only to be sniped at or have a burst of machine-gun fire rip through the air above you. The stark alternatives were to throw yourself down on ground that had not been cleared or make a dash for cover through the same uncleared land.

One of the bravest actions carried out by the sappers was when they were called upon to recover casualties from mined or booby-trapped areas. Although on many occasions fearless soldiers would try to rescue their injured comrades, if they in turn tripped further devices and became casualties, the situation simply got worse, and the difficult and abhorrent decision had to be made to leave the wounded until the area was safely cleared. The pressure to try and recover men wounded and lying helpless in the open was immense. On 29 May 1945 sappers from 625 Field Squadron RE were tasked to do just this, and had to clear booby traps from houses in Fontana Liri to enable casualties from the Royal Berkshires to be removed.

The Germans however did not have it all their own way. In one action 625 Field Squadron RE were called upon to lay booby traps in front of their brigade defensive positions. Some of these consisted of special beehive charges laid on their sides and fitted with tripwires. The beehives were special demolition stores using the hollow-charge principle designed to penetrate armour or produce bore-holes in rock. They contained a charge of 3 kilograms of high explosive. The beehives were laid on their sides and tripwires attached so that if the wire were tripped the explosive jets from the charges would be fired horizontally down the length of the wire. In one case a small field of such charges accounted for several German dead and many others wounded. As always, though, these types of trap are often indiscriminate. During November 1944 beehives were laid extensively both by 625 and 626 Field Squadrons RE for their respective brigades. One or two were set off by stray animals. One outpost reported seeing an old woman trip one beehive. Although knocked down by the blast, she was seen to pick herself up, shake her head and run into a nearby house. This apparent failure might be explained by the fact that some beehives were laid with their axes pointing down the track, i.e., at an angle to the tripwire, in the hope of catching not only the unfortunate who tripped the wire, but the other members of the patrol who were following.[21]

Another winter ploy which 626 Field Squadron RE were asked to consider by the 1st Guards Brigade was the use of explosive sledges. It was intended that these would be piled high with explosives and then would be pushed down a hill towards the unsuspecting Germans in their positions. It is not clear how the sledges would be steered, or the charges fired, but it was noted that the snow melted before the opportunity for testing them had presented itself, much to the relief of the sappers involved.

Fortunately not all the traps worked and some soldiers had the luck of the devil. An American Technical Report recounted the story that one cellar full of gin and whisky was so effectively booby-trapped that it had to be destroyed, despite the desperate efforts of the Commander Royal Engineers and one of his Bomb Disposal Officers to save the drink. The booby traps were first discovered when a soldier from a Highland Regiment was seen to emerge from the cellar flushed and happy with a full interior load and several bottles of VAT 69 (whisky) in his arms. When accosted by some local sappers, he pointed to his treasure saying that he:

> Couldn'a understand why all the bottles were tied with bits of string.[22]

Notes

1 PRO WO 204/5991, Bomb Disposal Intelligence Summary Number 14 dated October 1943.

2 Land Mines and Booby Traps, FM 31, War Department, United States Government Printing Office, 1943.

3 Pöppel, Martin, (trs. L Willmott) *Heaven and Hell, The War Diary of a German Paratrooper*, Spellmount, Tunbridge Wells, 1988.

4 PRO ADM 1/14567.

5 Landmine and Countermine Warfare, US Report 1972 – The Italian Campaign.

6 Hogben, Major Arthur, *Designed To Kill*, Patrick Stevens, Wellingborough, 1987.

7 Harpur, Brian, *The Impossible Victory*, William Kimber, London, 1980.

8 Wallace, Captain H Jamison, 'Achtung! Minen', *Infantry Journal*, November 1943.

9 *op. cit.*, note 5.

10 Jefferies, Lt Col J C, Account from Loyal Edmonton Regiment, 27 December 1943.

11 Notes on the experiences in mine laying and shelter construction. US Engineer Research Office January 1945.

12 Riordan, Thomas M J, *7th Field Company RE 1939–1946, The 'Shiny 7th' at War*, T M J Riordan, York, c. 1984.

13 Lee Harvey, J M, *D Day Dodger*, William Kimber, London, 1979.

14 PRO WO 204/12239, Sabotage Reports, HQ Allied Armies, Italy, 24 December 1943.

15 *op. cit.*, note 14, Main HQ Eighth Army HQ CMF, 11 October 1944.

16 *op. cit.*, note 14, Sabotage Reports, 45 US G2, Staff Document AP0 512.
17 Army Service Forces, Ordnance Department, Ordnance Bomb Disposal Center, Aberdeen Proving Ground MD, USA, Bomb Disposal Technical Information Bulletin No 44, dated 1945.
18 PRO WO 204/5998, Air Ministry Instructions to Bomb Disposal Units Number 1011, dated 29 November 1944.
19 Burhans, Lt Colonel R D, *The First Special Service Force – A War History of the North Americans 1942–44,* Washington DC, Infantry Journal Press.
20 *History of the First Division, Florence to Monte Grande, August 1944–January 1945.* Schindler's Press, Cairo, 1946.
21 *The Royal Engineers Sixth Armoured Division,* Tipografia Antoniana, Padova, 1946.
22 *op. cit.*, note 1, Bomb Disposal Summaries including reports of Aberdeen Proving Ground.

CHAPTER 6

Sabotage

*Your object is to embarrass the enemy in every possible way so as to make
it more difficult for his armies to fight on the main front.*

Partisan Leader's Handbook

No account of the malicious use of explosives would be complete without
addressing their use in sabotage operations. There is a mass of material on
this subject covering both the devices and their deployment. Once the
surface is scratched a myriad of plots and plans emerge from the secret and
shadowy world of the intelligence agencies, special forces and the resistance
movements they sponsored. To support them a wide range of explosive
stores and specialist weapons was developed and deployed. As is often the
case in war, the more complex the plan or more complicated the device,
the less likely it was that they would work. Equally there was often a dis-
crepancy between what could reasonably be done on active service and
what was proposed. Many of the backroom staff, although indispensable,
had no actual understanding of real operational requirements. A good idea
in the comfort and safety of a laboratory does not always translate into an
effective device for use on operations in hostile enemy territory. It will be
recalled that MD1 was sometimes known as 'Winston Churchill's Toy
Shop'. The view that the staff were designing deadly toys for the operatives
of SOE and the resistance movements suggests some sort of game. It was
not for those out in the field. The Germans regarded sabotage, even when
carried out by regular troops from the SAS or Commandos, as an act punishable by death.

There can be no doubt that the various agencies and resistance movements did impair German military power both materially and morally.
Without a detailed study it is impossible accurately to assess the impact of
attacks against the infrastructure and transport systems. And it must be
remembered that not all sabotage required the use of explosives. Mislabelled
rolling stock or misdirected trains could result in logistic delays with vital
equipment arriving in the wrong place, at the wrong time and miles from
where it was needed.

159

It is convenient to examine the subject now because during the Second World War, just prior to and after the Normandy landings, the German Armies of occupation right across Europe had to contend with thousands of sabotage attacks. In Russia, Yugoslavia, Greece, France and many other occupied lands, the Resistance, partisans or guerrillas, call them what you will, were becoming a growing threat to the Third Reich.

These fighters, with the exception of the Russian partisans later in the war, could never challenge the Germans directly. A group of fighters, often poorly trained and ill-equipped, was no match for any of the German divisions, even those, which were second rate. Four thousand Maquis discovered this to their cost during the uprising in Vercors in June 1944. The area, a great plateau southwest of Grenoble, consisted of some 300 square miles of wood and rolling countryside protected by rocky approaches that were considered defendable against the Germans. In the event the German 157th Reserve Division with the aid of Stukas and a small force of some 200 commandos who landed by glider wiped out some 650 of them, the remainder being forced to flee in disarray. Those that escaped reverted to the classic hit-and-run tactics, which proved so successful elsewhere.

In the East the Germans had to contend with attacks by the Russian partisans. Initially in some areas the Germans were welcomed and treated as liberators. However, the harsh and often murderous treatment of the population ensured that the resistance to occupation grew. The scale compared with that in Western Europe was immense; at its peak it involved some 250,000 partisans and 500,000 men in the Axis security forces. It rapidly became a ruthless and barbaric war. The partisans, eventually controlled by the Red Army, exercised total rule over the people in the areas they dominated. Collaboration with the Germans, even in the face of starvation, was punishable by death. The Germans for their part took brutal reprisals against the civilian population regardless of whether or not there was proof of guilt.

In the 'Battle of the Rails' behind the Army Group Centre Front the partisans, in the period from 1 September to 1 November 1943, are estimated to have carried out some 32,000 attacks on the railways. These attacks unquestionably caused problems for the Germans during their retreat to the Dniepr. In early 1944 there was a reasonably quiet period during which the partisans conserved their explosives for the biggest attack of the war which was against the German rear areas. This took place on the nights of 19–21 June to support the Soviet Belorussian offensive due to begin on the anniversary of the German invasion of the motherland on 23 June 1944. During the night the partisans brought all railway traffic to a standstill, often using chain demolitions, which destroyed long lengths of track. The

160

Germans estimated that in total there were 10,500 demolitions and that they recovered some 3,500 mines and traps. Although there were no demolitions, on the actual night of the offensive the damage was enough to prevent the Germans bringing forward desperately needed reinforcements.[1]

Booby traps were used, chiefly to delay the repair of damaged railways. Particularly effective were deeply buried delay charges designed to function hours, days and, in some cases, weeks after they were laid. These had electrical clock mechanisms, which allowed the partisans to target the nearest repair parties. The result was that simply sweeping for contact mines was not enough to stop attacks and prevent further delays and casualties.

The partisans also relied on the assassination of German soldiers, officials and collaborators to lower morale and deter other Russian civilians helping the enemy. Their greatest success was the killing of Wilhelm Kube, General Commissar of Belorussia on 22 September 1943. This was carried out by one of his 'intimate' serving girls who placed a mine in his bed and blew him up. Goebbels wrote of the occurrence:

> This shows what dangers leading National Socialists must face, especially in the occupied territories in the East. To remain alive in the present crisis one can not be too careful.[2]

It is inconceivable that this was the only such attack and that the partisans did not leave other devilish devices to trap and terrorise the German invaders. While all this activity did not prevent the Germans from controlling the key areas of the occupied territories it helped to undermine their military power. It did produce delays, inconveniences, a need to revise plans constantly and forced vast numbers of troops, albeit often second line soldiers, to be placed on guard duties around vulnerable points and to patrol in other areas to deter attacks.

In the West, SOE was, in Churchill's words, established to 'Set Europe ablaze'. If it were to do so it would require both the trained personnel in place and the necessary explosives and other specialist equipment to carry out the task. It was made clear from the start that as far as SOE were concerned irregular warfare was a no holds barred operation.

In north-west Europe, one of the problems was that because of the lack of an allocation of suitable aircraft, the necessary explosives and other stores could not be supplied in significant quantities. Even so in France in the year before D-Day effective action was directed against the railway system. French saboteurs, supported by the available SOE dropped stores, cut tracks, blew up bridges and destroyed locomotives. Between June 1943 and May 1944, 1,822 locomotives were damaged, 200 passenger cars destroyed and a further 1,500 damaged, in addition 2,500 freight cars were destroyed and 8,000 damaged. In the month after D-Day the attacks continued and were particularly effective in isolating the Normandy battlefield. During June a total of 486 rail cuts were reported. On 7 June 1944 26 trunk lines were unusable including the main lines between Avranches and St Lo, St Lo and Cherbourg, and between St Lo and Caen. All were sabotaged with multiple cuts.[3]

One of the most important stores used in the destruction of the railways was the 'British Igniter Fuze Signal Fog Mk 1'. Rather than just cut the railway it was designed to function as a train passed over it, the resulting destruction being a much more pleasing outcome for the saboteur. The device was a simple adaptation of a peacetime railway signal fog. These were needed in emergency to warn drivers to stop, and as implied by the name, were usually used in foggy conditions when signals could not be seen. They consisted of a small metal body with three internal percussion caps and some quick-match flash composition. In normal use the body is attached to the top of a railway line by a simple wire clip and when the train runs over it the percussion caps are fired, setting off the quick match which provided the necessary flash-and-bang to warn drivers to stop. The adapted signals fog had a detonator attached to the side of the body. This time when it was crushed by the wheels of the train, the percussion caps fired, ignited the quick match, which in turn set off the detonator. This would be linked by Cordtex to a main charge attached to the rails. In the early deployments the importance of ensuring that the detonator faced the outside of the line was not realised. After a number of failed attacks it was discovered that if the signal fog was placed on the line with the detonator inwards, then as the wheel of the train passed over it the percussion caps would be set off, but at almost the same instant the inner flange on the wheel would slice off the detonator before it functioned. This was simply remedied by ensuring the saboteurs attached the switch to the railway line with the detonator facing outwards. The number of failures then significantly reduced. Additionally, when deployed normally, two signals fog would be used. If the direction of an oncoming train was known then both would be deployed in advance of the charges. If it were not known which way the train would come then one signal fog would be deployed at either side of the line cutting charges. When correctly deployed and used in pairs this simple device proved reliable and effective in destroying trains.

The standard explosive charge produced by SOE contained 3 pounds of plastic explosive with a central primer tube. It was brick shaped measuring 10½ × 2½ × 2½ inches and wrapped in rubberised fabric. It could easily be split into two 1½-pound slabs to enable it to be deployed more flexibly. A

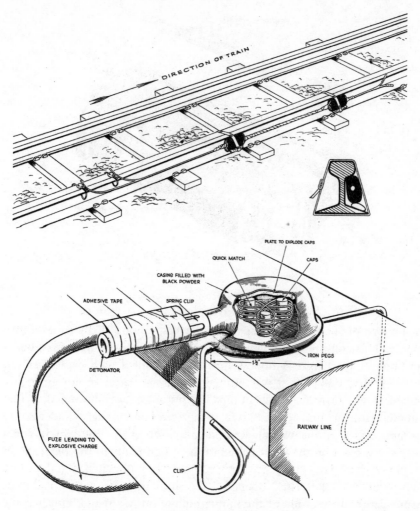

A railway line prepared for demolition

linear cutting charge, using the hollow charge principle, was developed for attacking girders. One of the most popular stores was the clam. This small, palm-sized charge was ideal for attacking machinery. It took the form of a rectangular box with rounded corners on the upper surface. At each end were powerful magnets securely fitted into their own compartments. In the centre there was room for a charge of half-a-pound of high explosive. Initiation was by time pencil or L delay which fitted into a slot in the top of the clam.

By 1945 MD1 and ISRB had developed a whole array of booby-trap and sabotage equipment, listed in a catalogue of special devices.[4] This detailed

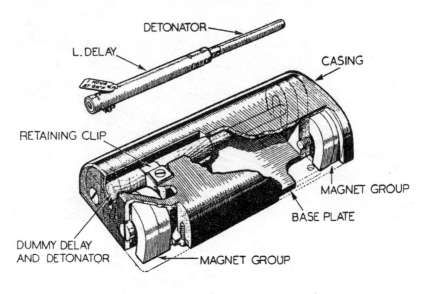

DETONATOR

L. DELAY

CASING

RETAINING CLIP

MAGNET GROUP

BASE PLATE

DUMMY DELAY
AND DETONATOR

MAGNET GROUP

Clam

a number of special victim-operated devices, among them an explosive pump. This consisted of an apparently normal bicycle pump with a built-in booby-trap charge. A hollow brass cylinder filled with explosives and fitted with a pull switch was pushed inside the barrel of an apparently normal German-issue bicycle pump. The piston rod was shortened, so that air could still be pumped into a tyre, two grooves on the side cylinder acting as air passages. A nut was soldered on to the top of the pull switch, and a screw was fixed on the end of the piston. When required to operate as an explosive device the piston was screwed on to the pull switch, and the safety pin withdrawn. The latter operation was done by removing a small brass nameplate from the side of the pump, pulling out a pin and replacing the plate. To use it, the saboteur would remove the enemy's pump and replace it with the armed explosive one. The next step was to deflate a tyre and retreat and wait for the owner to return. A soldier returning to his bike and finding the tyre flat would naturally remove the pump to re-inflate it. The action of pulling out the piston would of course operate the pull switch and it would not be the tyre that was blown up but the unfortunate soldier. In total some 138 of these devices were made.

Another device, which has been used on more than one occasion since by terrorists, is the explosive-filled torch. The SOE example could be used either as a grenade or a booby trap and was again manufactured from captured German equipment, this time torches. Two of the three batteries in the torch were removed and their place taken by a cylindrical, deeply

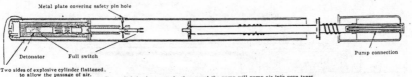

Metal plate covering safety pin hole

Detonator   Full switch

Pump connection

Two sides of explosive cylinder flattened, to allow the passage of air.
1. Using slightly shorter stroke than usual the pump will pump air into your tyres.
2. When the piston is screwed into the pull switch the device is then ready to operate as a booby trap.

The SOE explosive pump

grooved bomb filled with baratol (a mixture of barium nitrate and TNT). This was initiated by means of an electrical igniter and a short length of safety fuse connected to a detonator. The delay to initiation was 4–5 seconds. The normal switch on the outside of the torch was adapted so that the current could flow to the torch bulb, or, after the removal of a small safety pin, to the electrical igniter. This allowed for the torch to pass a casual inspection and operate normally if examined at a checkpoint. However once the safety pin was removed it would detonate if switched on. The reason for the short delay was to allow the torch to be used as a grenade giving the operator time to throw it before it exploded.

Even more bizarre were exploding droppings, stones and rocks. These utilised a store known as a tyre burster. This consisted of a small metal container made of two halves, each slightly smaller in size than a shoe-polish tin. It contained 70 grams of high explosive and a simple, pressure–activated, firing switch. These were produced in large quantities – by the end of the war over 1½ million had been manufactured. For camouflage the tyre bursters were built into various items. To imitate droppings successfully, distinguished experts such as Professor Julian Huxley, then secretary of the London Zoological Society, and experts from the Natural History Museum were enlisted as advisors. The droppings were made of papier mâché and painted by hand. The aim apparently was to allow a resistance fighter who might be driving a horse and cart to drop these devices in front of German cars or marching troops. The inventor seemed convinced that enemy drivers would get pleasure out of running over such piles of mess and would be blown up for their troubles. David Smiley, an SOE agent, used these stores to assist in the attack of some Germans in Albania. He set up an ambush on a bridge, in which a large explosive charge was laid and detonated via a command wire. The ambush party then spread a number of the tyre bursters, these particular ones camouflaged as mule droppings, on the bridge. Shortly afterwards two German vehicles arrived and stopped on the bridge after their tyres had been blown up on the dung. At this point the main charge was fired and the bridge, Germans and their vehicles disintegrated in the ensuing explosion.[5]

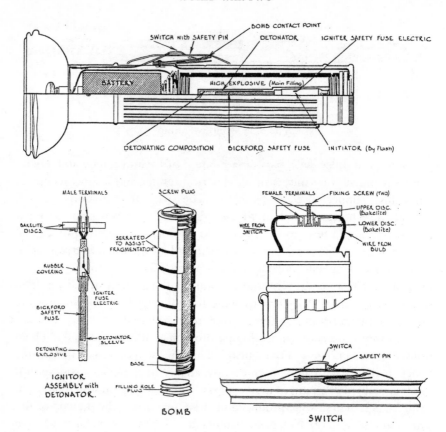

The explosive torch

The Germans, as we have already seen, used captured stocks of Ground Pistol Spikes (the No. 8 Switch) in Italy. They also used captured tyre bursters against their former owners. In August 1944 the War Office in London warned the Allied armies that the Germans were using tyre bursters disguised as stone, mud, rock or horse dung. These devices, it noted, were thought to be very unstable and great care was to be taken in dealing with them. Disposal was to be by demolition and carried out by the Royal Engineer Bomb Disposal Companies only.[6] It seems that the Allied forces in Italy were having captured SOE stores used against their soldiers and were attributing them to the Germans. Nothing appears to have been done to counter this impression. This may be because SOE was still so secret that no one knew they *were* their stores. Alternatively it may have been that SOE denied their use as they had many enemies at home who might use such information for political purposes to try and discredit their work.

166

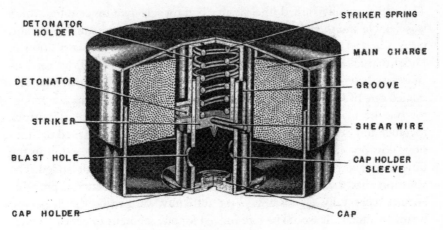

DETONATOR HOLDER

STRIKER SPRING

DETONATOR

MAIN CHARGE

STRIKER

GROOVE

BLAST HOLE

SHEAR WIRE

CAP HOLDER

CAP HOLDER SLEEVE

CAP

The tyre burster

Another bizarre store was the exploding rat. It consisted of a rat that had been gutted and then stuffed with plastic explosive and sown up again. Efforts were made to ensure that the resulting shape still resembled a dead rat. It could be initiated by a time pencil or could have a short length of safety fuse and detonator hidden under its tail. In the latter case the rat would be left near a boiler, in the coal used to fuel the fire. It was expected that the firemen would pick up the rat and throw it into the fire, where the safety fuse would be initiated and as a result the boiler would be blown up. SOE also produced small quantities of explosive charges camouflaged as coal, logs, and fishplates.

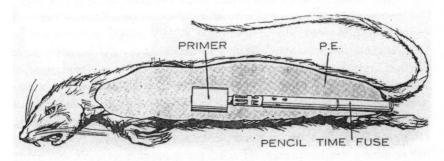

PRIMER

P.E.

PENCIL TIME FUSE

The explosive rat

For the destruction of aircraft in flight, an altimeter switch that worked on the principle of an expanding bellows was adapted. In operation the bellows would expand as the target aircraft climbed, and at a predetermined height, they would close an electrical switch and fire an explosive charge.

This was normally stuffed into an attached bicycle-tyre inner tube, which was flexible and therefore easy to slip into an aircraft. It was introduced into service in 1941. It has been suggested that the attempted assassination of Hitler that failed in March 1943 might have been successful if this particular device had been available. The attempt involved von Tresckow, who persuaded one of Hitler's entourage to accept a bottle of Cointreau as a present for one of his staff. It consisted of two captured magnetic clams stuck together and fitted with a half-hour time pencil. The device failed to function, possibly due to the cold slowing down the chemical reaction in the time pencil, and it had to be quietly recovered when the aircraft landed. The assertion that the barometric device would have been better is probably correct technically. But as always the difficulty was getting the device on board an aircraft. It would be rare indeed for any saboteur to get easy unauthorised access to any Luftwaffe aircraft, let alone Hitler's.

Another specialist bomb was designed to fit inside a ship's fender. This consisted of a metal cylinder containing a charge of up to 10 pounds of plastic explosive. It was fitted with a pressure-firing system in which a crushing force of over 150 pounds was required to make the charge function; there is no record that it was ever used.

In the main, SOE operatives and the Resistance did not make much use of the booby-trap switches supplied to them. A possible reason for this was the fear of reprisals. It seems that, at least in the early days, a broken railway line or a downed electricity pylon would not result in brutal retribution. However, blowing up soldiers in ambushes or shootings in close-quarter attacks would result in swift and lethal reprisals on the local population. There are, nonetheless, a few accounts of attacks made using booby traps.

One reference to the use of tripwires and mines (possibly tyre bursters) comes from E H Cookridge's book, *Inside SOE*. Phillippe de Vomécout, an SOE agent known as Major Paul, had arranged for the bombing of a German arsenal in Michenon in 1944. This was an old French army ammunition dump, which was taken over and used by the Germans. For a long time this had been a target the Resistance were keen to attack. However, it was well guarded and it was decided that the best way to destroy it was to call in the RAF. This was arranged for the night of 6–7 May 1944. During the bombing the Resistance arranged for a number of ambushes using mines and tripwires around the depot. When the bombing started, around 23:30 hours, German soldiers tried to save themselves from the inferno by fleeing the camp. In doing so they ran into the ambushes set up by the Resistance and set off mines and tripwire devices as they fled.

In Denmark the Resistance used a booby trap to try to kill a notorious Gestapo informer. The woman, Grete Lorte, had entrapped and betrayed

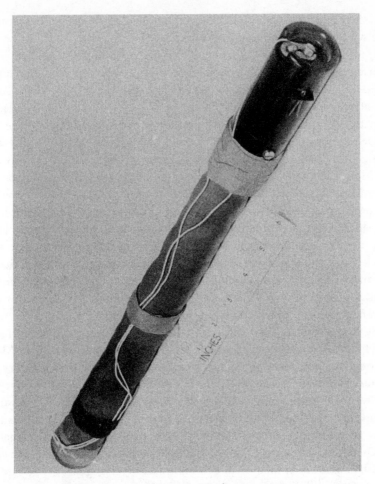

Altimeter switch

an SOE agent, Andy Larsen. His comrades decide to avenge him and, using Nobel 808 plastic explosive (which incidentally smells of marzipan), they made a small bomb wrapped in string disguised as a box of chocolates. Unfortunately she was out when it was delivered, but her current lover, who was a German sympathiser, greedily opened it. A heavy explosion occurred and he was killed on the spot. Although Grete escaped her fate the SOE men consoled themselves with the fact that another traitor had died.[7]

In another courageous and enterprising attack, which showed great initiative, a set of lock-gates on a canal were destroyed by a short-fuzed time bomb. A German guard was the interested spectator of a violent quarrel between two Frenchmen for possession of a suitcase. The smaller of the two, rather than the surrender to his apparent adversary, suddenly threw the case into the canal, at which point both men bolted, leaving a gaping sentry as sole witness to the resulting explosion.[8]

It is not clear if Churchill coined the phrase 'set Europe ablaze' because he had been briefed, early on in the war, on the work that was being undertaken by Section D to produce incendiaries. But the prospects of incendiary attacks on a large scale were to be a major part of SOE's planned activities. In this the bombing of London during the Blitz may well have influenced them. The Germans dropped hundreds of thousands of 1-kilogram incendiaries and these proved highly effective. When used in conjunction with high-explosive bombs they created massive conflagrations, destroying large parts of London and other cities. The SOE staff must have endured these raids in the early days of the organisation's existence, and perhaps it is not surprising then that they took a keen interest in fire-raising. The devices produced included incendiary cigarettes, arrows, fire pots, blocks, soap and bottles containing flammable mixtures. It is known that the Italian section requested the supply of the cigarettes and that they were supplied to the section in August 1942. In total some 43,700 cigarettes were manufactured and distributed.

SOE spent much time planning and preparing for a major fire-raising attack against the Germans, which was initially known as project Moon, although its name was subsequently changed to Operation Braddock. It called for special incendiaries to be dropped in their millions by Allied bombers for use by the masses of foreign and slave labourers working for the Reich's armaments industry. The devices were small moulded celluloid containers filled with an incendiary composition of either petroleum or white spirit gel and initiated by a time pencil. These incendiaries were taped to instruction cards, which detailed their method of operation in several languages. The card also acted as an aid to dispersion and an air brake, so that when dropped in bundles by allied bombers, the card slowed the rate of decent sufficiently to prevent the incendiaries being damaged on landing. When initiated they would burn, producing local temperatures of up to 2,000°C.[9] In total almost 4 million of these were manufactured and placed in store. Unfortunately the plan took little account of the Germans' hold over their workers and the likelihood of draconian reprisals if they were discovered carrying or using such devices. This consideration prevented political approval being given for the operation to be put into effect until late in the war, and even then there was some concern that the devices would simply be collected by the Germans and used against Allies as they advanced into the Third Reich. In the end the Americans dropped some 250,000 in southern Germany in September 1944. This caused the Germans to issue a series of warnings about them but there did not appear to be any major outbreaks of fire.

As always, if the Resistance set patterns by repeatedly attacking the same targets then they had to beware of ambushes or booby traps being left by the Germans to catch them out. In Greece it was reported that the Germans were fed up with saboteurs who were simply cutting down telegraph poles. As a consequence on one stretch of main line one in four poles was booby-trapped. Holes some 8 to10 feet deep were drilled diagonally down to the base of each of the poles. Into these holes 12 standard cylindrical 100-gram TNT charges were inserted. The bottom one of these was connected to a ZZ 42 igniter and a wire under tension ran from this to a plug at the top of the hole. Any attempt to cut down the telegraph pole would result in the wire being severed and the charge of a over a kilogram of high explosive functioning. This and wooden splinters from the pole would be more than enough to kill or maim the unwary saboteur.[10]

Attacks on shipping in ports and harbours were practised by all the combatants in the Second World War. The Italians in fact pioneered them in the First, when, 12 days before the end of the conflict, on 1 November 1918, a team of Italian swimmers mined and sank the Austrian battleship *Viribus Unitis* in Pola harbour. During the Second World War attacks ranged from swimmers attaching small limpet-type mines to the sides of merchantmen to midget submarines deploying massive side-mounted delayed-action charges to attack capital ships. Our concern is the specialist raiders.

Within the United Kingdom the Special Boat Section of the Commandos, later upgraded to become the Special Boat Squadron (SBS), was raised to carryout such raids. The first limpet operation against enemy shipping was carried out on the night of 21 July 1941. Sergeant Allan and Marine Miles in a canoe entered Bengazi Harbour from the submarine HMS/M *Taku* and sank a merchant ship with limpet mines. During their exit from the harbour they holed their canoe on a jagged rock and were both captured. Fortunately they escaped Hitler's decree on the treatment of such men and survived the war as PoW.[11]

The development of the first British limpet mine has already been described. Throughout the war the design continuously evolved. The Type 6 limpet produced in three different marks was the most used and some 38,500 of these were manufactured. They contained a charge of just over a kilogram of plastic explosive. Switches known as AC delays initiated them. These worked on the same principle as the McAlpine delay already described in chapter 2, although the design was improved upon. To increase reliability two AC delays were used with each limpet.

To get the best performance out of the limpet it had to be placed about 6 feet below the water line. Then it would blow a hole about 3 feet across in most merchantmen. To do this a special collapsible rod was developed.

In the event of the saboteurs being discovered, or a mine being spotted, a brave enemy diver could simply pull the limpets off the intended targets and drop them in a safe area where they would explode harmlessly. To prevent this a booby-trap anti–disturbance fuze was designed and fitted to the Type 6 Mark II Limpet. This had a water-armed delay to ensure the safety of the saboteurs and was fitted into the underside of the mine. When in place a trigger in the base of the fuze rested against the target ship's side. After it had been armed, any attempt to remove the limpet would result in the trigger operating and the mine being detonated. This also had the benefit that when more than one mine was placed on a ship, as the first one functioned, if the shock wave was sufficient to blow off any of the others, they would also explode.

There were many attacks using limpet mines. Probably the most famous was operation Frankton, led by Major H G Hasler RM, against shipping in the Bassen-Bordeaux area of France.[12] The audacious plan called for six pairs of Royal Marines to set off in canoes from a submarine and over a period of three nights paddle some 60 miles up the Gironde river. On the fourth night they would attack shipping with limpet mines and afterwards they would escape overland. In calm and clear conditions the operation was launched on the night of 7 December 1942. An unfortunate accident seriously holed one canoe and it could not be launched, but the other five set off. Despite their brave efforts only two crews, one led by Hasler, managed to reach Bordeaux, where they successfully mined several ships. Only Hasler and his number two managed to escape back to Britain. The other successful crew, Corporal Laver and Marine Mills, escaped but were later betrayed, arrested and shot. Of the others, four were captured and eventually shot by the Germans on 23 March 1943. One was drowned and the final crew member was recorded as missing.

The most successful attack using limpets was launched from Australia against the Japanese in Singapore harbour in September 1943. Ivan Lyon, a regular Captain in the Gordon Highlanders, who was operating with SOE led it. Designated Operation Jaywick, a team of saboteurs used captured Japanese fishing boats to get close to the harbour. Under the cover of darkness the team launched three two-man canoes which made their way into the harbour and attached limpets to the ships that were there. The result was spectacular; seven ships totalling some 30,000 tons were sunk or badly damaged. The canoes and saboteurs all returned to their mother ship and two weeks later were back in Australia. The following year a further raid by 28 men ended in disaster when the Japanese spotted them. The saboteurs were either killed in action or captured, the prisoners subsequently being executed in July 1945.

172

The Italians who pioneered this type of warfare were heavily involved in attacks in the Mediterranean. They used speedboats, swimmers and chari-oteers (riders on the 'human torpedoes'). Since 1935 they had been exper-imenting with all manner of methods and devices under the auspices of Commander Belloni. He ran a force known as X Flotilla that developed both surface and underwater attack systems. Early in the war in December 1941 the battleships HMS *Queen Elizabeth* and HMS *Valiant* were damaged in underwater attacks.

When using swimmers to place charges, instead of using magnets the Italians designed devices with clamps to attach the bombs to the bilge keel of ships. They also utilised a dual initiation system. This could either be a mechanical timer or a propeller-driven system. The latter could be set for a specified number of nautical miles travelled. The advantage of this was that the device would explode while the ship was at sea. Ships sunk in shallow harbours sometimes simply settled on to the bottom and were salvageable. This clearly would not be the case for a ship out in open water.

The Italians also developed a mine that used a compressed air cylinder and a rubber tyre to attach it to the bottom of a ship. The diver would swim with the mine, which would have neutral buoyancy, and position it under-neath the target ship. When in the correct position a cylinder in the centre of the mine containing compressed gas would be opened which would inflate the tyre and pin the mine to the bottom of the ship.

The Italians ran particularly successful operations against shipping in Gibraltar, the first ones used crews and chariots despatched from the sub-marine *Scire*. Although unable to penetrate the harbour defences they managed to attack three merchant ships outside. Two of these were badly damaged and the third sunk. Later the Italians set up a top-secret operation in which they established a land-base in Spain only some 4,000 yards from the Gibraltar frontier, near western beach. Frogmen operating from the villa attacked merchantmen with some success in July 1942 when four ships were damaged. Later in September another small ship was disabled. While these attacks were being organised another even more inspired and ambitious plan was being hatched. A scuttled Italian tramp steamer, the *Olterra,* lying off the port of Algeciras in Spain was covertly converted into a chariot depot ship by cutting underwater holes in her sides. The chariots were secretly smuggled in to Spain overland from Italy in the guise of industrial gas cylin-ders. From their new base in the *Olterra,* an attack was launched on Force H in December 1942. It included the aircraft carriers HMS *Furious* and HMS *Formidable* and the battleships HMS *Nelson* and HMS *Renown.* The courageous attempt failed and two of the chariot crews were killed by depth-charges and gun-fire while and the third escaped. Despite their losses the brave Italian frogmen launched further raids and were successful in attacking merchantmen outside the harbour in May and August 1943. Neither the Spaniards nor the British discovered the source of the attacks until after the war.[13]

The surface section of the X flotilla used high-speed, low-profile boats packed with some 300 kilograms of explosive, known as *barchini esplosivi* (explosive motor-boats). They used a single crew member, known as the pilot, who aimed his craft at the centre of the target ship. When close enough to ensure the speeding boat would not miss, the pilot locked the controls, pulled a lever and was ejected backwards out of the boat with a collapsible raft. Once in the water he clambered on to this to prevent shock injury from the underwater explosion when his boat struck its victim. The pilot then paddled back out to sea hoping to find a rescue ship.

The Italians claimed to have sunk HMS *York* in Suda bay in Crete in March 1941 using these boats. In fact the cruiser was badly damaged, beached and then finally destroyed by German bombers. Closer to the mainland the Italians planned a night attack on the shipping in the Grand harbour in Malta in July 1941. This was to be accomplished by a combination of two chariots, and eight *barchini esplosivi*, which were towed into an attack position by a mother ship. Unfortunately for the Italians, the force was spotted on radar and the defences fully alerted. When the craft were heard approaching searchlights were turned on and the guns opened up on the craft in sight. With surprise lost, the others turned back but were later set upon at daybreak by RAF Hurricanes. In total 15 of the Italian special forces died and 18 were made prisoner.

The Germans of course also had their own sabotage organisations. There was *Abteilung II* (Department II), which was part of the *Abwehr* (Defence) and controlled by Admiral Wilhelm Canaris and the Reich Main Security Office (*Reichssicherheitshauptamt* – RHSA). This latter organisation was based in Berlin and within it *Amt VI* (Office VI) run by Walter Schellenberg was responsible for external sabotage and espionage. Between them they undertook many operations and produced a number of devices. They attacked targets, particularly shipping, whenever and wherever they could. In March 1941 the SS *Tacoma Star*, a refrigerating ship, arrived in Liverpool. A dockyard worker accidentally discovered a large incendiary device disguised as a tin of frozen eggs. This was almost identical to all the other tins of eggs, but contained an incendiary mix and a J Feder 504 timer. It seems probable that the device was placed on board in Shanghai when a saboteur arranged for the substitution of a tin of genuine eggs while in transit from the consignors to the docks. In another incident in January 1943 a large explosion occurred in the hold of the ship the SS *Ravenspoint*, which caused

174

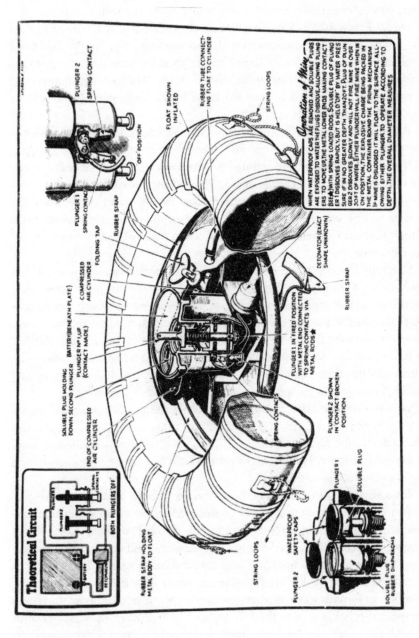

Diagram of an Italian pneumatic mine

serious damage. The investigation into the incident indicated that a bomb was built into a case of oranges and that this was again substituted at some point while being delivered from the consignor to the ship.

On 10 February 1944 another similar device hidden in a crate of onions was discovered near Northampton. It was rendered safe by the late Lord Rothschild who was closely linked to the security services.[14] In it, two J Feder 504 long-delay clockwork timers with attached detonators and primers were embedded in two blocks of plastic explosive. Ten blocks of cast TNT surrounded these.

When interrogated after his capture Otto Skorzeny, the famous leader of the glider-raid to rescue Mussolini, described visiting the RHSA–Amt VI/F's offices in Berlin. He claimed he was shown many devices that made use of a new explosive called nipolit. He said that in addition to the ordinary nipolit camouflage charges there was an ink-stand made from the explosive. This was 9 inches long and 5 inches wide and held two inkwells. There were also cartridge pouches and some bases of radios made out of the explosive.

Skorzeny also described a photoelectric fuze made from selenium, which could be set to function if light was shone on it or if it suddenly went dark. Furthermore this incorporated a self-destruction system which would detonate should the battery for the photoelectric switch begin to run down. Skorzeny reported that there were 10 to 15 of these devices. He also claimed to be responsible for the design, a fact that his interpreters knew to be untrue. At this time the Germans were also experimenting with magnetic and land based acoustic igniters and radio–controlled systems.

Skorzeny also said that all the larger charges (22 pounds or above) incorporated booby traps. The most important of these was the anti-lift pressure release device the *Entlastungzünder (EZ 44)* which will be described in detail in the next chapter. He also went on to describe many new experimental grenades and other munitions.[15]

Towards the end of the war the Germans formed raiding detachments known as the SS *Streifcorps*. Many of the men in the corps came from the Brandenburg Division, which besides its combat soldiers had a large number of specialists skilled in languages, sabotage and counterintelligence. The Division had been heavily engaged in the battle against Tito's forces in Yugoslavia where it had suffered many casualties. It was disbanded in October 1944 with its combat troops being sent to regular army units, and the specialists being sent to the SS *Streifcorps*. There were SS *Streifcorps* units on both the eastern and western fronts and their mission was to commit acts of sabotage and espionage. The unit exploited foreign personnel including Spanish and French who could operate behind enemy lines, and if stopped could claim to be escaped forced labourers. They were trained at a combat sabotage school in Tiefenthal.

The Americans captured some of these men in late 1944. There were four teams of three men each. They consisted of Frenchmen who were former members of the Legion of French Volunteers and some militia. Their specific task was to sabotage vehicles and fuel dumps, especially petrol trailers and railway tank cars. They were dressed in American uniforms and armed with hidden pistols, bombs, incendiaries and grenades. The method of operation was for the teams to contact an Allied outpost, claiming to be forced labourers who had just escaped through German lines. To support this they all carried the necessary papers and supporting documentation. With their disguised boxes of explosives they also carried a can of genuine rations, which they offered to the Allied soldiers. Obviously if as a result of this goodwill gesture the can was opened normal *Wehrmacht* rations would be discovered. The other cans all outwardly looking innocuous contained the following: a magnetic demolition charge very similar to the allied clam; a flexible detonating cord some 2 metres long; an unknown delayed-action initiating system and an incendiary compound, tubular in shape with a slow burning fuse connected to a friction igniter.[16] The charges could be used separately or as a combination, where the explosive would be used to breach a container with the incendiary composition guaranteeing it would be set alight.

From an Allied point of view the German use of raiders and sabotage attacks had no significant impact on the course of the war. The main reason for this was that they were defending occupied territories, the populations of which became more and more hostile towards them as the war progressed. There were of course localised successes that caused jitters. When the Germans launched their offensive through the Ardennes in the Christmas of 1944 they made use of about 150 of Otto Skorzeny's specially trained troops who dressed in American uniforms and used captured vehicles. They did initially cause some panic among the ground troops which went as far back as Eisenhower's HQ. The alarm however rapidly subsided and the Germans were swiftly rounded up and those wearing American uniforms were, in accordance with the rules of war, executed.

The Germans had to contend with resistance growing against them as the war progressed. While the commitment and courage of the men and women involved is not in doubt there is question over the operational efficiency and cost-effectiveness of the more exotic devices. The Braddock incendiaries were produced in vast quantities but in the end very few were dropped, and then with no positive results. The only exploding rats deployed were, according to SOE records, discovered by the Germans in a

177

container before they could be used.[17] This apparently had some impact on the Germans who displayed them at all their German Military Schools and also caused wide-ranging searches to be carried out. The other stores, the torches and the bicycle pump do not seem to have been used. The camouflaged explosive logs, coal and fishplates were despatched to the German section of SOE, but there is no record of their use. Limpet mines were successfully deployed, but only in a few highly specialised operations. The classic pull, anti-lift and pressure switches although supplied in their millions, do not seem to have been much used, although the tyre bursters seem to have found favour in some quarters and of course by the Germans. The main tools of the saboteurs were simple demolition charges and clams, fired using command wires in ambushes or time pencils, L delays and signals fog. These items were eventually supplied in large quantities. The Americans alone by 22 June 1944 had produced a total of 12,000,000 time pencils most of which were shipped to England.[18] As will be seen in later chapters many of these switches, and indeed German booby-trap igniters, were used, but in the post-war period.

Some consider that in setting up SOE the lid was opened on Pandora's Box. SOE, and later the OSS, set about unconventional warfare with no holds barred. Their task was to harass and terrorise all the occupying Axis forces and any methods were acceptable. They would talk to and train anyone who would fight the Germans, Italians or the Japanese. They published and distributed thousands of copies of a pamphlet entitled *How to Use High Explosives,* clearly written and well illustrated. It was translated into most European and some Far Eastern languages and distributed widely. In doing so it sowed the seeds, and established the principal methods of operation of terrorist and guerrillas forces which have been in constant use around the world ever since. In terms of equipment, some of the booby-trap switches designed for SOE were, until recently, still manufactured and used in the former Yugoslavia.[19]

Notes

1 Cooper, Mathew, *The Phantom War*, Macdonald and James, London, 1979.
2 *op. cit.*, note 1.
3 Harrisson, Gordon A, *Cross Channel Attack*, series *United States Army in WWII – The European Theatre of Operations*, The Office of the Chief of Military History, Washington DC, 1951.
4 Descriptive Catalogue of Special Devices and Supplies, volume 2, compiled and issued by MO1 (SP), The War Office, 1945.

5 Seaman, Mark, *World War II Secret Agent: Directory of Special Devices*, PRO, London, 2000.

6 PRO WO 204/12239, Sabotage Reports.

7 Cookridge, E H, *Inside SOE*, Arthur Barker, London, 1966.

8 PRO HS7/125, French Resistance, Railway Sabotage, 1944.

9 PRO HS/6/720, Braddock I and II, 1942–1945.

10 Army Service Forces, Ordnance Department, Ordnance Bomb Disposal Center, Aberdeen Proving Ground MD, USA, Bomb Disposal Technical Information Bulletin No. 45, dated February 1945.

11 Courtney, G B MBE MC, *SBS in World War Two*, Robert Hale, London, 1983.

12 Lucas Phillips, C E, *Cockleshell Heroes*, Pan Books, London, 1957.

13 Jackson, Sir William, *The Rock of the Gibraltarians*, Associated University Press, London, 1987.

14 Rothschild, Lord, *Meditations of a Broomstick*, Collins, London, 1977.

15 PRO WO 204/12362, Security of Material: Sabotage, 1943 February–1946.

16 PRO WO 171/5956, Works Section 383, 1945 March–December.

17 PRO HS 7/49, History and Development of Camouflage Section, 1941–45.

18 Brunner, Dr John W, *OSS Weapons*, Phillips Publications, Williamstown NJ, 1994.

19 King, Colin, *Jane's Intelligence Review*, volume 7, no. 2, 1997.

CHAPTER SEVEN

The Liberation of North-West Europe

Lucky escapes are over-publicised and are not nearly as common as generally supposed.
Engineer Intelligence Report 45, dated 8 November 1944

By late 1943 the Germans were effectively encircled and being attacked from all sides. Fortress Europe was under assault; from the Russians in the east, the Allied armies in Italy in the south, and an air bombardment of ever increasing intensity from the RAF and USAF from the west. It was clear that the opening of the second front was inevitable and both sides were making preparations for the coming battle. The landings on 6 June 1944 marked the beginning of the final phase of the war, but the battle was not going to be an easy one.

Despite their setbacks, the Germans were still an imposing and treacherous foe. With their backs to the wall and an influx of young fanatics being thrown into the fight, every means at their disposal was used to hold up the Allied advance. One of the major developments on the Axis side was the introduction into service of a new range of mines, many of which were non-metallic and difficult to detect: they were made of wood, glass or Bakelite. They also introduced new anti-lift booby traps, which were considered impossible to render safe. As resources dwindled, improvisation became the order of the day. For example, stocks of German aircraft bombs were available for use by the ground forces because towards the end of the war, the Luftwaffe bomber fleet had been either shot out of the sky or grounded for lack of fuel. The battle against these new devices, and many improvised mines and booby-trapped munitions, started at the water's edge and on the glider landing grounds.

Rommel, having recovered his health, had taken responsibility for the coastal defences in western France in November 1943. He quickly realised that mobile defensive operations without air superiority would be almost impossible. He concluded that the best defence would be based on fortifications and field defences. The battle would, he considered, have to be won on the beaches and within the first 48 hours of any landings. He also thought that landings would most likely be made at high tide when the distance the assault troops would need to cross would be kept to a minimum. Because of the limited time available he decided on a series of resistance nests with the gaps between them filled with mines and other improvised explosive devices and obstacles.

He stressed in particular the importance of laying mines and introduced the use of these on obstacles to sink Allied landing craft as they approached the beaches. In Normandy, hedgehogs and tetrahedral barriers, types of anti-tank obstacles, were moved from their inland locations to the beaches most suitable for landings. The intention was simply to cover the beaches between high and low watermarks with obstacles, mined where possible, which would prevent any flat-bottomed craft having a free run at the beach. In addition all fields suitable for glider landings were to be closely studded with poles so that no glider could land between them. These poles were also to be trapped with mines.

General Meise, Rommel's engineer expert, informed him that there were enough captured explosives in France to manufacture 11 million anti-personnel mines. Rommel on 13 January demanded that 2 million mines per month be made available. Later the required figure was raised to 200 million mines. Despite his own determination and drive to get things done, when Rommel inspected the air-landing obstacles on 18 May 1944 he was deeply disappointed at the rate at which preparations were advancing. Only a few stakes had been planted and of these hardly any were mined because of the lack of supplies. To remedy this he ordered that 13,000 shells be provided which could be fitted with pull switches and tripwires and attached to the anti-air landing stakes. Fortunately for the Allies, the millions of mines that Rommel estimated he needed never materialised and, at the time of the Allied landings, the defences, although still perilous, were largely incomplete. There was no central plan, decisions on obstacles seemed to rest at divisional level and depended on the whim of the commander and his engineering advisor. Furthermore those devices that were laid below the high watermark were subject to the rigours of the Atlantic Ocean. The difficulty in laying and maintaining underwater obstacles on the Atlantic coast should not be underestimated. Winter and spring gales could easily shift, uproot or destroy them. When mines were used waterproofing was essential, but even then the cumulative effects of the waves and corrosive action of the salt water rapidly rusted any exposed components. Sometimes this would make the mines more sensitive and sometimes inoperative. In most places it was decided that these would not stand the onslaught of the sea for a significant period and they were therefore not deployed in quantity until end of the winter.

The Allies realised at an early stage that the problem of clearing a safe passage for ships, landing craft and assault forces during combined operations against enemy coasts was of the highest importance. To be successful both reconnaissance of beaches and extensive trials were carried out to establish what the obstacles were, whether they were mined or trapped and how they could best be defeated. This was a continuous process evolving as new obstacles were deployed. It lasted right up to D–Day itself.

To counter the threat detailed information was needed. This could be gained from two main sources: aerial photography and physical reconnaissance of the beaches. The former could provide an overview of the types of obstacle and their density and even show mines on top of posts. The latter was needed to confirm the detailed construction of the obstacles and whether they and the beaches themselves were mined. A key question, for example, was whether the Tellermines on top of the posts were simply fired by pressure, or were they deployed using the built-in booby-trap sockets in conjunction with pull switches and 'snag lines' between pairs of posts. If this was so, the mine would function not only if it was struck by a landing craft, but also if a craft snagged the lines running between them.

Operation Tarbrush was set up to get this intelligence and involved landing small teams of experts on the French beaches at night to obtain information on the defences. On the night of 16–17 May 1944 at Bray Dunes Plages, a specialist sapper search team set off to carry out a detailed reconnaissance of the beach. The party consisted of Lieutenant Groom RE, the commander, Sergeant Moffat, who had a mine detector and a signalman. A Motor Torpedo Boat (MTB) took the trio to a point some distance offshore where they disembarked into a small rubber dinghy and set off through the swell towards the hostile shoreline. They were aiming for the remains of a small wrecked ship which would provide some cover. On touching down they leapt out of the dinghy and dragged it clear of the water. Simultaneously they saw a sentry sitting 140–150 yards away to east, lighting a cigarette. Despite this Sergeant Moffat proceeded cautiously up the beach using the mine detector. Lieutenant Groom followed, laying tape to enable them to find their way rapidly back to the back to dingy should they have to depart in a hurry. The beach was covered in small seashells, which crackled when they walked on them and which was quite unnerving. On the port side of the wreck they found a post with a mine attached to it and carried out a detailed examination of the assembly.

On investigation the post was found to have a baulk of timber 46 inches in length and 10 inches in diameter on top. This was fastened to the post by three lashings of cordage. A Tellermine 42 was fixed with wire to the top of this. The wire was in a figure-of-eight pattern, so that it would not interfere with the operation of the pressure plate. The mine was sloping 45° to seaward at about 8–9 feet above ground. The sand round the post was scoured by the action of sea. Examination showed that the Tellermine was waterproofed with plastic grease and the auxiliary detonator hole which could be used for booby-trapping was blocked with cork. This was good news as it meant there were no trip or snag lines. Unfortunately, because of the sentry on the beach, still only some 150 yards away, any thought of recovering the mine had to be abandoned. Having gained all the information they could, and with time running short, they followed the tape back to their dinghy pushed it out through the surf to a depth of about 4 feet and scrambled in. They paddled back out to rendezvous with the MTB and thence back across the Channel. This was just one of the several successful Tarbrush covert landings. The skill, expertise and endurance of the men involved should not be underestimated. It was no mean feat, disembarking into a dinghy in the middle of the night and paddling through the waves of the cold winter sea to the shore, not knowing if the enemy might see them or that they would set off an unseen mine. The reconnaissance itself required a calm and systematic approach and then as cold and tiredness began to bite there was the long haul back out through the surf into the darkness to search for a blacked-out MTB.[1]

Much work on obstacle demolition had started as a result of the disastrous raid on Dieppe in August 1942 when both men and tanks struggled to get off the beaches or past concrete obstacles that obstructed the roads into the town. In July 1943 a requirement was established for a self-propelled device carrying a charge of 2 tons of high explosive for beach wall demolition. The range was to be 600–650 yards and speed at impact some 60 mph. The result was the Giant Panjandrum.[2] This consisted of two massive wheels 10 feet in diameter, in between which was an 8-foot-long cylinder that would contain the explosive. The wheels had a series of slow-burn rockets attached to them near the rims. Like a Catherine wheel, when lit, these rockets would propel the Panjandrum up the beach. The aim was to launch the Panjandrum down the ramp of a landing craft and for it to be rocket propelled until it hit an obstacle upon which it would explode. Trials were carried on Westward Ho! beach but proved less than successful. Firstly some of the rockets burst, causing unbalanced thrust which forced the Panjandrum off course. A second problem was that the rolling Panjandrum would have to cross a shell-cratered beach and not smooth sand. During trials therefore mines were detonated to produce the required craters. Sadly these caused the whole device to prove very wobbly and quite unstable often with catastrophic results. In one trial, which was attended by a number of VIPs, the belching fire monster took off, went out of control and headed for the distinguished guests causing them to scatter into the dunes. Fortunately the Panjandrum toppled over at the last moment and as it lay on its side in its final death throes the rockets burnt themselves out. Sensibly the project was cancelled.

Other trials included the use of torpedoes fired at the beach, ramming experiments, rockets from Typhoons and Bangalore torpedoes on the front of landing craft. It was also established that small-arms fire could destroy the mines on the stakes but the difficulty was hitting them from a tossing and turning landing craft.

In the British landing sectors obstacle clearance teams were formed from a mix of Royal Navy and Royal Engineer personnel. The units called Landing Craft Obstruction Clearance Units (LCOCU) were responsible for clearing beach obstacles between the high and low water marks. They were in Landing Craft Assault, (LCA) which were armoured against small-arms fire and had a half-inch of steel plating welded on under the hull. The teams worked in lightweight swimsuits in water 10 feet deep up to the waters edge. They used charges of 20, 30 or 40 pounds in weight. These had to be placed two-thirds of the way down obstacles to destroy them. Some LCA also had 50-pound depth-charges for disrupting obstacles, but these could only be used if the landing craft was able to retreat for short distance. These were mounted on chutes at the front of landing craft. After the initial assaults the teams cleared obstacles working mainly when the tide was out.

The Royal Engineers formed the 1st Assault Brigade to clear the obstacles on the British beaches above the high-water mark. They had a mix of special assault tanks, including the Armoured Vehicle Royal Engineers (AVRE). These were Churchill tanks armed with the Petard mortar in addition to which they carried 3-pound hand-placed sausage charges. The Petards fired short-range demolition charges, often known as flying dustbins. These were high-capacity, high-explosive shell weighing some 40 pounds. The first breaching teams had to deal with high sea walls impassable to tanks, steel obstructions, set in the beaches and often booby-trapped, streams, anti-tank ditches, barbed wire and road blocks, all of which were covered by fire. Despite the intelligence gathering, prior to the landings there were many concerns about the obstacles to be faced. Just before D-Day some concern was expressed about some large box arrangements, which possibly contained bulk explosive, which could be trembler or pressure operated. Alternatively these boxes could simply be spikes set in concrete to sink landing craft. It was concluded that one round of 75 mm high explosive fired on the day would soon allow the engineers to discover which.[3] On D-Day itself the LCOCU and the Assault Engineers did much brave and valuable work clearing the obstacles, suppressing fire from pillboxes and clearing routes through minefields to assist the assaulting infantry. Two LCOCU cleared 2,400 obstacles in three days in Normandy, many of the obstacles were trapped with German and French shells rigged with a variety of pull and pressure igniters.[4] This work was not without cost and there were many casualties from both the defenders' fire and from the mines and traps themselves.

The Americans too carried out much work on beach obstacle demolition. Their interest went beyond Normandy as they also had the Japanese to contend with. Victory against them would require the assault and capture of many Pacific Islands. The bulk of this work was undertaken by the Destruction of Obstacles for Landing Operations Committee (DOLOC) at Fort Pierce in Florida. It was a joint Army and Navy venture and dealt with the destruction of underwater mines and obstacles. It established that hand-placed charges were difficult, slow and dangerous to use if under fire or at night. On 15 February 1944 a number of high-priority trials started, all using large, high explosive demolition charges. A whole range of ideas was tried including floating charges, radio-controlled boats and short-range high-capacity torpedoes. Like the British, the Americans also undertook trials using pole charges held forward of the landing craft and rockets. Another possibility that was considered and worked on theoretically was a tidal-wave device. This involved charges in ships ranging from 2,000–5,000 tons, which would be sunk offshore and then detonated.[5] The aim was to create a massive tidal wave to destroy the beach defences. Despite all this good work none of these systems were tried or deployed during the D-Day landings. In some cases this did not matter: for example on Utah beach the obstacles proved ineffective. It had been planned that the engineers and naval demolition parties would follow the assault infantry and blow 50-foot gaps in the German beach obstacles. In the event defences were sparser than expected and all were quickly overcome within an hour of the engineers landing.

It was a different story on Omaha beach. The initial failure of the assaulting infantry to neutralise the shore defences had severe repercussions. The 6th Special Engineer Brigade and the naval demolition parties were unable to blow gaps in the beach obstacles as planned. Furthermore, the weather was on its limits for landing operations which resulted in many demolition parties either not disembarking at all or landing in the wrong place. Casualties among the engineers were among the highest of all units on the first day, running at 40 per cent. They were even higher in those engineers' units in the initial assaults. The rising tide meant that valiant attempts to clear and mark lanes were largely unsuccessful and only one gap was blown; even then it could not be marked because many of the necessary marker buoys had been lost. Fifteen officers and men from the demolition parties were awarded the Distinguished Service Cross for their valiant work on that grim, stormy morning.

On the shoreline groups of riflemen led by fearless officers, NCOs and even individual private soldiers eventually began to get off the beaches. At 10:30 hours two landing craft courageously steamed full ahead into the obstacles firing all weapons and managed to reach the beaches. Their action proved how ineffective the obstacles were and their covering fire gave the pinned-down troops much needed morale support. At the same time two destroyers closed on the shoreline and opened fire. Under cover of this engineers of the 37th and 146th Engineer Battalions managed to make two gaps in the wire and minefields and slowly the German resistance began to crumble. Once through the coastal crust, the engineers continued with their task of dealing with mines and booby traps.

Early on in Normandy the US engineers attached to the 82nd Airborne Division encountered many Polish and Georgian soldiers whose morale was poor and who were more than willing to surrender. Having done so the prisoners disclosed much valuable information on the German use of mines and methods of booby-trapping. Many, particularly the Tellermine, were employed with considerable ingenuity. The 82nd reported some mines were buried three deep in such a way that the second and third mines were not visible when the first or second were removed. An inexperienced team sweeping for mines would remove one but leave the others in place. Some of the Tellermines were buried upside down or sideways and fitted with either a pressure igniter, which would turn the mine into a massive anti-personnel device, or they were buried on their sides with a pull igniter and tripwire leading from them.

A new type of igniter was discovered in June 1944. This was known as the 'Buck igniter', deriving its name from the original manufacturer. It was meant to be an instantaneous chemical igniter designed to have a very low metal content and therefore be difficult to sweep. It relied on a thin glass phial of acid which was surrounded by flash powder enclosed in a thin aluminium capsule. Someone treading on the capsule would crush the glass ampoule allowing the acid and flash powder to mix and ignite. The igniter was fitted to several different mines, the most common being a small pot mine. This was manufactured locally in occupied countries to supplement normal production. The igniter was also used to adapt French 50mm mortar shells into improvised anti-personnel mines.

The igniter failed to live up to its manufacturer's expectations and some were apt to be 'lazy' in firing, having delays of one to two seconds between actuation and the detonation of the explosive filling. In the case of the small charge in a pot mine this would often be enough to prevent serious injury. However when the 50 mm mortar shell was used there was still the lethal fragmentation.

The familiar S mine was also encountered, now often laid with an anti-lift wire. The procedure for this was quite simple and was detailed in German military publications. The mine would be placed on a standard German 200-gram charge which itself was on a stake that had been driven into the ground. A ZZ 42 igniter was attached to the charge with a wire running from the safety pin on top to the side of the mine. Any attempt to lift the mine without cutting the wire would result in the safety pin being withdrawn from the igniter and the charge being detonated.

Delayed-action devices were encountered; in an ammunition dump on the outskirts of Cherbourg a 4-day delayed-action device was recovered. Other specimens of 6- and 80-day delayed-action timers based on the fuzes of naval mines were also recovered, although none had been actually set in charges. It is possible that these were intended for use in the port itself, with the intention of detonating as clearance work was in progress, with a view to further delaying the eventual return of the port to use for Allied shipping.[6]

At about the same time captured documents revealed that the Germans had been investigating ways of using the standard long-delay time bomb fuzes, the El AZ 17 A and B series, to initiate delayed-action demolitions. These fuzes used a robust clockwork mechanism. When used in an aircraft bomb, on impact an electrical igniter initiated a small heating collar which contained a tube of thermite; this in turn melted a wax pellet and released a spring-loaded plunger, which on rising allowed the clockwork mechanism to begin running. The German report detailed two possible methods of using these in the ground role. Firstly the fuze could be charged from the normal aircraft systems or by using a battery. Once this had been done, striking the fuze sharply on its side would start the clock. The fuze would then have a gaine attached and it would be replaced in the normal fuze-well of a bomb, or on to a demolition charge. The other method was to remove the clockwork mechanism from the fuze and manually take out the heating collar, which surrounded the clockwork action and prevented it running prematurely. With this removed, the clock could be set, the fuze re-assembled and the whole assembly replaced, as before, in the normal fuze-well of a bomb. It was noted that once in position there was no indication that the bomb was armed and the clock running down. Consequently any bombs found in bomb dumps with El AZ 17 fuzes fitted had to be checked with a stethoscope to ensure the clock was not ticking and they were safe.[7]

The Germans placed great emphasis on booby-trapping their anti-tank mines to make their removal more difficult and so delay their clearance. This principally relied on the use of pull igniters, which were employed using built-in sockets. These, however, were not difficult to clear manually. In 1944 a new purpose-built, specially designed and self-contained anti-lift device appeared. It worked under a pressure of more than 2 kilograms in weight. Technically it was easier and quicker to lay but, more importantly from a clearance point of view once armed it was effectively impossible to clear without causing the mine above it to detonate. It therefore posed new problems for the mine clearers. Designated the *Entlastungzünder 44 (EZ 44)* (Anti-Lifting Igniter 1944) it was used to trap a proportion of the mines in a minefield. Once this device was located in a minefield, it was ordered that clearance was to be by destruction *in situ* rather than by making any attempt to render them safe or remove them. This ruling would indicate that the device had already caused several Allied casualties.

It was constructed out of metal and consisted of a flat, cylindrical casing containing a clockwork arming-delay mechanism, a spring-loaded striker held in the cocked position by a detent and a 200-gram explosive charge and detonator assembly. The striker was also secured by a safety wire, which was connected to the clockwork mechanism to prevent it accidentally arming. The detent was operated by a spring-loaded pressure piece in the top face of the casing. A safety strip passing externally into a slot in this pressure piece prevented its upward movement before the device was armed and, at the same time, passed internally through the casing to engage the clockwork and prevent rotation. A rubber cap was placed over the pressure head as waterproofing.

Before use the EZ 44 had to be wound up by means of a key. It could then be installed under a mine. It was armed by withdrawing the safety strip either directly or by attaching a pull-cord to the ring provided. On arming the pressure piece of the igniter was held down only by the weight of the mine and at the same time the clockwork mechanism proceeded to unwind, withdrawing after about one minute the internal safety wire from a hole in the striker and thus fully arming the device. The striker was then only held by the trigger mechanism and was dependant upon the continued pressure of the mine. Cleverly, if the system was deployed under a mine which was too light, it was impossible to withdraw the safety strip and so release the clockwork mechanism.

Once armed release of the pressure would cause the EZ 44 to function and the 200-gram charge would be sufficient to detonate the main filling in the parent anti-tank mine. For those deploying the device it was clearly a nerve-racking business and the German army introduced measures in which the soldiers laying the mines had to hand over the safety strips to prove that they had armed the anti-lift switches.

These may have been used in an incident which also involved delayed-action traps in mines in Normandy in July 1944. It was reported by 60 Engineer Combat Battalion that they encountered a roadblock of Tellermine 35s on 13 July. This consisted of two rows of six mines each. Two centre mines were first pulled by cord and exploded immediately; four mines were then observed to be smoking and exploded some two or three minutes later. After a waiting an unspecified time nothing else happened. The remaining mines were deactivated by hand. All these were fitted with ZZ 42 igniters that were either grey or sandy in colour.[8] Booby-trapping was not always an isolated event, in another incident in July in the village of Lessay, Engineers from the US VIII Corps reported removing more than 300 booby traps.

The Americans were not always on the receiving end of the malicious use of explosives. As the US 6th Armored Division were advancing through towards Brest they indulged in a little extra military activity. The 9th Armored Infantry Battalion purchased a truck which they modified to run remotely along a railway line. The 'Doodlebug', as it was called, was loaded with 750 pounds of captured explosive and fitted with a crude improvised crush-switch attached to the front bumper. It was set off one night under its own power at 25 mph to cross the thinly manned front line to intercept a nightly German re-supply train. At about 23:00 hours a terrific explosion was reported to have been heard from about 3 miles behind the German lines. Unfortunately it never proved possible for the 9th Armored to check the results of their work.

During the fighting in Normandy the Allied dominance in terms of air power and artillery (including naval gunfire support) meant that the Germans were always subjected to heavy bombardment. An officer with the 12th SS Division described a local counter-attack against the Canadians in Buron:

> It was bought to a standstill mainly by the artillery of the invasion
> fleet. Because of this concentrated fire, such as he had never seen
> before on any battlefield, both officers and men became demoralised
> and were forced to dig in.[9]

This perhaps accounts for the deliberate targeting of Forward Observation Officers (FOO) with booby traps. An obvious location for such traps being anywhere with a panoramic view over the battlefield. The 1st Battalion of the Gordon Highlanders fought around the village of Percy en Auge during 16 August 1944. The battalion had dispersed in and around the village and got under cover in farm buildings. Major Martin Lindsay serving in the battalion was talking to the CO when there was a tremendous explosion from the church some 50 yards away. The whole edifice came crashing down in clouds of dust and smoke. As the air cleared Lieutenant Colonel Maurice Burnett, the CO of the supporting Field Regiment Royal Artillery, emerged from the rubble covered in dust from head to toe. He had been standing in a porch by the church when the explosion occurred. Fortunately the arch had withstood the blast and protected him from falling masonry. Captain Alan Brookie, the FOO, was killed. He had gone up into the tower to try to get a better view of the surrounding area and set off a booby trap with a large explosive charge, specifically designed to catch out those controlling the Allied guns. It was a sad day for the battalion as Brookie was one of the old sweats that had fought alongside the Gordons through the whole of the campaign in the desert.[10]

A whole range of booby traps was reported as being used in France. Typical of these was a steel helmet on the ground that covered a standard German 200-gram demolition charge. This was staked to the ground and had a ZZ 35 pull igniter inserted with the pull wire attached to the helmet. Anyone lifting or kicking the helmet would initiate the charge, the steel shell of the helmet itself providing the shrapnel. A booby-trapped rifle was discovered in which a small explosive charge was hidden in the butt which would explode when the trigger was pulled. This is an interesting report, because manufacturing such a booby trap would take considerable effort. If a doctored round of ammunition was used it would be fairly straightforward. However, building a charge into the butt of the weapon and designing it to be safe to construct, yet to function when the trigger was pulled, would require a high degree of innovation and engineering skill. As always with this type of trap, once laid there is no control over who will pick it up and cause it to function.

The sappers continued their outstanding work clearing mines and traps, but with all the demands placed upon them, particularly construction work, there was never enough of them to go round. As in Italy, within infantry battalions it was the assault pioneer platoons who often took responsibility for the clearance of mines and booby traps. They did sterling work, beyond all praise, in the most difficult and dangerous circumstances. They were always on the job, methodically and conscientiously testing every place that might be mined or trapped. In many battalions it was a matter of pride with them never to ask for Engineer assistance. Brigadier T Hart Dyke DSO wrote of their work:

The pioneers always had to find detachments to accompany the forward companies. They were thus subjected to enemy small arms fire in the attack, enemy artillery fire as they cleared the way for our vehicles when everyone else was under cover, and then there was always the tricky business of dealing with enemy mines when discovered. For the enemy had a low degree of cunning when laying his mines. Anti-personnel mines were attached to anti-tank mines so that when the latter were being lifted the personnel were blown up. Again, anti-personnel mines were attached together so that when one was being dealt with another detonated.[11]

It was not without a cost. During the advance through Holland, near Roosendal on 5 November, C Company of the York and Lancaster Regiment had their ration-truck blown sky-high by a mine. The battalion pioneer officer, Lieutenant Hawkins, accompanied by Corporal Ellis and a section of assault pioneers, set out to clear the area around the truck of mines and other traps. During this there was a devastating explosion, which killed Corporal Ellis and badly wounded Hawkins in the eye. With a grand sense of duty, Hawkins went back to battalion headquarters to explain what had happened. He suspected that they had encountered some new German device, and the next day the Royal Engineers were sent to investigate.

Brigadier Hart Dyke recorded the sad loss of Corporal Ellis:

> It was he who had got a bridge constructed under fire on the River Vie and who had saved the bridge into the docks at Le Havre. He was always at Hawkins' side when there was a sticky job to do. His courage was proverbial and he had already been awarded the Distinguished Conduct Medal for conspicuous gallantry.

Clearly the prompt dissemination of technical information about all new munitions was vital if casualties were to be prevented. By now systems were in place to circulate information to specialist units. The British Army and RAF Bomb Disposal units had, respectively, *Bomb Disposal Intelligence Summaries* and *Air Ministry Instructions to RAF Bomb Disposal Units*. The Americans used *Bomb Disposal Technical Bulletins* that were issued by Aberdeen Proving Ground every two weeks. All these reports were distributed to provide proper and speedy technical intelligence and included details of new mines and booby traps. It is doubtful however that this information got down to the likes of Corporal Ellis and the assault pioneers.

One of the major concerns about the occupation of Germany was the fear that all civilians would be intensely hostile and would use booby traps and sabotage devices to attack the rearguards of the advancing Allied armies. Every soldier was prepared to face a violently hostile people who would kill and maim at every turn. Hitler and his increasingly repressive regime still held sway over them. Even mentioning defeat could result summary trial and execution. The slick German propaganda machine spewed out misinformation and daily prophesied a dramatic change of fortune, with mythical weapons and phantom armies coming to the Führer's rescue and reversing the endless series of defeats. As a consequence, during the fight for and the final occupation of Germany the use of booby traps and sabotage devices set by the local population had to be considered a real threat.

The reality, as far as civilians were concerned, turned out to be different. There were only a few isolated attacks and in the main, the advancing Allies found most of the German civilian population silent, sullen and going quietly about their daily tasks, oblivious to the events unfolding around them. Where booby traps had been laid by the military the local German population were sometimes more forthcoming. In Aachen, many devices were encountered in the town and the importance of information from local German civilians became invaluable. Booby traps of a purely harassing nature were encountered, for example, doors wired to explosives hidden in their mailboxes. One small area was found to contain no less than 25 booby traps, most of which were pull wires with grenades. One particularly clever German soldier had arranged two grenades in such a way that either tripping or cutting the wire would activate the device.

Of 22 reports that came to Engineer HQ, no less than 10 were from civilians. In every case these reports were verified and proved correct. A policy of careful interrogation was pursued throughout the operation in the town with gratifying results. It is thought that these German civilians were not trying to sabotage their own countries war efforts, or trying to help the Allies, they were basically concerned with doing what they could to accomplish the removal of a danger to themselves.[12]

The importance of mines and booby traps as casualty producers was made clear after the battles in and around Aachen in an *Engineer Intelligence Report* written in November 1944. It stated that compared to other casualty producing weapons possessed by the enemy, mines and booby traps caused the highest mortality rates. Furthermore the wounded were nearly always seriously or very seriously injured, suffering the loss of limbs and badly maimed bodies. Shelling, bombing and small-arms fire, though serious, produced casualties with a far lower mortality rate. In terms of mines and booby traps, it noted, lucky escapes were over-publicised and were not nearly as common as generally supposed. The need was for constant vigilance backed up by sound intelligence and thorough training. These provided the soldier on the ground with the best possible protection. It concluded that luck and good fortune were not measurable factors.[13]

Prisoner interrogation also proved valuable in establishing whether booby traps or long-delay devices had been left, although objective judgements had to be made on how reliable information might be. Certainly some die-hard Nazis talked of booby traps and hidden devices simply to frighten their captors. Many others, however, were glad that their war was over and openly volunteered information. In November 1944 a series of messages between the operations branch at SHAEF and the War Office department responsible for prisoner interrogation revealed the lengths the staff would go to discover the truth behind rumours of delay devices

It began on 12 November when SHAEF requested help with information stating that extensive demolitions were in place in Flushing but had been disarmed for sake of the civilian population. On 13 November it was requested that the recently captured garrison commander, Commandant Rheinhardt, be interrogated. On the 15th it was reported that Rheinhardt had been moved to the UK and could not be found. On the 18th Rheinhardt was located and quizzed about the reports and said that no such demolitions were in place. He then stated that the Allies should interrogate a PoW, Batzen, who would have put in charges if they were there. Perhaps this was to cover his back if some charges were subsequently discovered. On 20 November Batzen was interrogated and stated that he did not lay charges. He did, however, say that the Divisional Pioneer Officer may have more information and that a Hauptman Winter should be traced. The final signal shows that Hauptman Winter was being looked for in the PoW system. There the records end, and no information is available on whether or not Winter was ever found or if any demolitions were laid. It is probable that events on the ground simply overtook the need for the information, but it does show a system in place, designed to assist the forward troops and possibly provide vital life saving information.[14]

The importance of gathering technical intelligence as the Allies advanced into Germany has already been described. This covered not only mines and traps, but all aspects of German weaponry from nerve gas to the latest jet designs. The collection of this technical intelligence became a key priority and a formal organisation was established to prevent important materials and documents being destroyed, and to collect and collate the information. This became known as T (Target) Force.

Their role was to advance closely behind the attacking infantry and seize specified targets of technical interest as they were uncovered. The infantry were to guard these sites until they could be fully examined by technical investigators.

In January 1945 some of the Royal Engineer Bomb Disposal Companies were attached to support T Force. Their task was to examine the targets for booby traps and prepared charges and to neutralise or remove them as necessary. Having done so they would pick locks, force entrances, and blow open safes to seize important intelligence. To support this fascinating new role courses were arranged in the UK and attended by many of the Bomb Disposal Officers.

19 Bomb Disposal Company RE were allotted to T Force, and in Hanover in April 10 days were spent searching for and blowing safes. This must have been a fascinating task and one which would test the integrity of the participants to the full. At the entrance to an underground ordnance store at Hanigsen, civilian workers said that the lift, the only way into the depot, was booby trapped with a large charge set to go off as it descended into the store. The only way to confirm this was to descend in the lift and bravely (or perhaps foolishly) the officer in charge decided to do just that. The charge was found as described, but fortunately had not been connected up. For this action the Officer was recommended for an MBE.

Despite their hopeless situation the Germans, particularly the SS, fought on. As they fell back, the supply system crumbled and they had to make use of all available munitions to stop the Allied soldiers. Aircraft bombs, sea mines and torpedoes were all surplus to requirements and could be used in conjunction with booby-trap switches to make traps and long-delay devices. Lieutenant Colonel Mark Henniker recorded that at every culvert under a road an aircraft bomb would be found, often detonated by a delayed-action fuze. These demolitions kept the sappers hard at work bridge-building. On one occasion a submarine torpedo was so well concealed under a culvert that it was not seen. It was detonated by a time-switch and blew up an Allied tank.[15]

In a similar manner Ian Hammerton, a flail tank troop commander in the XXII Dragoons, recalled the destruction of an Assault Vehicle Royal Engineers (AVRE). In one town they came across there was a thick concrete roadblock on either side of the road into the middle of which a cylindrical concrete block had been rolled. This resisted normal tank-high explosive fire and therefore a Churchill AVRE with a Petard was requested to assist with the demolition. Using this the block in the centre of the road was reduced to rubble. Hammerton was invited to go through the breach, but couldn't because the flail attachment was too large. It was decided the Petard-armed AVRE would go through and widen the break from the other side. It had just got through the gap when there was a tremendous explosion, and the 40-ton tank was shattered and thrown into the air. A jeep, which had nipped in behind the tank, simply vanished in the explosion. A naval mine with some 300 pounds of explosive had functioned under the tank, which also set off the remainder of the Petard rounds carried inside it. Hammerton thanked his lucky stars for the wide flail jib.[16]

SHAEF in May 1945 issued a document, which gave some indication of the types of trap that had been encountered on march into the Third Reich.[17] These, of course, still presented a threat to Allied soldiers and German civilians even after the armistice. It covered a wide range of traps and finally made some reference to the elusive booby-trapped water bottle, although not quite in the format previously described.

In this case a standard American aluminium canteen and cover was found attached to the pistol belt of a dead American soldier. The bottom of the canteen was cut with a sharp chisel like tool and folded inwards. About three quarters of the canteen was packed with a cream-coloured putty like plastic explosive, in the centre of which was enclosed a booster charge and detonator. From this a cap and fuze extended out through a hole in the base of the canteen cover. A friction-type igniter was used and attached to a 5-second delay fuze. The igniter was pegged into the ground with a nail or wooden peg. Moving the body, or removing the pistol belt, would be enough to cause the friction igniter to function and the charge in the water bottle would explode 5 seconds later.

In other cases the enemy booby-trapped the bodies of their own dead soldiers using egg grenades in their pockets. Lines were attached to the actuation cords on the grenade igniters and tied to pickets set in the ground. Moving the corpse, to search for documents or loot, would cause the igniter to be pulled and the grenade to function. It may be thought that it would be possible to detect the presence of the trap by the resistance felt when the corpse was moved. However, the dead weight of a body is such that the few extra pounds force required to initiate the igniter would not be felt by the looters or searchers.

As always attractive items were easy to trap and often caught out the gullible or incautious. In one incident a bicycle leaning against a wall was trapped using an S mine and a pull igniter with a cord attached to the rear wheel of the bike. When moved by an unwary soldier the mine functioned with devastating effect causing 15 casualties.

A trap with a large explosive charge, which fortunately failed to function, involved an abandoned 88 mm flak gun. The muzzle of the gun was sealed with a wooden plug and the barrel elevated to an angle of 45 degrees. A wire was fastened to the inside of the plug and ran down the length of the barrel to a charge located near the breach. The charge consisted of four containers, each with a total charge of some 30 pounds of high explosive. The firing switch was a standard German pull igniter and was attached to the top charge. The trap could be activated in one of two ways. If the breach was opened then the weight of the charges was enough to drop out of the barrel and thus pull on the wire attached to the plug. This would have been sufficient to activate the pull igniter. Alternatively, if the barrel was lowered and the plug pulled out the charge would also detonate. Sadly no information was given on how the trap was discovered, but presumably, if the barrel was lowered before opening the breach, the booby trap could have been discovered without it functioning.

An odd sabotage device consisted of an incendiary built into a mess tin with a false bottom and food on top. The false bottom contained a mixture of thermite and a long-delay timer. Quite how this would be used is unclear: if left lying around an inquisitive soldier would no doubt have a look at it, and possibly take or test the food and in doing so discover the hidden incendiary device. He would be very unlucky if the timer ran out at the exact time he picked up the mess tin. If used for sabotage, it would look very out of place anywhere other than in kitchens and mess halls.

Many other ploys were reported. One involved the use of misleading signs. In one instance a lane was marked with white tapes, and a notice saying 'Mines Cleared' was found by engineers. As 'Mines Cleared' was not the normal designation, the area was swept and found to contain both box- and *Schu* mines. Instances were also reported of the Germans leaving signs bearing the inscription 'Verges Swept' along mined roads.

Like the British in 1940, the Germans did try to establish their own system of stay-behind parties similar to the auxiliary units and they set up a sabotage organisation. Initially, Goebbels used this for propaganda purposes. A general appeal was made to all Germans to resist the invader by clandestine means, but as we have seen, this did not work, and in the main the civilian population went about their business without any attempts to attack the Allied forces. Himmler, however, did set up a guerrilla movement, which was also known as 'the Werewolves' and was established by Obergruppenführer Prützman. It is not clear exactly what the aims of the Werewolf organisation were. Under interrogation some agents admitted that they were to harass the Allies, particularly their lines of communication. They were also to liquidate Germans who collaborated with the Allies. In this they had one notable success, when on 24 March 1945 one of their units assassinated the newly appointed German mayor of Aachen. Other agents admitted that they were to fight on after the fall of the Third Reich. However there was a dilemma for the Nazis in setting up the organisation because in doing so it tacitly admitted that they were losing the war. There were very few Germans, military or civilian, who in late 1944 and early 1945 would have dared to discuss openly the possibility of the defeat of the thousand-year Reich.

It was intended that each German *Wehrkreis* (district) would set up their own organisation and report to Obergruppenführer Prützman. In some areas quite considerable initiative was shown, but in others (particularly those furthest from the front) little was done. Allied reports later confirmed this; they noted that since January 1945 German sabotage and espionage agencies had constructed a number of underground dugouts that were to be used by the stay-behind parties. These dugouts were equipped with bunks and other living accommodation to support four men. Dugouts were found in the area of Roer and it was believed there were others in the Eiffel region. There were also warnings that the enemy hides, sabotage dumps or caches might be booby-trapped to prevent unwary examination or entry. There were other warnings about disguised explosives and other stores. As well as using their own sabotage and booby-trap switches, the Germans used a lot of captured SOE items, for example, clams, incendiaries and time pencils. Where supplies of these were insufficient some were copied and manufactured by the Germans.

There were some acts of sabotage. In one incident a jeep was booby-trapped with a British No. 77 white phosphorus grenade. The vehicle had been left unattended by the driver for an unknown length of time. During this period the grenade, that had had some form of German detonator attached to it, had been wrapped in paper and was wedged under the accelerator. When the driver returned it was dark and he could not easily see the trap. He climbed into the vehicle and when he put his foot on the accelerator it would not move. Rather than looking he kicked the pedal, fortunately for him this caused the detonator attached to the grenade to fall off and roll under his foot where it exploded when he stepped on it. Had it set off the grenade it would almost certainly have killed him.[18] In another incident it was reported that a billet left by one unit was re-occupied by another about an hour later. In this interval it had been booby-trapped.

A report from the intelligence branch at 15th Army Group HQ revealed that 50 pounds of high explosive were hidden in a room in a building which was suitable for a divisional or corps command post. The charge was prepared for firing and had an electric detonator inserted into it. Leads ran out to a road 150 yards distant from the building. It is presumed that Werewolves were to detonate the charge by connecting leads to a battery if and when the building in question was used by Allied troops. There were also concerns that retreating German pioneers would emplace large charges at key locations and link them up to the long delay J Feder 504 timers. Intelligence indicated that these would not be set running, but would be left for the Werewolves to start at a later date. There was however no physical evidence to confirm that this ever happened. In the end the German collapse was so complete that the Werewolf movement came to nothing, and its members simply slipped away.

When the guns fell silent at the end of the war in Europe, it did not, of course, signify the end of the killing and maiming. Mines, booby traps and unexploded ordnance continued to, and still do, take their toll of lives. The task of dealing with the remnants of war was enormous. In France 13 million mines were cleared between 1945 and 1946 with 2,217 killed and 3,630 other casualties. In Russia 58.5 million mines and 122 million other items of ordnance were removed from Soviet soil. In Aachen in two years 1,340 German PoWs cleared 760,000 mines at a cost of 108 killed and 112 wounded. In Guernsey in two months 300 PoWs cleared 67,000 mines with 8 killed and 14 injured.[19] There is no information available which gives a breakdown of what actually caused the casualties, but no doubt booby traps and booby-trapped mines were responsible for some casualties. The figures do however support the earlier report by the engineers on the lethality of mines and traps. The figures show that the ratio of killed to wounded is very high.

Notes

1 PRO WO 205/200, Reports from Operation Tarbrush.
2 PRO ADM 116/5248 Admiralty Miscellaneous Weapons Development Department: Beach Obstacle Demolition.
3 PRO WO 171/1807, 79 Assault Squadron RE, War Diary.
4 Ladd, J D, *Assault from the Sea 1939–1945*, David and Charles Ltd, Newton Abbott, 1976.
5 PRO DEFE 2/1069, The Destruction of Beach Obstacles.
6 PRO WO 204/5991, Bomb Disposal Intelligence Summary No. 13 , issued by Chief Engineer Allied Forces.
7 PRO WO 204/5997, Instructions to RAF Bomb Disposal Units, Air Ministry Instruction 946 dated 1 October 1944.
8 PRO WO 219/792, SHAEF messages.
9 McAndrew, Bill *et al.*, *Normandy 1944: the Canadian Summer*, Art Global Publications, Montreal, 1994.
10 Lindsay, Martin Lt Colonel, *So Few Got Through*, Collins, London, 1946.
11 Hart Dyke, Brigadier T DSO, *Normandy to Arnhem,* Green and Thompson Ltd, Sheffield, 1966.
12 PRO WO 205/1180, Appendix A to SA Engineer Intelligence Report dated 8 November 1944.
13 PRO WO 205/1180, Engineer Intrep 45 Dated 8 November 1944.
14 *op. cit.*, note 8.
15 Henniker, Mark, *An Image of War*, Leo Cooper, London, 1987.

16 Hammerton, Ian C, *Achtung! Minen*, Wild Hawthorne Press, 1980.
17 PRO WO 219/3446, Watch Out for Booby Traps!! Notes on German Booby Traps, May 1945.
18 PRO WO 204/12239, Sabotage Reports, Allied Force HQ G2, report dated 22 March 1945.
19 Croll, Mike, *The History of Landmines*, Leo Cooper, London, 1998.

CHAPTER EIGHT

The War Against Japan

Even the touchy job of disarming bombs, mines and booby traps, normally becomes an individual or small group project and captures only passing interest in the midst of an island conquest.
Saipan: The Beginning of the End, Major Carl W Hoffman

Like the other theatres of operation, during the early stages of the war in the Far East and Pacific little use was made of either mines or booby traps. The Allies, stunned by the attack on Pearl Harbour and the subsequent successes of the Japanese army, whom many had arrogantly considered an inferior foe, were thrown back in disarray on all fronts. In the initial retreat through Burma time and a lack of suitable supplies prevented the use of these devices as part of the organised defence other than some hasty demolition. For their part the Japanese, trained to attack on every occasion, and sweeping all before them, had no need for such methods. As well as a clash of arms there was a collision of cultures and military codes. To the Japanese surrender was intolerable, death for the Emperor an honour. Disturbingly as the conquering Japanese forces spread through the Pacific and Burma tales of atrocities and cruelty percolated down among the Allies. Stories of the merciless bayoneting of the wounded and humiliating, inhumane treatment of prisoners were abundant. From an Allied point of view surrender to the Japanese meant at best harsh treatment and at worst death from starvation, beatings and illness. Not surprisingly the fighting between the two sides rapidly degenerated to a point where quarter was rarely given.

In Burma by early 1944 the Japanese advance had slowed as their lines of communications were extended. Conversely, the Allies, falling back on their own depots and receiving a higher priority for stores and equipment, were able to plan and execute a more determined and co-ordinated defence. The Japanese remained largely on the defensive until March 1944 when they launched their so-called invasion of India. As the Indian 20th Division retreated towards Imphal and India, a vast depot at Moreh containing food, ammunition and stores had to be abandoned. It fell to the sappers of the Division to deny its use to the Japanese and much was destroyed with some

201

of the remainder being booby-trapped. The final task was setting fire to the oil storage tanks and departing. Despite this, during their advance, the Japanese still captured a wide range of weapons, equipment and stores. Many of these, particularly the explosives and demolition stores, were to be used against their former owners.

In the Pacific the US Navy stopped the Japanese in their tracks at the battle of Midway in June 1942 and they were forced on the defensive. Like the Germans, as the tide of war turned against them the Japanese were compelled to reconsider their tactics and methods To some senior Japanese officers, but by no means all, it became clear that attack under any conditions irrespective of the chances of success in the face of heavy firepower would result in the squandering of lives for no practical gain. Unfounded self-confidence arising from the tradition that they had always won was not a sound military principle. If Japanese soldiers, sailors and airmen were to die then their courage should not be squandered and their lives had to be traded at the highest price. The arrival of the kamikaze pilots amply demonstrated this principle. But these tactics were not restricted to aircraft. There were also sea and land kamikaze. In 1945 the following slogan was published:

> One plane for every warship
> One boat for every ship
> One man for ten of the enemy or one tank.

For the Japanese soldier on the ground it meant fanatically defending positions, often to the death, using every method of defence. To help him a range of suicide weapons was designed. At the same time the use of mines and booby traps was reviewed.

Although the Japanese employed anti-tank mines and beach mines, they never mass-produced or used pressure-activated anti-personnel mines. To begin with, in the advance, there was no need for such devices, and later, when retreating, pressure-activated anti-personnel mines could not be deployed effectively in the jungle with its dense undergrowth surrounding dispersed defensive positions. In this environment trip wires were much more effective. In one engagement in Burma the Japanese deployed grenades tactically on a large scale to improve a defensive position. They attempted to block off the approach to a centre of resistance by installing booby-trapped grenades in a jungle-covered area 100 yards wide and 200 yards long on a high and narrow mountain ridge. Within this area more than 100 British 36 grenades were employed. Tripwires attached to long vines and creepers were used in rigging the grenades in the very heavy undergrowth. The Japanese were able to use ordinary telephone wire and made no attempt to camouflage either the wires or the grenades other than that afforded by the natural dense vegetation.

The Japanese did produce a number of switches specifically designed for booby-trapping and initiating long-delay charges. Very little was known about these standard Japanese firing devices until the end of 1944. Very few purpose-built switches had been recovered in the field and most of the information about them came from captured and translated documents. Some of the devices, particularly the time-delay and the pressure igniters, appeared to be rough copies of the British and German traps.[1] In addition the Japanese used many crude, locally produced firing switches, for example, a simple electrical igniter consisting of a very basic switch built into a rubber tube. In it an insulator separated two electrical contact plates. Anyone or anything putting pressure on the tube would force the contact plates to touch and so close an electrical circuit and fire an attached detonator. The actuating pressure for the switch was unknown.

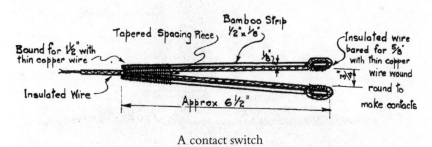

A contact switch

Both the Japanese Army and Navy produced long-delay demolition devices; these employed either chemical or mechanical clockwork delays and were of sound construction. None of these ever seems to have been mass-produced and so they did not present a significant problem to the advancing Allies. In addition, at this stage of the war, particularly in the Pacific, the very high rate of interdiction (interruption of supplies by aerial bombing) meant that deliveries of all stores were restricted and possibly prevented stocks of the switches getting to the front lines.

Thus the Japanese often had to improvise using whatever stores or munitions were at hand. Unlike the Germans, they had little detailed planning and training in the use of mines and booby traps. We have already seen that in Burma grenades were employed tactically to strengthen defensive positions using simple activation techniques and that more often than not trip-wires were used. Another good example of this improvisation was a trip suspension method using a percussion activated 97 or 91 grenade to which

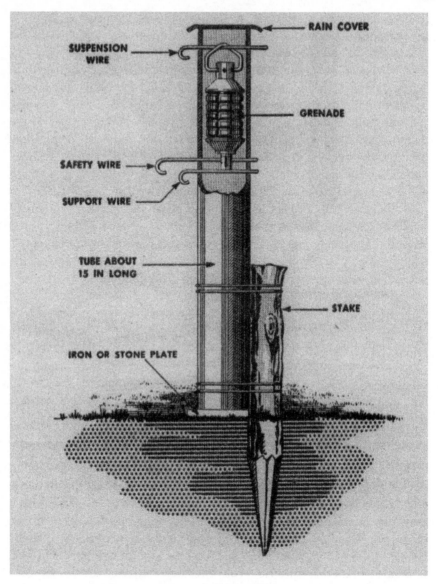

A Japanese trip grenade in its case

additional explosive had been added. This was suspended in an empty cartridge case by a simple wire pin attached to a tripwire. Anyone tripping the wire would pull the pin out and allow the grenade to drop on to the base of the cartridge case causing it to function. The cartridge case itself would provide additional fragmentation. The key requirement was to ensure that the drop was sufficient to initiate the grenade's percussion cap.

Typical ruses encountered in the Pacific included booby-trapping Japanese Samurai swords which many considered to be prize possessions. Some were rigged with fine wires attached to grenades so that when they were picked up the grenade would function. More devious was a report of a booby-trapped handle which contained a small explosive charge. Simply grasping the handle was enough to cause the charge to function.[2] This could possibly have used a variant of the electrical contact-switch previously described.

In another trap two freshly killed fowl were suspended from a tree hanging down from wires, inviting the unwary soldier to pull the birds down. Doing so would have activated a charge hidden in the tree and killed the hungry man. The old bird trap idea was also prevalent. This consisted of a 75 mm or 105 mm shell with an improvised fuze that was underneath a heavy plate or stone propped up by a stick. A simple tripwire was attached to the stick so that if tripped the stick would fall and allow the stone to drop on the exposed striker. A brave, or foolish, man, however, would need to lay these types of trap if they were to work effectively. This was because whichever way it was set there were inherent risks. If the stone or plate were placed in position first then the insertion of the shell would have to be done with great care, as catching or knocking the stick would result in a premature explosion. Equally, if the shell was positioned first, then the setting and balancing of the weight on the stick would also be a delicate act. Next there would be the attachment of the tripwire, again a risky business with both the weight and shell in position. It was not a task for a tired or clumsy soldier.

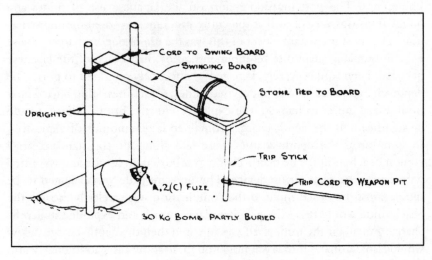

Bird-trap device

205

Fighting and dying did not prevent the bodies of Japanese soldiers, and particularly officers, being further utilised in the name of the Emperor by being booby-trapped by their retreating comrades. Grenades were often placed in a dead man's armpit and the limb wedged under his body. The pin would then be pulled from the grenade and the defenders would depart. Any movement of the body could result in the grenade becoming dislodged and functioning. On Saipan a wristwatch on the arm of a dead officer was attached to a pull switch and a hidden charge. A soldier lifting the arm to remove the watch was seriously injured in the subsequent explosion. On Iwo Jima similar traps were laid utilising large prefabricated charges in rough pine boxes containing 24 pounds of explosives. These had two friction lighters inserted into holes in the tops of the boxes, which were secured by twine. One end of a pull cord would be attached to the rings on the friction igniters and the other secured to a body. Anyone moving the body without checking first would initiate the friction igniters and via a short length of safety fuse detonate the main charge. 24 pounds of high explosive would be more than enough to kill anyone moving the body and any others close by.

On Tarawa concrete obstacles were placed on the beach with barbed wire interlaced between them. Attached to the barbed wire and the obstacles was tripwire connected to buried charges. As the wires were fairly obvious it is probable that this trap was intended to destroy any vehicles attempting to breach the obstacle by moving the blocks. It could be anticipated that the charge would be of some considerable size.

Evidence to support this comes from Luzon during the liberation of the Philippines. The post-invasion report on the Japanese use of mines and booby traps was very clear that the entire program was based on improvisation. The most important aspect of this was the use of depth-charges. These were presumably surplus to requirements, as by then much of the Japanese navy had been sunk, severely damaged or effectively confined to port. The depth-charges were used as improvised mines, sometimes being buried next to ordinary mines to increase the explosive effect. This, of course, would be significant as the depth-charges contained large amounts of explosives. In some areas the depth-charges were laid alongside the standard small conical beach mines. The depth-charge was buried on its side and was fitted with a pressure-plate firing device. The pressure plate was arranged to be snug against the beach mine. If the combination was carelessly moved, the beach mine would drive the pressure plate inwards and explode the depth-charge. Equally if the mine itself was initiated then the depth-charge below would also detonate. If that was not enough, in some cases additional drums of fuel or alcohol were placed by the depth-charge to give a blast incendiary effect as well. Depth-charges were also fitted with pull switches and then buried on the approaches to pillboxes or other emplacements. The switches would have wires that led back to the positions and the charges could be simply fired by pulling the wire. Normally there was a 7- to 11-second delays between pulling the switch and the charge exploding.

In a similar manner both Japanese bombs and shells were used as improvised charges. In particular 50 and 30 kilogram bombs were used in conjunction with pull or trip lines. Some bombs with electrical fuses were converted so that they could be fired using standard blasting machines or batteries at the end of a command wire. In one incident in a hospital at Sangley Point a 250-kilogram bomb with a modified fuze was found which had been wired into a light switch. Throwing the switch would cause the bomb to function.

The Japanese also made good use of failed US ordnance, particularly aircraft bombs. On the Marianas in the Hansa Bay area two booby traps set up in dumps were discovered. In both cases the enemy incorporated dud US 23-pound parachute fragmentation bombs. In one, four of the bombs were arranged under a sheet of galvanised steel. The sensitivity of the armed American fuzes attached to the bombs was such that moving the steel would cause the trap to function. The second booby trap had three US parachute fragmentation bombs and a Japanese 50-kilogram bomb. The Japanese bomb was hidden in a dump of cordage. From this ran a length of Cordtex instantaneous fuse. This had a plain detonator attached, which was in turn connected to a short length of safety fuse and a pull switch from which ran a tripwire. Three branch lines of Cordtex ran from the main length of instantaneous fuse to the three American parachute fragmentation bombs. Fortunately the wire was not tripped and the trap was rendered safe. Traps with such large interlinked charges were designed to kill not only the unfortunate man that tripped the device but also any of his companions close by.

On Okinawa, because of the nature of the terrain, the Japanese elected to abandon certain areas but left behind many traps. At Kiska a radio was booby-trapped. The battery compartment was filled with high explosive and it was arranged to fire if it was switched on. As a result warnings went out cautioning all troops about the possible dangers of booby-trapped electrical equipment. Any vehicle, light circuit or other electrical gear that could be rigged to fire when switched on needed close examination. Proving nothing is new, just as in Gallipoli in the First World War, a phonograph was booby-trapped so that anyone moving the needle arm would complete a circuit and fire a charge hidden under the floor. Another trap at Kiska utilised an apparently abandoned field gun. This gun, left behind by the Japanese, had anti-tank mines placed both in front and behind one of the carriage wheels. To increase the effectiveness the mines were set on top of boxes of picric acid. Any attempt to move the gun either forward or backward would result in the mines and additional charges being initiated.

Although not booby traps *per se,* suicide weapons do fall outside the normal parameters when considering the use of munitions and explosives. Usually the munitions designer makes every effort to protect the user but clearly this is not the case with suicide devices. Quite where they sit is difficult to determine even today. Some consider that suicide bombers are more akin to guided weapons since the bomber himself guides the explosive device to the target. The Japanese had a range of such weapons; of course, the most important were the kamikaze pilots who attacked American shipping. They also designed kamikaze fast-attack boats but, although they were deployed at dusk when they would be hard to detect, they were significantly less successful than the aircraft. On the ground the Japanese soldiers also had suicide weapons. The lunge mine, for example, was designed for ambushing tanks. It consisted of a cone-shaped hollow charge mine with about 6 pounds of TNT fired by a simple striker system. This was fitted on to the end of a 6-foot pole. Using bayonet-type drills, the Japanese soldier would advance on the approaching tank, preferably from a flank, and lunge at it, thrusting the mine on to its armour. The striker would fire the mine, disabling the tank, but of course also killing the Japanese soldier. Equally, Japanese soldiers, particularly the wounded, would as a last resort use concealed grenades to kill themselves and any approaching enemy rather than be captured. From an American viewpoint, no chances were to be taken when encountering Japanese wounded or surrendering soldiers. The advice given in a naval booby-trap publication in 1944 was quite simple:

Make him strip or shoot him.[3]

Most seemed to prefer the latter option.

It is worthy to note that, by now, the Americans, at least in the Navy, had adopted a much more informal style when writing about booby traps. The British produced detailed technical pamphlets aimed more at the specialist mine and bomb disposal units, which of course needed such information. The Americans, in addition to producing good technical detail, also set about providing information in a more readable and digestible format for their front-line soldiers. It was intended that this more simple approach would enable the basic lessons to be learned by all soldiers, without reams of unnecessary technical detail, and therefore would be more effective at reducing casualties. The pamphlet produced for the Navy, and hence the

Marines, entitled *Booby Traps*, written in 1944 used a style much more familiar to the soldier and provided examples of real attacks. Simple statements like 'remember your first mistake will be your last' were designed to hammer home the lessons.

Meanwhile, back in Burma the British were also forcing the Japanese back. A study of the monthly reports by the Commander of the Royal Engineers of IV Corps provides a fascinating insight into the sort of traps that were encountered and how they were dealt with.[4] For example, a Japanese position known as 'Bare Patch' on the Vaona spur was examined by an unknown Lieutenant Colonel of the 17th Division on 15 February 1944 after it had been cleared by 70 Field Company RE. He concluded that the defences were well planned and constructed showing a good degree of engineering skill. When they abandoned the position it was booby-trapped, but not very well according to his report:

> The position on being evacuated was booby-trapped. The booby traps were on the whole of a very simple nature consisting of our 36 grenades attached to tripwires or under boxes, or Japanese grenades placed under some object on which a pressure might be exerted, and so ignite the percussion cap. It seemed unlikely that they would operate unless a really heavy weight was placed on them. One British shrapnel mine was found in a trench attached to a tripwire. A large booby trap was found in a gun position, which consisted of one shell attached to a wire on top of a pile of star shells.[5]

In the March 1944 Intelligence Summary, another IV Corps report illustrated that the Japanese use of grenade-traps did not always fail to work, although in this case fortunately they did not cause casualties. A section of sappers in a forward position were present at the unearthing of buried Japanese equipment in the Nakdara area. The officer in charge of the operation, again unidentified, made the following comments about exploring the abandoned Japanese position:

> In a covered in passage of a Jap position it was noted that one side of the passage had a revetted side. In conjunction with infantry officers I started to dismantle the revetment. As the revetment moved earth began to slide and suddenly one of the infantry officers saw a 36 grenade, which had previously been held in position by the earth against a second wall of revetment, had now sprung loose. He gave a warning and a rapid evacuation of the vicinity was effected by everyone. The grenade went off without causing casualties. As we were getting up, a second grenade went off. This was later discovered to

have come from a spot approximately 10 yards away from the first one and was also presumably held in place by a revetment. It is not understood quite how the second grenade was set off by the first. It was placed however in a position where a person might reasonably expect to lie down if he was escaping from the first booby trap.

On returning to the position after a short time interval, a tunnel was found behind the revetment. But now being very wary of booby traps it was decided to dig down through the top of tunnel some distance from the entrance. Having done this and got into the tunnel a small store was found. However, great caution was taken because of the confined space and the fear of further traps. A wide range of military equipment and stores was recovered including many British rifles and explosives. The final note in the report highlighted in red pencil stated that:

It is very noticeable that nearly all the stuff here is our own. Jap booby traps are fixed up with our own grenades in many cases, although quite a considerable number of Jap grenades have been found.

The IV Corps reports continued to give examples of Japanese traps. The following were found in Potsangbam area near Imphal on 23 May 1944. A Japanese light machine-gun was discovered with a tripwire attached to the cocking handle and connected to a British-pattern pull switch. From this, instantaneous fuse led to British Nobel 808 explosive stuffed into the fuze cavity of a British Mk IV mine, all of which was which was buried. Nearby a Japanese medical pannier with a 36 grenade positioned beneath it with the pin removed was discovered and made safe. Although no further traps were discovered it was again noted that many British-pattern pressure and release switches and No. 27 detonators were recovered. Also found was box of Japanese Type 93 mines in full packing. It noted that the full box held 20 mines but worryingly 6 were unaccounted for.

By now the Allied forces through hard physical training and mastering the necessary jungle skills were able to infiltrate behind the Japanese lines and lay ambushes. Traps were used in these ambushes. These, however, did not always go to plan. The post-action sapper report on Operation Knock gives a vivid description of how things can go wrong. The intention of the operation was to lay an ambush on the Japanese lines of communication and to attack their re-supply vehicles. The ambush group consisted of a company of Ghurkha Rifles, a section of 70 Field Company RE, and a Forward Observation Officer from the artillery. The method was to infiltrate behind the Japanese lines and then for the sappers to block and booby-trap the road. Once the enemy soldiers in the vehicles had been killed, the sappers were to destroy the vehicles with incendiaries.

On the first night the ambush was not effected and most of the ambush force withdrew leaving only one platoon of Gurhkas and an officer and four sappers. The sappers retained:

2 × 10-pound charges of high explosive (Nobel 808).

120 yards of Cordtex.

18 × No. 36 Grenades.

6 × incendiaries fitted with safety fuse.

2 × time incendiaries.

The grenades were ready for fitting to pressure and release fuzes using instantaneous fuse and detonators. In addition there were pull switches, tripwire and tree charges.

On 26 February 1944 the ambush was set with Ghurkhas at either end as cut-off groups. In the centre section the sappers prepared the ambush charges. On one side of the road there was a steep bank and on the other a steep, noisy scree slope which dropped away into the jungle. One sapper set about preparing a tree for demolition and a tripwire across the road. Another buried a 10-pound charge and connected it using a tripwire. The third buried the second 10-pound charge 40 yards from the first and connected it to the former with Cordtex. The fourth sapper laid the grenade booby traps between the two charges. This work was done rapidly and all but the second sapper finished laying their charges. At this point one of the sappers accidentally set off a booby-trap grenade, but fortunately was not injured. Everyone thought that they had been attacked by the Japanese and set off for the pre-planned rendezvous point. After a while when nothing else happened they returned to the ambush site where the sappers carefully finished the laying of the second charge. All now retired to wait for the first Japanese vehicles. These arrived in the darkness and for some reason stopped short of the tree with the tripwire fired charge. Other vehicles arrived until about eight were stopped at the block and the drivers went forward to examine the road. In unison the Ghurkhas opened fire and killed them all. At this point there seems to have been some confusion as to the exact location of the other booby traps and in light of the recent events, it was decided it was too dangerous to close in, examine and destroy the stationary vehicles.

The ambush party withdrew some distance and a Japanese patrol of about platoon strength was observed approaching the scene. Shortly afterwards, the two 10-pound charges were heard to detonate as the enemy patrol reached the vehicles. Later at least one enemy soldier could be heard groaning. As they departed the ambushers put down mortar fire on the block and this was answered by rifle and machine-gun fire. Shortly afterwards two grenade traps were heard to function. The ambush party finally withdrew after 07:00 hours.

The post-ambush report concluded that the infantry had to know exactly where the booby traps were, how they were set and what was a safe distance from them. It was also agreed that more booby-trap switches should have been carried and that as much of the fastening and cutting of wire should have been done before the sappers moved down to the road actually to lay the traps. The importance of camouflaging both the large charges and the Cordtex link was also emphasised.[6]

Reports on booby traps feature in the IV Corps records right up until the final surrender. Towards the end most of the traps seem to have consisted of a sandbag with 4–5 pounds of picric powder with a pull switch and a detonator inside. Some were sited for firing from a nearby foxhole by pulling a length of string. Others had photographs or other odds and ends in the bag in the hope that a greedy soldier or looter would pick them up. These bags were considered very dangerous if detonated, but were quite easy to disarm.

The report concluded that the principles of booby-trap delousing were no different from those taught on the 1944 divisional pioneer course. But owing to movement and the many routes that were used it was impossible to travel with 100 per cent security, as that would limit the rate of advance to a crawl. The most important detector for mines or booby traps was the eye, with a prodder or bayonet used for verification. Except when deliberately gapping deep fields of mines, the electric detector was no better than the prodder. If speed of advance was vital this could be increased if Royal Engineer mine-clearance teams were to the fore.

SOE also operated in the Far East and from March 1944 took on the name 'Force 136'. Two major operations were mounted, one into Burma and the other into Malaya. SOE supplied many of their devices to those operating with Force 136. In Thailand David de Crespigny (codenamed Smiley) described an incident he had with one of the SOE incendiary cases:

> I had with me a briefcase made by the special effects people at SOE. It had 6 pounds of thermite in the bottom and could be used as a booby trap. You could leave it and whoever opened it would blow themselves up or you could destroy secret documents with it. These were put in the case and a button pressed and about five seconds later it would explode. When packing the case with codebooks and various signals it exploded. It must have been a short circuit. I was

extremely badly burnt on my hands knees and face. These produced very painful wounds, which finished up maggot infested. It took three weeks in Siam to recover.[7]

With the recapture of Rangoon in May 1945 a wide variety of Japanese sabotage equipment including disguised charges came to light. These were fully reported in both British and American publications. It seems probable that these charges may have been destined for clandestine use in India, but no evidence to support this has been found. Equally no evidence has been discovered to indicate that these devices were used against the advancing Allied forces. Intriguingly many of these sabotage devices are remarkably similar to items manufactured by the Germans or by SOE, for example, explosives hidden in food tins and explosive coal. It is clear that SOE's Force 136, which operated in Burma, was supplied with much specialist equipment and it is probable that some of this fell into Japanese hands.

Photographs and a report credited to a United States Navy Liaison Officer detailed the items found in Rangoon.[8] In addition to the coal and food tins, incendiary cylinders, incendiary bricks and Bakelite battery containers were recorded. These items all look remarkably similar to SOE stocks, but whether they were captured stores or copies is not known. The ordinary soldier in the advance would have known nothing about the activities or stores produced by SOE.

In a separate US Navy report other interesting sabotage items were noted. They included tubes of toothpaste and tins of food, which all contained explosives. The toothpaste type tube was a metal foil tube with no markings, which was filled with approximately 4 ounces of an RDX-based explosive. This had to be used with an igniter system which consisted of a small tube containing an igniting composition, a delay and a detonator. This had to be screwed into the tube of toothpaste and then to light it, it was struck like a match on a rough surface. Three types of food cans were discovered, the main difference between them being the labels, which concealed the true nature of the cans. They were Libby's strawberries, Libby's 'fancy pineapple' and Del Monte 'mixed salad vegetables'. All contained approximately 1.37 pounds of an RDX-based explosive. These could be used either for sabotage or booby traps, depending on the initiation system that was used.

Another interesting item which may have been a booby trap, but was more likely a close-quarter assassination weapon, was a gun built in to a Ronson lighter. It consisted of an excellent imitation of a standard Ronson encased in a chromium-plated cover and as far as external details go was complete down to the dummy sparking-wheel and wick. The only point likely to arouse suspicion was its weight, which was more than normal. US trials with the gun proved that it worked as designed and that in principle an unwary soldier picking it up and using it could inadvertently shoot himself or a comrade.

Thus far, throughout the whole book, while examining the use of booby traps, the emphasis has been on the military implications of deploying the evil contraptions as a weapon of war. What must also be remembered is that, like anti-personnel mines, booby traps once laid know no ceasefires and will maim or kill anyone or anything that trips the firing system. Much has been written about the long-term effects that mining and booby-trapping have once the guns fall silent. It is not my intention to enter this debate. That these devices cause misery on an unprecedented scale is not in doubt, and others have argued the case against the use of them much more eloquently than me. Battle-hardened soldiers are not immune to the suffering of the local population and can be adversely effected by the death or injuries caused by booby traps, particularly where the local population are liberated and are keen to help the cause. Of all the accounts I have read the following illustrates best the harrowing nature of such events.

James Allen fought with the 2nd Green Howards against the Japanese in the Arakan. One night his battalion had reached a delightful spot to stop for the night. It consisted of two small *bashas* (huts) and a well surrounded by low hills. Having settled his men in positions around the area he went exploring and discovered that one of the bashas was occupied by a man his wife and two small children, a boy of about ten and a girl of about five. The adults were shy but the children were soon adopted and spoiled by the men who gave them sweets and made them toys. In return the children became self-appointed water-carriers filling bottles for the men and carrying water to the cooks. Allen continues:

> One mid-morning I was on my hill when there was a tremendous bang down below, silence and then terrible screams from a child. Like everybody else I rushed down to find a scene which lives in my memory still.
>
> Part of the well wall had disappeared and all around was blood and parts of a small human body while the little girl lay writhing on the ground, covered in blood and dirt and emitting a high pitch keening that was not a scream but sounded infinitely worse. The first man there picked her up and we saw she had lost her left arm as well as suffering other injuries. Many of the men, including the one carrying the child, were crying as they bore her towards the MO, who was now running over. As he took the little girl in his arms the parents arrived and the mother tried to snatch her daughter but was

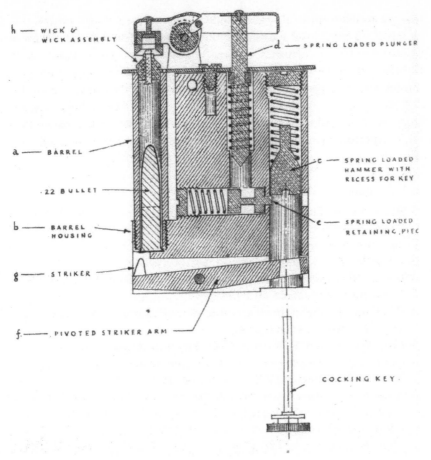

h — WICK &
    WICK ASSEMBLY

d — SPRING LOADED PLUNGER

a — BARREL

.22 BULLET

c — SPRING LOADED
    HAMMER WITH
    RECESS FOR KEY

b — BARREL
    HOUSING

e — SPRING LOADED
    RETAINING PIECE

g — STRIKER

f — PIVOTED STRIKER ARM

COCKING KEY

Booby-trapped lighter

restrained by her husband. The couple followed the doctor with the woman crying piteously but neither seemed to be concerned about their son – I am sure they had not seen the horror at the well.[9]

Some men led by the pioneer sergeant took on the ghastly task of returning to the well to recover the remains of the little boy, which were placed in a small, swiftly constructed, wooden box. Allen could not bear to watch and left the scene. A short while later the parents emerged from the MOs tent bearing a small bundle and it was obvious that the little girl had also died of her wounds. When the pioneers had finished their grisly work the CO took the remains to the parents in their basha and handing them over tried, through an unofficial interpreter, to express the battalion's sorrow at what had happened. It then transpired that the parents believed that the battalion had deliberately killed their children. The Japanese, they said, had left some time ago and therefore it was not their doing. An investigation pointed to a Japanese booby trap, which had been placed on the far side of the well, which was seldom used by the men or the children. All this time the trap had been lurking there waiting for the right action to fire it. This too was explained to the devastated parents but still they refused to accept it. The final twist in the whole horrible tale was that as parts of the boy's body had been blown into the well it could no longer be used.

Notes

1 Army Service Forces, Ordnance Department, Ordnance Bomb Disposal Center, Aberdeen Proving Ground MD, USA, Bomb Disposal and Technical Information Bulletin No. 41, 1 December 1944.
2 PRO WO 203/5865, Reports on Operation OBOE.
3 Booby Traps (NAVPERS 16110),Bureau of Naval Personnel, Navy Department Washington DC, 1944.
4 PRO WO 203/5869, Intelligence Summaries, Japanese Mines and Booby Traps, February 1944–July 1945.
5 PRO WO 203/5869 IV Corps Chief Engineer Reports
6 *op. cit.*, note 4, Sapper Report on Operation Knock.
7 Imperial War Museum, SOE Transcripts, 12096.
8 Army Service Forces, Ordnance Department, Ordnance Bomb Disposal Center, Aberdeen Proving Ground MD, USA, Bomb Disposal Technical Information Bulletin No. 58, 15 August 1945.
9 Allen, James R, *In the Trade of War*, Parapress, Tunbridge Wells, 1994.

PART THREE

Post World War Two

CHAPTER NINE

Government Surplus

When Superintendent Bird GM MBE of the Aden Police was asked by the Imperial War Museum to suggest items for an exhibition of terrorist weapons and devices, it was pointed out that 80% would be British.
Survey of Terrorist Methods and Devices 1938–1967

The total commitment in the Second World War to defeat fascism in Europe and the Japanese in the Far East had two major implications which have affected the world ever since. One, which is clear for all to see, is the beginning of the collapse of the empires. The defeated nations, Japan and Italy, were stripped of their former territories. Germany had lost hers at the end of the First World War. The British, French and the Dutch, all with significant interests across the world, had not the strength to hold on to theirs. Independence was what the people wanted and rarely was the transition peaceful. The second implication is perhaps less clear. The need for total war with no holds barred encouraged the spirit of resistance and an independent manner. In the dark days of 1940–1943 SOE concluded that anyone who would fight the Axis forces was welcome no matter what their politics. Later they were taught and supplied with all that was needed to harass the common enemy. The SOE, the American OSS (Office of Strategic Services) and the NKVD (People's Commisariat for Internal Affairs) in Russia had all encouraged, supported and condoned violent acts, which the Germans at least branded as terrorism. At the end of the war some of these same resourceful and independently minded men and women saw no reason not to use the same tactics and methods to gain their own political ends. In Malaya, for example, in the closing stages of the war, the anti-Japanese communists even considered killing all the SOE officers from Force 136 attached to the various guerrilla units and seizing power in Malaya.[1]

When examining booby traps, the period between the end of the Second Word War up to the involvement of American troops in Vietnam can be divided into two distinct sections. The first is the Korean War which was a limited action using conventional forces. Within this framework mines and booby traps were used in much the same manner as they were in the Second World War. To avoid duplication only a few of the many incidents will be described and some issues relating to the importance of training.

The other conflicts tended to be 'police actions', internal security or counter-insurgency operations. These campaigns, in Palestine, Aden, Cyprus and Malaya, saw the emergence of modern terrorism with bombing becoming one of the principle forms of attack. Initially many conventional military mines, booby traps and explosives were used as the post-war world was awash with surplus military stores and equipment. As time progressed and supplies of these explosives and purpose-designed switches ran out, the development and use of home-made explosives and improvised devices became more commonplace. These, when designed to be activated in a victim-operated manner, were called booby traps and indeed meet the definition of such a device. Today technically they are referred to as 'victim-operated improvised explosive devices' (VOIED). Even the use of a terrorist time-bomb left without warning could be considered a booby trap when judged against the current definition. Protocol II of the Inhumane Weapons Convention of 1981 states that booby traps include 'manually-emplaced munitions or devices designed to kill or injure which are actuated by remote control or automatically after a lapse of time.' The main emphasis of this book is the use of military booby traps. However, those responsible for bomb disposal in the early post-war period rapidly learnt that they had to deal with a wide variety of devices, many of which were improvised in nature.

The police actions, internal security operations and counter-insurgency campaigns that followed the Second World War were clearly lesser conflicts. In Palestine, for example, at the height of the bombing the official Engineer Reports regarding incidents refer to them as civil commotions.[2] And, in truth, for seasoned front-line soldiers who had just finished fighting the Third Reich or the Japanese, they were much less dangerous campaigns. However, they placed new stresses and strains on those soldiers that fought them. In unfamiliar countries, far from home, soldiers kept the peace in tense and uncertain atmospheres where danger lurked in the shadows. Violence, swift and sudden, would erupt, leaving young soldiers or civilians dead or mutilated and, as abruptly as it had started, the mayhem would stop and peace would reign again. In most campaigns the intensity of the violence grew steadily, as did the skill and determination of the terrorists. While recognising that one man's terrorist is another's freedom-fighter, and the end justifies the means, for simplicity these fighters shall be referred to as terrorists. Most employed methods which many, particularly at the time, considered intimidating and cowardly. The tactics which are sadly familiar to us all now included ambushes, close-quarter attacks with pistols and grenades, snipers and, of course, all forms of bombing including booby-trapping. What is extraordinary, considering how soon after the war some of the actions started, is the tone of the reports into some of the incidents. There are the expressions of contempt, shock and horror that such devious and dastardly methods could be used. But used they were, and with the possible exception of Malaya all have been successful.

In the months that followed the end of the Second World War, the Jewish community in Palestine turned increasingly to active resistance and open revolt to British rule. Attacks against the British continued until their final withdrawal from Palestine in 1948. During this period the Haganah, the Irgun and the Stern Gang struggled continuously against the British Mandate until the UN resolution on partition in November 1947. During this period there was a campaign of assassinations, ambushes, bombings and kidnappings. The worst attack was on 22 July 1946, when a bomb destroyed the King David Hotel in Jerusalem killing 91 British, Jewish and Arabs and injuring 41. Many of the other attacks involved the use of booby traps.

On 20 January 1946 a device was placed against the wall of the Mount Carmel Radar Station control hut. It consisted of two 50-pound packs of explosive fitted with both time-delay and anti-handling switches. The time delay consisted of four British L delays or time pencils all of which apparently failed to function. After half an hour the terrorists informed the station by telephone of the presence of the device. Subsequently it was disarmed and it was discovered that in addition to the time delays there were three pull igniters and one book-type release switch (No. 3 Switch). The pull switches were designed to operate if the lid of the top box was opened; the book release switch was set to function if the top box was moved.

Attacks of all natures continued throughout the period, but the terrorists had a notable success on 9 November 1946 when a booby trap was set in a disused building in the David Quarter of Jerusalem. A pamphlet produced just after the event noted that:

> This incident is included for its illustration of the extreme methods which Jewish Terrorists may employ when planning deliberate murder.[3]

The attack was in fact a simple 'come on' which today is a well-known terrorist tactic. Then, it was an outrage, which seemed totally unjustified.

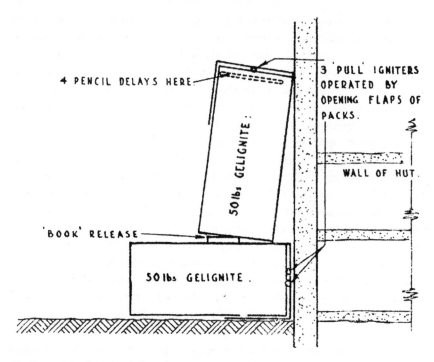

4 PENCIL DELAYS HERE

3 PULL IGNITERS OPERATED BY OPENING FLAPS OF PACKS.

WALL OF HUT.

50 lbs GELIGNITE:

'BOOK' RELEASE

50 lbs GELIGNITE.

Booby-trapped device left at the Mount Carmel Radar Station, 20 January 1946

It seems that, while acceptable in general warfare, this type of attack was considered inexcusable in peacetime.

The incident started with a series of anonymous telephone messages and letters, which were received by the Jerusalem District Police HQ. These indicated that a derelict building was being used by terrorists to hide an arms cache. On the first two occasions that the police searched the building nothing was found. On the third occasion the warning was accompanied by a plan purporting to show the exact position of the cache. This time a party of British-born Palestine policemen was sent to the building to investigate the matter. The officer in charge of the party entered the premises at approximately 06:15 hours and made a preliminary investigation. He examined all the rooms and scratched the floor in several places, but moved and found nothing. A second party then entered the building and were heard to be moving some masonry. Moments later there was a devastating explosion. Three of the party died instantly: two of them were blown out of the building and one was flung against a wall. A fourth received fatal stomach wounds and died later and a fifth was injured.

Afterwards a platoon commander from 253 Field Company RE and two sections of sappers examined the scene. The building was extensively damaged but a search was carried out to recover the bodies and to establish the type and position of the charge and the means of initiation. The exact location and size of the charge was not established, but a pressure mechanism was located close to the position of the cache marked on the map. It was thought that this was linked to improvised mines located in different parts of the building.

It rapidly became clear that normal police and military methods were inadequate when engaged in operations against the Jewish terrorist organisations. Their use of improvised mines and booby traps, particularly in follow-up operations after a contact, caused needless casualties. It became necessary to provide advice to ordinary soldiers and policemen when dealing with such incidents. The broad principles that were developed by the army and the Palestinian police in the event of an incident involving a device or an explosion hold good to this day. They may be summarised as follows: clear surrounding buildings and place a cordon around the danger area; limit the number of persons required to work in this area to an absolute minimum with only one man actually approaching and dealing with a device; treat every incident as something new and take nothing for granted on its first appearances; when actually dealing with devices, having discovered one means of initiation, look for another and then a third, for initiation systems were seldom used singly.

Warnings were given about booby traps and the need to suspect everything and touch nothing until it was clear that the course of action chosen was the correct one. Demolition stores were to be taken by specialists. It was concluded that only experts would be required to disarm mines or traps, and then only in the most urgent of circumstances, or when in pursuit of essential information. These experts were mainly Sappers, and later some members of the Palestinian police.

For a short period, the Jewish resisters targeted the railway and communications systems using improvised railway mines, some of which were booby-trapped with built-in anti-handling systems. The report into the first few incidents recalls that one of the interesting features of the device was that apart from the main essentials, the explosives and the detonators, all the components were from everyday articles available from any household; all that was needed was a small workshop with a lathe to produce the devices. The railway mine operated on the passage of a train over the rails and the resulting depression of a sleeper. This was made possible by means of an adjustable plunger secured to a battery box placed underneath the sleeper. The booby trap consisted of a separate anti-lift switch, which was positioned in such a manner that a spring-loaded plunger was held under compression by a stone wedged between the rail and the buried bomb. Removal of the device released the top plunger which, under the influence of a spring, moved up and completed a secondary booby-trap circuit. The whole system had to be very carefully positioned and disguised. It was most probably first encountered on 17 November 1946 when a railway mine was discovered at Petah Tiqva. In removing the main charge Captain J M Newton RE, 6 Airborne Division, was killed when the mine exploded and an accompanying NCO injured. It was a bad day for the British Army as seven other soldiers were killed and eleven injured in two separate mine attacks. The following day there was a further tragedy when Captain Adamson RE was killed by another booby-trapped railway mine at Ras El Ein.

As a result of these incidents, 6th Airborne Division HQ issued further instructions in a signal regarding the procedures to be adopted when dealing with mines on the railways. Surface mines were to be pulled but because of the booby traps, all buried mines were to be destroyed *in situ* irrespective of the damage that they caused. Precautions against other booby traps were also to be intensified. This included reiterating the rule that all this work was to be done as a one-man risk. The signal pointed out that casualties and loss of life had occurred because of direct disobedience to these orders.[4] As the attacks on railways and trunk communications continued further warnings about booby traps were published. Another 6th Airborne Brigade HQ report noted that saboteurs had taken new measures to slow repair parties by the concealment of booby traps and mines. If, under any circumstances, it was thought that the failure of a trunk telephone line was due to the work of saboteurs then fault parties were required to be accompanied by a Royal Engineer representative qualified to deal with mine and booby trap threat. All personnel were warned to take the utmost caution in handling mines or suspect booby traps.

Many of the attacks used British explosives and switches: for example, on 17 January 1947 three suitcases each with 492×4-ounce sticks of Nobel 808 were found by Palestinian Police at the Alliance School at Tiresias. Later, on 13 February, limpet mines were used to sink an army launch in Haifa harbour.

An important element of the Palestinian campaign was the beginning of detailed forensic investigations into the incidents which aimed firstly to establish what had happened and why, and secondly to recover good forensic evidence to convict the perpetrators within the framework of the law. In the early days the investigators had little other than basic ballistic, explosives and booby-trap training. A call to a scene of an explosion or the find

224

of a booby-trap device would, more often than not, result in the investigator walking to the scene and simply having a look. Most devices were relatively simple but it was correctly predicted that the future would bring much more sophisticated designs. A remarkable Police Officer's name emerges in Palestine, which is to crop up again in Kenya, Cyprus and Aden. This was F W Bird who was to retire in the early 1970s as a Superintendent with a GM and an MBE. He dealt with a wide variety of devices but perhaps his greatest contribution was utilising his Criminal Investigation Department (CID) background to set about establishing systems to properly investigate bombing attacks. This included the recovery and detailed forensic examination of devices and components from explosions. The work was not only restricted to bombs but also covered the use of firearms. His work in Palestine was cut short with the withdrawal of British troops in 1948.

In the same year, but across the world, in Malaya, a communist insurrection began. It was mainly a shooting war with assassinations and close-quarter ambushes being the preferred methods of engagement. Although explosives were used they do not seem to have been utilised to the same extent as in other similar actions. One area of interest in Malaya was the doubtful practice of using booby-trapped ammunition by government forces. Although not a new tactic it was fraught with danger because control of the booby-trapped rounds is lost at the point that they are left for the enemy to find. In Malaya there is evidence that this practice was actively pursued. In Operation Purvey, some 10,000 rounds of .303 were doctored with high explosive. On firing, either from a rifle or a Bren light machine-gun, such a cartridge would detonate, burst the barrel and kill or severely injure the firer. There was some concern about the legality of such actions, but General Templer, the GOC, dismissed these. A further 50,000 rounds were ordered which were filled with a thermite incendiary composition. These when fired would simply melt and seal the breaches of the enemy weapons. The advantage of these was that if the enemy discovered the doctored rounds and managed to get them back into the British supply system they would not kill the British troops. The SAS also doctored weapons such as Lee Enfield rifles, which were left for the communist terrorists (CT) to find.[5] It wasn't only the SAS that were involved in such activities. Roy Follows joined the Malaya Police and spent much time fighting the CT. In one incident he recorded that he was summoned to the Officer Commanding Special Branch and given a bandolier of .303 ammunition. He looked at it and on being asked what it was stated that it was the normal ball ammunition. He was then told that in fact the rounds had been doctored and the propellant, a low explosive, had been replaced with high explosive. Follows was then told to leave this ammunition where it was probable that the CT were likely to find it. He recorded that, several weeks after he had left the ammunition, there was an ambush by the terrorists in which it was reported that, as they opened fire, there were a number of breach explosions, which resulted in the ambush being abandoned.[6] If true then it was a very effective way of demoralising the opposition. The SAS also used booby traps when they located vacant CT jungle hides. The normal procedure was to lay ambushes, a far more effective way of killing. However, in cases where it was not possible to wait for the CT to return, the camps would, on some occasions, be sown with traps using British switches and grenades. Of course the problem with this action was that once the CT became aware that this was happening, rather than falling for the traps, they disarmed them and then used the stores used against their former owners.

Still in the Far East another and altogether different war started on the 25 June 1950 when North Korean forces poured over the 38th parallel and invaded the South in a surprise attack. The fighting yo-yoed up and down the peninsula before stalemate was reached in 1951 with both sides digging in and fortifying their positions back on the approximate line of 38th parallel. Korea's predominantly mountainous landscape tended to channel the forces along valleys and strongly influenced the fighting.

The first booby traps deployed in significant numbers by the North Korean Army were used during their retreat from the Pusan perimeter. Initially these were simple devices. They were not particularly effective and, crucially, according to reports, were often easy to locate. As the campaign progressed, however, the enemy became a much more prolific and proficient booby-trapper. Most of the traps were pull, tension release or pressure activated, although some incorporated time delays. Fortunately for the UN soldiers, there seemed to be a lack of understanding of the basic requirements of an explosive train as many of the devices failed to function correctly. It was discovered that the commonly issued Chinese stick grenades were often used to initiate larger, hidden charges. Trials by American Technical Intelligence teams showed that, when used to try to detonate TNT filled stores, the grenades were not powerful enough unless they were placed in intimate contact with the TNT and the actual filling of the grenade exposed. If this was not done, it resulted in the grenade functioning but the detonation wave not propagating through to the main charge, which consequently failed to detonate, thus significantly reducing the effectiveness of any trap.

When on the defensive Soviet and Chinese doctrine dictated the saturation of abandoned areas with mines, booby traps and delay devices. The

North Korean Army mirrored these tactics as they fell back towards the 38th Parallel. Traps were sown in abandoned foxholes, field telephones, dead branches, scraps of timber, discarded equipment and the bodies of the dead. In Seoul most of the important intersections were mined and many western-style buildings sown with traps.

The UN forces continued their push up the Korean peninsula with the intention of destroying the remnants of the North Korean Army. As they approached the border with China, they were almost overwhelmed when on 25 November 1950, 180,000 Chinese soldiers launched a surprise attack. The UN forces fell back in disarray first to the 38th Parallel and then they were forced to abandon Seoul for the second time before stabilising the front at the end of January 1951.

In appalling winter conditions in February 1951 during operations Killer and Ripper (they didn't mince words in those days) the communist forces were driven back to the 38th Parallel. During these operations the communist use of mines and booby traps became a significant factor in delaying the UN forces.

A common ploy was to booby-trap the many peasant huts that lay just off roads and on the hillsides. In this they took advantage of the natural construction of the huts and their unusual heating systems. Heat from a small fireplace at one corner of the building was ducted under the floor via a series of channels, thus warming the whole hut. The booby trap consisted of placing charges or grenades in these channels and linking them to an initiator hidden in the base of the fireplace. Advancing UN troops naturally took shelter in these huts during the freezing nights. Soon after a fire was built to warm the quarters the heat generated would set off a detonator linked to the hidden charges and the hut would be destroyed.

Another favourite winter scheme taking advantage of the soldiers' need for warmth was trapping loose timber, branches or scrap wood with grenades. These would be placed under the wood and then the safety pins would be removed. Anyone lifting the timber would release the fly-off levers and allow the grenades to function. A variation of this consisted of a cone-shaped cardboard container filled with explosive and fitted with a pull switch. This would be buried under a branch to which a wire linked to the pull switch was attached. Picking up the stick would cause the trap to function. In some instances the traditional Korean ceramic jars were filled with explosive linked to trip-wires. Disturbing the wires or moving the jar fired the trap. Again in Seoul large buildings were also often booby-trapped with pull switches attached to windows and doors and linked to significant charges of up to 300 pounds, more than sufficient to reduce the structure to rubble.

A commonly encountered controlled mine was a 55-gallon drum filled with eight pounds of TNT and surrounded by rocks. Some of these were fitted with electrical detonators and command wires which were fired by concealed soldiers, often hidden in well-camouflaged foxholes situated close to the roads. Other 55-gallon drums encountered by attacking or advancing UN troops were used in conjunction with short lengths of safety fuse which was lit and the drums then rolled down hills into the path of the advancing soldiers. The effectiveness of these must be questioned, firstly because the directional stability of the drum, once released, would be in the lap of the gods, and secondly it would be difficult to get the timing of the fuse right so that it detonated as it reached the troops. Nevertheless, if it *did* reach the right place at the right time it would cause casualties and if not, any drum rolling down a hill would be likely to cause alarm and despondency among the UN soldiers.

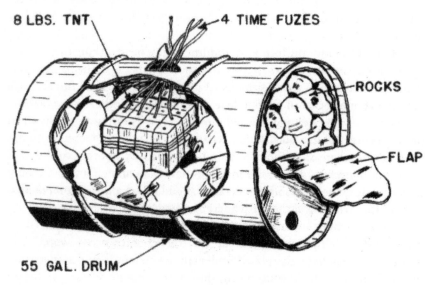

Sketch of a 55-gallon rolling mine

Some traps were quite complex. In the village of Pyonchang, an entanglement of electrical and telephone wires was found spread across the road. On closer examination it was discovered that many grenades of various types were anchored in the roadbed and also on the shoulders of the road. A wire fastened to the safety pin or pull ring of each grenade led back to the maze of wires on the road. Had the entanglement of wires been disturbed then one or more of the hidden grenades would have gone off, spreading lethal fragments across the area.

When nuisance-mining, Chinese engineers would dig a hole anything from 2- to 6-feet deep and in it lay a number of mines. On the fuze of the top mine they would place a piece of timber or log that was cut to size so that the top of the wood was just below the surface of the road. Once correctly set the hole would be filled in. No matter how good the minesweeper they would not detect the mines hidden deep below the surface of the road, but the first tank or vehicle crossing the top of the log would set off the mines hidden below. The use of several mines ensured that the tank would be immobilised.

The Americans in particular quickly recognised the need for effective training in order to preserve lives and save equipment. Many of the casualties that occurred early on were considered avoidable if the proper care and caution had been exercised. Investigations showed that being careless or cocky contributed to the success of the North Korean traps. The simple expedient of marking and reporting a possible mine or a trap to a squad leader was considered the most sensible way of reducing casualties. The key was to remain alert when travelling on foot or vehicle through territory previously occupied by the enemy. In addition to basic training on all mines and booby traps, the issue of simple booklets proved to be valuable in reducing casualties. The Engineer Office of Eighth United States Army in Korea published a pocket-sized guide to the most common mines and traps. The sound, but basic technical detail in this booklet was supplemented by a series of cartoons showing typical traps.

In the stalemate that followed the UN advance back to the 38th Parallel both sides fortified their positions First-World-War-style with narrow trenches, deep bunkers and barbed wire. In addition minefields were prolifically sown in front of the trenches. Patrolling became a key function and both sides set about ambushing each other. Finally in July 1953 a cease-fire was signed, which brought the hostilities to tense and anxious close.

Back in the Middle East, by 1950 Britain had left Palestine and pressure was building to withdraw from Iraq, Jordan and Egypt. It was considered essential however that Cyprus remain as a key base in the Middle East for the foreseeable future. Cyprus itself was a mixture of Greeks and Turks. With Greek support Archbishop Makarios began a movement to rid the British from the Island. The architect of the campaign was General Grivas who set up the EOKA (National Organisation of Cypriot Fighters) guerrilla movement. From the start he recognised that they would need to win through a process of attrition by continuously harassing, confusing and exasperating the British enemy. The methods chosen were sabotage of government installations and surprise close-quarter attacks. Initially EOKA were short of munitions, and supplies were obtained from sunken ships around the coastline – recovered munitions had their fillings steamed out for use in bombs. Others were smuggled in from Greece and explosives were stolen from local quarries. Later EOKA manufactured large numbers of pipe bombs which were often initiated by German or British booby-trap switches or time delays.

Booby-trapping became commonplace as the campaign progressed. Grivas recalls how Cyprus youths were recruited and participated in the battle of the flags. In this pupils would raise Greek flags on the roofs of their school buildings. These would be seen by British soldiers on patrol who would naturally go in and pull them down. Of course, the next step was to attach a booby trap to the base of the flag and a soldier trying to remove it would be killed or injured.[7]

As far as the British Army was concerned, in these counter-insurgency type operations (not in general war like Korea) there was also a shift in the responsibility in dealing with the devices from the Royal Engineers to the Royal Army Ordnance Corps (RAOC). The Corps called upon Inspecting Ordnance Officers (IOO) who were ammunition trained and Ammunition Examiners (AE) who were warrant officers and non-commissioned officers to help investigate incidents. These men received extensive technical training in all aspects of explosives and ammunition design, which provided sound background knowledge on which to base their investigations. Although well versed in the destruction of stray ammunition, in the early days the IOO and AE had little if any technical training on dealing with improvised devices. Most simply got on with the job learning as they went. Establishing how the shift in responsibility from the Royal Engineers (who historically seem more suited to the role) to the RAOC came about is unclear. It seems that when there was a need for detailed explosives investigations the British sponsored police services called upon the IOOs and AEs for advice and technical assistance. In Cyprus these men were actually seconded as Government Explosives Officers to give advice to the local police and assist army units. In this capacity they both dealt with devices and investigated explosions. As a result a link was established in which army units needing help with terrorist devices naturally called upon officers and men from the RAOC. In Cyprus Major W C Harrison RAOC undertook the lead role.

EOKA used the full range of terrorist tactics, which included targeting and killing bomb disposal personnel. One such booby trap killed Staff Sergeant J A Culkin RAOC who was attached to the Brigade HQ at Limassol. On 23 September 1956 the Limassol police received a telephone message allegedly from a shepherd who had seen two or three men acting suspiciously carrying a heavy box into a cave at Ayia Pylasksi. This information was passed to the local military and a number of soldiers from the Royal Norfolk Regiment went to investigate. Shortly afterwards, Staff Sergeant Culkin and a Detective Sergeant (DS) Chippendale from the CID went to the scene. On arrival they were told by a Major in the Royal Norfolks that the suspect cave had been found and searched by some of their soldiers. Against one wall of the cave, near the entrance, a large wooden box was discovered which was surrounded by stones and brush-wood. As this appeared suspicious it was left alone until the arrival of the two sergeants. Initially they both entered the cave together searching the ground and walls for booby traps as they went. When they arrived at the box Staff Sergeant Culkin knelt down to examine it and the area immediately round it for wires or other protruding objects. According to DS Chippendale this action was done in a thorough and very careful manner. It appears that Culkin was satisfied that no such objects were present. At this stage he turned to DS Chippendale and advised him to leave the cave for his own safety. Some 30 seconds after Chippendale left there was a violent explosion. Culkin was immediately evacuated to hospital, but was pronounced dead on arrival; indeed it was the medical officer's opinion that he had been killed instantly.

Major Harrison went to the scene and recovered a number of fragments; from these and, after questioning, it appeared that the box was approximately $24 \times 18 \times 10$ inches and made from white pine. It had contained some form of electrically initiated booby trap. Further searches at the scene revealed two further boxes in a cave close by. These, like the one Culkin had examined, were covered with stones. The boxes were of metal construction and placed next two each other. It was decided that no purpose would be served by giving these boxes a critical examination and it was decided to use a small disruptive charge to blow them open. The result was a massive explosion which collapsed the whole of the cave.

The report into the affair highlighted the dangers of investigating items in caves. It was suggested that wherever possible these should be collapsed and destroyed before they could be used for terrorist purposes. Under no circumstances should security forces wander around caves unless all possible precautions had been taken to clear them of booby traps. It also revealed a weakness in the disposal policy, in that dismantling items without proper diagnostics, for example, X-rays, was bound to cause casualties. The report concluded that Staff Sergeant Culkin had carried out outstanding work as an AE over the previous 12 months safely disarming a large number of sabotage devices.

On 24 November 1958 another AE was called to the village of Khlorakas after soldier of the Durham Light Infantry found a booby-trapped pipe bomb. The bomb, made from 3-inch water pipe, had a hole drilled in the side and into this was fitted a German ZZ 42 igniter. This could have been arranged to fire by pressure or by withdrawal of the safety pin by a trip wire. No attempt was made to remove the igniter and after photography the bomb was destroyed *in situ*.

On 11 March 1958 Sergeant Perry RAOC went to the Port Security launch *Penguin* in Paphos on which a bomb had been found. This was a standard EOKA pipe bomb filled with dynamite to which iron rivets had been added to act as shrapnel. The initiator for the bomb was a 1941 vintage No. 9 L delay. Sergeant Perry disarmed this device by removing the delay. This was just in the nick of time because it functioned shortly afterwards. The original report states that Sergeant Perry 'visited' the launch rather than being 'ordered' to it or 'tasked'. It may just be the writing but does suggest a very low-key response to an item clearly identified as a device. Sadly another AE, Sergeant R Kirkby, was killed helping the police investigate a number of home-made mines. He had disarmed two and was examining a third when it exploded and killed him.

During the 1960s the Inspecting Ordnance Officers and Ammunition Examiners trade was reclassified, and they became Ammunition Technical Officers (ATO) and Ammunition Technicians (AT). With this new classification, they served in Aden and were responsible for dealing with terrorist devices. Between 1964 and 1967 they dealt with a total of 1,503 terrorist incidents. During this period the teams required to deal with the devices consisted, at any one time, of no more than one Major Senior Ammunition Technical Officer (SATO) and two ATs. During the operations only one AT was injured and that was by a hand grenade thrown at him while he was dealing with an incident. The Royal Engineers also carried out disposal work but this seems to have been restricted to route and area clearances. The types of devices encountered in Aden varied considerably and were ingenious in their construction and design. They included drainpipes to fire mortars remotely and rockets using conduit piping to launch grenades (mainly British 36 grenades). By using clothes pegs, watch or clock timing systems and simple torch batteries, the terrorist produced a variety of booby traps. Photograph albums sent through the post, thermos flasks, ashtrays, children's satchels, parcels and tins were all used to disguise devices. As in Cyprus many of the these used British stores including booby-traps, switches and time pencils.

In January 1966 F W Bird arrived in Aden and began the process of setting up a laboratory to carry out technical forensic work. As well as microscopes and cameras there was an order for an x-ray machine costing £480. This item was considered most important and was to be for the rapid

and positive examination of suspect bombs or booby traps and most importantly would eliminate the 'blind' approach then in place when dealing with
such devices. Bird, because of his experience in Palestine and Cyprus, also
set up a training scheme to teach the local police in methods of bomb-
detection as well as instigating basic precautions against the bombers. He
delivered a number of lectures to the military and the police on the importance of his work and how in the long run it would help reduce casualties.
The subjects covered included:

What forensic science can achieve.
The need to protect exhibits.
Why the co-operation of soldiers in the field is vital for this work.
Terrorist methods of weapon-concealment and hides in dwelling houses
    and in the open.
Terrorist bombs and sabotage devices.
Booby traps, where they were most likely to be found and their methods
    of operation.

In retrospect this shows remarkable insight and is as valid today as it was
then.

The campaign also saw the appearance of Warsaw Pact mines and booby-
trap switches, most supplied via Egypt. On 28 February 1967, a British
political officer, Anthony Ingledow, was attacked in his home. An Arab
servant, who subsequently fled, had set up a mine behind a cabinet in the
sitting room of his house. This detonated in the middle of a dinner party
and killed two women and injured a further 11 guests.[8] Initially it was
assumed to be a booby trap but investigation by F W Bird revealed that a
Czechoslovakian bounding mine, based on the German S mine, had been
rigged to fire electrically using a watch and battery.

In an earlier attack on 19 September 1966 a boat used by the British
forces was booby-trapped near a checkpoint in little Aden. The boat, which
was out of the water, had a grenade and blocks of Russian TNT hidden
under the keel. The grenade with the safety pin removed was arranged so
that the fly-off lever was held in place by the weight of the boat. Some 3–4
seconds after the boat was lifted the grenade functioned but fortunately, as
in Korea, the attached TNT blocks failed to detonate. Had they done so
there would have been serious casualties.

The violence ended with the withdrawal of the British forces on
30 November 1967, but again across the world another terrorist campaign
was in full flow. Hong Kong was a long-standing British colony, but with
the communist take-over in mainland China, there were from time to time

riots and other forms of unrest. However, in the summer of 1967 the situation became more serious. Over the next year terrorists deployed over 8,929 suspect devices. The majority of these, some 6,859, turned out to be hoaxes, although 253 devices exploded while the rest were dealt with by bomb disposal teams.

In a heavily populated area, placing one device on the streets was sufficient to bring traffic to a standstill and seriously disrupt the life of the colony. In general the devices, mainly using black powder from the local firework industry, were not designed to cause massive casualties among the civilian population. In terms of the use of military booby-trap switches, this was the last campaign in which vintage Second World War designs were used, although only in limited numbers. The items used and recovered were mainly restricted to time pencils and L delays and a few pull, pressure and release switches. In the main the Chinese used improvised victim-operated switches. Although the terrorists did not set out to cause massive casualties there were many deaths and, as always, bomb disposal personnel were considered fair game.

A Sergeant CC Workman RAOC was killed in September 1967 at Lion Rock Hill when examining yet another booby-trapped flag. The device exploded and he fell some 200 feet down the hillside. Another casualty was from 9th Independent Field Squadron RE. A device was being examined by an officer from the company when it exploded and he lost several fingers from both hands in the explosion. At that time the responsibilities for bomb disposal were split between the RE and the RAOC. All agreed that the RAOC would be responsible for bombs in Hong Kong and Kowloon, and that 68 Field Squadron RE would undertake the task in the New Territories.[9] At the beginning of the campaign this seemed to be a very acceptable solution. A letter from the Engineer-in-Chief dated 25 September 1967 noted that:

> In the city, so far, we have been very little involved. Ordnance (I think rightly) are dealing with terrorist devices and we are ready to reinforce as necessary.[10]

This pragmatic approach was not universal and a very long and acrimonious dispute developed between the RE and the RAOC over the responsibility for the disposal of terrorist devices in peace-keeping operations. This vexed question resulted in many staff meetings, none of which managed to resolve the issue satisfactorily.

The official guidance on the issue given in *Keeping the Peace,* a pamphlet dated 1963, did not help resolve the matter.[11] In essence it stated that, as is normal in the field, the responsibility for the detection and clearance of booby traps, mines and explosive devices rested primarily with the REs and the assault pioneers of infantry battalions. In addition infantry rifle companies were recommended to get basic training. The detection and neutralisation of booby traps required, it noted, knowledge of enemy engineering techniques and so the Sappers should do the work. However, the report also concluded that from an investigative and passage-of-information point of view, ATOs and ATs were expert in all matters concerning ammunition and explosives, including disarming and dismantling explosive devices. This was of vital importance when it came to obtaining information on how the devices operated and disseminating this information to the troops on the ground. There was also a need to provide evidence to police officers investigating attacks to support prosecutions.

It became a protracted and increasingly bitter struggle, which still rumbles on today. Both sides accused the other of undermining their case, with the RAOC fighting strongly to retain the role and the Engineers trying to take it off them. The RAOC position was that ATOs and ATs were specially trained to render safe devices, they said:

> RE personnel are not specially trained to dismantle complicated explosive devices and normally they clear the devices in situ having cleared the area and taken precautions to minimise effects of an explosion. The resultant damage must be accepted in the interests of safety.[12]

In private the Engineers took a very haughty line; Brigadier Richard Clutterbuck OBE wrote:

> There is no doubt that the RAOC are doing all they can to build up a case for taking over this responsibility completely, worldwide. This is clearly impracticable and I know you are resisting it strongly. Nevertheless I think we would loose some sympathy if we were to emulate their intrigues and try to deprive a non-operational corps of their 'ewe lamb' of danger.[13]

Equally in private they admitted that they were not providing the necessary attention to the subject and that more training and the development of new techniques and equipment was required. At that stage the RAOC placed too much emphasis on the dismantling of devices and recovering evidence. The RE concluded that manually dismantling devices for intelligence purposes rarely justified the risk. In this they were right, and the

235

RAOC were to pay a high price for the failure to develop remote techniques in the early days of the Northern Ireland campaign.

It must not be forgotten that both the Navy and the RAF also used specially trained personnel to assist with the disposal of bombs and booby traps. The death of Lieutenant Ferminger in Sicily has already been recorded. In Hong Kong they also carried out such work. The London Gazette entry for 26 July 1968 records the award of the BEM for gallantry to Petty Officer (PO) Anthony Charlwood on operations in Hong Kong:

> On 13th August 1967 accompanied by another rating, PO Charwood was called upon to render safe several live bombs on the road junction in the Wanchai District. A large hostile crowd collected surrounding the ratings. And while engaged in preparing to detonate the bombs, a grenade was thrown from the crowd injuring PO Charlwood in the leg. Although in great pain he continued at the site and completed the task of rendering the bombs safe.

The bombing in Hong Kong ended almost as abruptly as it started, and for the British army there was a short period of comparative peace before the outbreak of the 'Troubles' in Northern Ireland. These were to claim the lives of many soldiers including bomb disposal officers in terrorist booby-trap attacks. The Americans however were fighting a very different war in Vietnam in which booby traps were to play an important role.

Notes

1 Short, Anthony, *The Communist Insurrection in Malaya 1948–1960*, Fredrick Muller, London, 1975.
2 PRO WO 261/253, HQ Chief Engineer Reports for Palestine and Transjordan.
3 Palestinian Pamphlet, Terrorist Methods with Mines and Booby Traps, December 1946.
4 PRO WO 275/42, HQ 6 Airborne Division.
5 Jones, Tim, *Postwar Counter-insurgency and the SAS, 1945–1952*, Frank Cass, London, 2001.
6 Follows, Roy and Popham Hugh, *The Jungle Beat,* Blandford, London, 1990.
7 Grivas, General George, *Guerrilla Warfare and EOKA's Struggle*, Longman, London, *c.* 1964.
8 Paget, Julian, *Last Post Aden 1964–67,* Faber and Faber, London, 1969.
9 PRO WO 32/21550, Chief Engineer Tour Notes from Hong Kong, 4–7 September 1967.
10 *op. cit.,* note 9.

11 Keeping the Peace, part 2 ,Tactics and Training, dated 16 January 1963.
12 *op. cit.,* note 9.
13 *op. cit.,* note 9, letter to Major General Bowring CBE, MC, dated 1 December 1967.

CHAPTER TEN

Vietnam

When the Americans came to Vietnam, they didn't bring with them a
hatred of the Vietnamese people, but we had it for them.
Colonel Huong Van Ba, North Vietnamese Army

The tunnellers from the First World War would not have envied the work
of the American tunnel rats in Vietnam. Sergeant James Lindsey was one of
that very brave and special breed of American soldiers who volunteered to
investigate these dark, dank and dangerous places. His duties required him
to descend into and explore the hundreds of miles of secret tunnels and
underground chambers that the Viet Cong had dug in the Cu Chi district
of Vietnam. It was a nerve-racking, solitary and perilous occupation,
squeezing through the tight, fetid, stinking tunnels in the sinister shadowy
half-light, with a pistol in one hand and torch in other. There was the ever-
present danger of being suddenly shot, stabbed or blown up by a hidden
booby trap with no immediate help at hand.

Sergeant Lindsey died in such a tunnel on 4 April 1967. He tripped an
unseen booby trap and was killed in the resultant explosion deep underground.[1] He was a victim of the Viet Cong who had proved to be a brave,
cunning and savage foe. They made use of every method to attack the
Americans and their allies and used booby traps to kill, wound, harass and
frustrate their enemy. They had had plenty of experience, having fought
both the Japanese in the Second World War and the French in the 1950s.
When the French withdrew the country was divided, and war broke out
with the North trying to take over the South.

At first the Viet Cong fought a limited war, but by 1960 this had developed into an all-out insurgent campaign. In 1964 regular North Vietnamese
Army units joined the fight with the intention of securing a rapid victory.
The US at first provided support and advisors to the South, but, in response
to the arrival of the North Vietnamese Army, complete American Units
were deployed. As the campaign intensified, more and more American
troops were thrown into the fray. It must be understood that the ground
they were to fight over was completely foreign and unforgiving to the US

forces. Additionally the direction of training at the start the campaign was focused on a European war, and this was fundamentally incompatible with what the troops would experience in Vietnam. In the early days the North Vietnamese Army and Viet Cong took the view that they could defeat the US in face-to-face combat in major engagements at times and places of their choosing. In such actions, however, the US soon brought to bear technical excellence and formidable firepower from artillery and fixed- and rotary-wing aircraft. The communists suffered a series of defeats. Once they recognised the futility of battling against such overwhelming might they reverted to avoiding combat except were the odds looked particularly favourable. Now their object was to kill as many enemy as possible at the smallest possible risk to themselves.

Geographically, South Vietnam was ideally suited to guerrilla warfare. The land is 75 per cent covered in brush and jungle, about half being true rain forest. In the south of the country the Mekong Delta formed a huge natural series of waterways, with mangrove swamps and flooded rice paddies. Jungle-covered mountains surround the small deltas, and the central highland areas had zones of dense forest interspersed with areas of tall elephant grass.

What the Viet Cong and the North Vietnamese Army lacked in the way of firepower they made up for in ingenuity. Booby traps were extensively employed by them in all phases of their operations from combat to sabotage. They were used to disrupt the mobility of US forces and they forced resources to be used for static guard duties and other clearance operations. In action they were a key component in pre-arranged killing zones and often an integral part of ambushes. In these they either triggered the action or were themselves brought into play by snipers or remotely controlled claymore mines.

The nature of the war in Vietnam was such that detailed records and after-action reports were kept and much operational analysis carried out. Various studies, including the use of records kept on primitive computers enabled problems to be studied and solved with minimal clerical effort. These proved that that mines and booby traps accounted for a high proportion of American casualties. The extent of the problem can be gauged from the following reports of attacks. From 1 March to 10 June 1968 a total of 817 incidents were reported. Of these 512 were mines and 305 booby traps. More importantly, of the booby traps less than half were detected before they functioned. Grenades were also favoured for booby-trapping and 71 per cent of the victim-operated devices used these.

To put this into perspective Captain James M Cox of the 1st Battalion 52nd Infantry wrote a report on mines and booby traps on the completion of his tour:

In the five months that the 1st Battalion 52nd Infantry have been in Vietnam emplaced mines and booby traps have caused the greatest number of casualties. Of the 77 men wounded due to hostile action, 71 have been wounded, some minor, some seriously, by these weapons which the Viet Cong have mastered so well. In the same respects 16 of our 23 men killed in hostile action have died because of mines and booby traps. Percentage wise this is 92% of all wounded and 70% of all killed. To say the least the percentages are rather high. The purpose of this report, therefore, will be to establish some means of avoiding, detecting, or applying immediate action should an element find itself in a mined of booby trapped area.[2]

The use of booby traps also had a long-lasting psychological impact on the US forces and in part helped alienate them from the civilian population that in any event could not be easily distinguished from combatants. In some cases, the fear of booby traps seems to have been so great that units in the field were under stress the whole time. This is reported to have caused severe mental fatigue on both the commanders at platoon level and individual soldiers.

Another US report recorded from January to June 1965, that booby traps and mines caused 11 per cent of all fatalities and 17 per cent of all wounds. To give one historical example, C Company of the 1st Battalion, 20th Infantry sustained over 40 per cent casualties in 32 days. They scarcely saw the enemy and took casualties mainly from booby traps and snipers. The effect on morale was such that these losses in men, and particularly of nearly all the NCOs was said to have been more than partly responsible for the massacre that occurred at My Lai.

It wasn't just the Americans that suffered: the Australians too were shocked at the effectiveness of Viet Cong traps. During Operation Iron Triangle they noted mines and booby traps had been the real killers. They presented a physical and psychological hazard of immense proportion. Like the Americans, by skilful and quick reactions they could counter sudden contacts with the Viet Cong, but the toll taken by booby traps was relentless. The Australians, who were under command of the US 173 Brigade, recorded that when it became clear that the Viet Cong knew the general direction of a sweep, they would lay booby traps in the soldiers' paths. They would use guides as they withdrew to take their own soldiers through safe lanes and draw the Australians on to the traps. At night they returned to re-lay traps in areas that had been cleared the day before. A combination of oppressive heat, heavy-going through the dense undergrowth, constant sniping and the extreme concentration needed to search for booby traps took a heavy mental and physical toll on the soldiers of the Royal Australian Rifles, as their official history recorded:

> Advancing under these conditions took great individual courage and determination. At one point B Company were ordered back into a spot they had been relieved to vacate the day before. A forward scout, Private Ross Mangano, had lost a leg and badly injured another on a booby trap which also wounded his section commander, Corporal Terry Loftus. Now the Company was required to silence enemy small arms fire from the area prior to a helicopter lift. Following an alternative route to avoid the booby traps of the previous day, McFarlane's company used a guide from C Company, but he to was blown up on a booby trap.[3]

Why then were the Viet Cong and North Vietnamese Army so good at booby trap and mine warfare? And why were the Americans and their allies so vulnerable? To understand, it is necessary to 'know thine enemy', examine what traps were laid, how they worked and what actions were taken to counter the devices.

The Viet Cong and the North Vietnamese Army were mainly a peasant force, equally at home in the jungles, paddy fields and villages that provided the background for their ambushes and traps. They had been at war for nearly a quarter of a century, with the Japanese, the French and later the Americans. Accordingly patience, cunning and resourcefulness, combined with in many cases a justified loathing of western culture, made them a determined and ruthless enemy. Add to this indoctrination by an often-brutal communist regime and it can be imagined that here were a terrified people determined to rid themselves of the Americans at any cost. Colonel Huog Van Ba of the North Vietnamese Army said:

> We had such a hatred for the enemy and such devotion to our noble cause of liberating our suppressed people that we felt we could overcome any difficulty and make any sacrifice. We didn't have any kind of humanitarian feeling about it, as the Americans did.[4]

Even if they could not engage in direct combat with the Americans, or had no mines or explosives, they could lay simple traps using local materials such as *punji*, simple bamboo stakes, sharpened and driven into the ground; everyone had a part to play. One wrote on how easy it was to kill Americans:

Not only guerrillas but old men and peasants following the guerrillas fought, women laid mines, wives and children of the peasants carried supplies with which the peasants and guerrillas could fight the Americans. Everyone was enthusiastic and confident. The guerrillas and compatriots fought till they ran out of supplies of mines and hand grenades.[5]

People with such a loathing of the enemy seemed to enjoy booby-trapping. The devices themselves can be broadly broken down into those which were explosive and those that were non-explosive. Although the former were by far the most numerous and the most successful casualty-producers, the latter had a significant psychological impact and are worth examination.

Non-explosive booby traps are medieval in concept and, in western eyes, chillingly menacing. The thought of being speared by an arrow, tipping into a pit lined with sharpened stakes or being crushed and skewered by a swinging log was enough to make the bravest man wary. With the exception of simple *punji* stakes these traps were much more time-consuming to construct, harder to trigger and camouflage and were, after the arrival of flak jackets and steel re-enforced boots, much less effective at causing casualties when compared to explosive traps. However, their value lay in their considerable psychological impact. Many forms of non-explosive traps were laid and all took advantage of local materials and camouflage. Non-explosive traps were often employed in conjunction with other explosive traps or mines at ambush sites. Muddy roads, jungle tracks and trails provided the necessary camouflage for all manner of devilish devices, and heavy vegetation to their sides provided cover for a multitude of other ingenious snares. Open grassy areas were not immune, as spiked plates and pits could be used. Streambeds were also suitable for non-explosive traps, particularly at fords where troops were likely to cross.

Some were used just once, but others were encountered on many separate occasions. Although crude, the devices were successful in their primary purpose of causing casualties. *Punji* stakes were the most common and were extensively used. They were designed to injure or kill personnel who stepped or fell on them. Often the pointed ends were treated with human excrement or other poisons so that the wounds they inflicted, even if minor, stood the chance of becoming infected and going septic in the hot humid conditions. The Viet Cong often employed the stakes on potential landing grounds where heavily laden troops could expect to be wounded as they jumped out of helicopters. In this they proved effective as recorded by Brigadier General S L A Marshall:

Already, without a shot being fired, four men had been lost to the company. Two of them had keeled over on the LZ [landing zone] – downed by malaria. The others, in jumping free, had come down on punji sticks and had their legs ripped open by these ever-present and nastiest of the enemy's strange devices. Hundreds of these sharpened bamboo stakes had been set in the elephant grass; saving the company heavy loss was the torrential rain of the evening before, turning the clay setting to mud, so that when the men brushed the sticks they toppled over.[6]

The stakes were also used as obstacles to protect Viet Cong defensive positions. They would be placed along the banks of gullies or streams where it would be likely that troops might jump from one side to another. At ambush sites they would be hidden in the grass behind fallen logs or other similar locations, which provided cover from view and cover from fire. When the ambush was sprung any man diving to avoid the fire risked being impaled on these simple, short vicious little stakes.

In addition to the liberal use of *punji* stakes simply planted in the ground, the Viet Cong manufactured numerous other non-explosive traps. A small selection of some that were encountered by the Americans during their time in Vietnam have been illustrated (see plate section). Many of these used sharpened *punji* stakes to inflict penetrating wounds. When sited alone, spike boards and mantraps were located where an individual's attention would be likely to be focused on something else. Careful reconnaissance of a trail for a tripwire might result in a man falling prey to a spike board or pit-type trap.

The Viet Cong also made use of poisonous reptiles and insects. Once again these seemed to be of limited effectiveness, but had a massive psychological impact on the American soldiers. One of the most unsettling traps reported was detailed in a US pamphlet entitled *Viet Cong Mine Warfare*; it described the following:

> An infantry man was walking into a cave in the central highlands feeling his way, wary of the variety of dirt traps the Viet Cong plant. Suddenly, something from above lashed at his cheek. Something else at his shoulder. A third something at his neck. He had walked into a curtain of snakes tied, like sinister stalactites from the caves ceiling. Hungry, angry, frustrated, they bit the soldier furiously. Bamboo kraits, they call them. Deadly poisonous.[7]

The Vietcong also made use of venomous snakes in their extensive tunnelling systems. These snakes would be left in the tunnels in areas where an unwary American tunnel rat might put his hand. Alternatively they were tied in place with a piece of wire which the Viet Cong could pull, and so lift the snake out of the way. A more menacing method involved tying the snake into a piece of bamboo, as recounted by an experienced American tunneller Lieutenant Jack Flowers:

> They would take a snake, we used to call them one-step, two-step, or three-step, and they were bamboo vipers. They weren't very long, but they had a very potent bite; once bitten you could only take one or two more steps. The Vietnamese somehow tied the snake into a piece of bamboo with a piece of string and as the tunnel rat goes through he knocks it, and the snake comes out and bites you in the neck or face and then the blood gets to your heart very quickly. You had to make sure when you went through a tunnel you not only looked at the sides with your flash light, but also you looked at the ceiling.[8]

In the tunnels the Viet Cong in another incident used a box of scorpions as a booby trap. The scorpions were held in a box attached to the ceiling of the tunnel and arranged with a tripwire which opened the box when moved. This resulted in the scorpions being tipped on to the unsuspecting tunnel rat below. Although not fatal they had the desired effect. One of Lieutenant Flower's men got stung in such a manner. He came screaming out of a tunnel absolutely terrified and shaking with fear. He never went back in again.

Although all these non-explosive traps contributed to the overall campaign against the Americans and had a frustrating and draining effect on morale, they were not that effective or the real killers. As we have seen, mines were the biggest casualty-producer, followed by booby traps. Most of these used grenades; the Viet Cong proved to be the most imaginative and cunning users of these, although, as is often the case, it was often the simple trap cleverly concealed which proved the most effective.

A common sight in Vietnam was a gate in the fence or wall that surrounded a variety of Vietnamese villages and farms. Equally common was the Viet Cong habit of booby-trapping the gates. Two methods were used: in one a grenade with a pull wire attached to the safety pin was hidden with the other end of the wire attached to the gate, so that when the gate was opened the pin would be withdrawn from the grenade and it would function. Alternatively, the grenade less safety pin was wedged under the gate so that when it was moved the fly-off lever was released. As with all the Viet Cong traps both grenade and wire (if used) were extremely well camouflaged.

In a departure from the normal horizontal tripwire a vertical wire was laid in the middle of trails. This used a bamboo arch placed across the trail with a grenade, sometimes with its delay element removed, secured to the top of the arch. A tripwire was extended from the safety pin to the ground. Any contact with the wire would pull the pin from the grenade and cause a detonation. The location of the grenade achieved a much better dispersion of fragments compared to one on the ground. The Viet Cong often employed this device at night to protect their positions and to provide a warning of approaching enemy. During the day the tripwire would be either removed or loosened and moved out of the way to allow the safe movement for their own troops.

By custom the Vietnamese flew many flags and banners and as we have seen in conflicts from the First World War onwards, these are always like red rag to a bull. The Vietnam War was no different, and the Viet Cong, counting on the fact that US and South Vietnamese forces would have a tendency to dismantle or remove all flags supporting the communist cause, would booby-trap them. Often signs or slogans insulting or infuriating to American soldiers would be left inviting their swift removal. Such actions of course proved fatal.

On 15 November 1970 the 3rd Ordnance Battalion (EOD) responded to a call from an American Advisor in the Bien Hoa sector at Long Thanh. On arrival the team discovered a sign made out of heavy cardboard which was placed on the side of the road through a hamlet. This had derogatory comments about the Vietnamese administration. Examination of the sign revealed a battery pack, wiring and a thread leading back to what appeared to be a paper cup. The area was evacuated and the wires cut and the sign moved remotely. This revealed an electrical pull switch that was connected to a modified American cluster bomb unit.

The Viet Cong recognised that under some circumstances American forces would destroy dwellings by setting fire to their thatched roofs. Where this was a strong possibility they would plant grenades in the thatched roofs that had had their pins removed and the fly off levers tied down with string or strong rubber bands. When the roofs were set on fire, the string or rubber would burn through and the grenades would explode injuring any troops close by. This, of course, was easily countered by never standing too close to buildings once they had been set on fire.

Vehicles were also attacked using grenades. One method was to drop these into fuel tanks. The grenades would have their pins removed and the fly-off levers held down by plastic adhesive tape. The adhesive on this tape rapidly lost its properties in contact with petrol and so allowed the fly-off lever to be released and the grenade functioned. Using different amounts of tape would vary the time delay. This, of course, could be simply prevented by using a locking device on the petrol cap.

Grenades were also used intentionally to trick teams searching for mines with mine detectors. A grenade would be buried with enough scrap metal to register clearly on a mine detector. The grenade would be lodged among the metal in hard-packed dirt with the pin removed. When a detector team discovered the suspect site the normal procedure was to use a prodder or bayonet to loosen the earth and uncover the mine. That act would break up the packed earth around the grenade releasing the fly-off lever and it would detonate.

The Viet Cong also used the old trick of finding or stealing American grenades, removing the delay element and then allowing the grenade to be found or placed back in the enemy supply system. Thus when a soldier threw it, it detonated instantly. This not only killed or maimed the soldier throwing the grenade, but also destroyed others confidence in their weapons and equipment.

The claymore-type mine was fully utilised in Vietnam by both sides. These could be either command-detonated or set up as a booby trap. Directional mines normally consisted of a high-explosive charge, often in sheet form, into which metal fragments were embedded. The Americans used the M18A1, while the Viet Cong used captured American stocks and locally manufactured improvised designs of their own. On detonating the charge the fragments would be hurled laterally in a dense pattern, cutting a swathe through anything in their path.

During the conflict the Americans pioneered the use of helicopters *en masse* for inserting and extracting troops, evacuating wounded and providing fire support. Of all of these the ubiquitous Huey was the American workhorse, but it was vulnerable to attack, particularly during that critical phase of flight when going into the hover above or touching down on a landing zone. The Viet Cong naturally focused their attention on these areas and targeted the helicopters with a variety of rockets, directional claymore mines and traps. The most lethal deterrent was the directional mines hidden all around the landing ground which would be command-detonated when the helicopter entered the lethal zone. Sometimes, if the helicopter did not enter the lethal zone, debussing troops would move into it. During operation Cedar Falls in January 1967, A Company, 1st Battalion 26th Infantry recorded:

As the point squad moved forward from the landing zone towards its designated blocking position tragedy struck. Two command-detonated claymore mines exploded and two men fell. A large booby trap mounted in a tree exploded and its fragments downed two more men.[9]

Grenades were also cleverly used in command-detonated anti-helicopter ambushes in a modern and more deadly version of the old fougasse. Firstly potential landing sites were located and then a charge of TNT buried in the centre of the site in a funnel-shaped hole 2 feet in diameter and 2½ feet wide. The charge was primed and then tamped with earth to within a few inches of the surface. A 2-foot square board was placed over the charge, to which grenades had been secured. The grenades were held in place by nails, which also prevented the fly-off levers being released. Once in place all the grenade safety pins would be removed and the trap was set. When a target helicopter approached the landing site the charge would be fired. This would both destroy the board and hurl the grenades into the air to a height of some 300 feet where they would all detonate producing a deadly concentration of pattern of fragments. If timed right these could inflict serious damage on the helicopter and injure its crew and passengers.

If remote control was not an option then the landing site could be trapped using the grenades-in-cans method. Bamboo poles were placed on the ground to form a large cross with a tin can attached horizontally to the top of the pole. Grenades with their pins removed were then placed inside the cans and attached to wires stretched between the poles. When the helicopter landed the wires would be pulled and the grenades, tugged from their housings, would drop to the ground and function.

Even the wash from the helicopter's rotor blades was used against them. It was noticed that when landing in small clearings the down-draught from the helicopter would blow the thinner branches of the trees in all directions. It was a simple matter therefore to place directional mines in the trees which, when detonated, would propel deadly shrapnel across the landing zone. These would be initiated by pull switches which had wires connected to the smaller branches of the tree. As the helicopter hovered just below the tree line, the thinner branches would be blown outwards and pull on the firing line, trigger the pull switches and fire the mines. Another method was to place grenades under light sheet metal and then remove the pins. The metal would be sufficiently heavy to hold down the fly-off lever, but a landing helicopter would produce sufficient down-draught to blow the metal off the grenade and it would detonate.

The Viet Cong made abundant use of captured or failed munitions, including aircraft bombs, artillery shell, mines, mortars and grenades. In some areas they had teams of spotters who would plot the fall of shells or sticks of aircraft bombs. After an attack they would go to the area and recover any failed ordnance. To put this in perspective, roughly 2 per cent of all shells fired failed, and 5 per cent of all bombs dropped by B52s. The result was that in 1966 alone 27,000 tons of dud bombs were available for the Viet Cong to recover and use. The larger munitions, for example air-craft bombs, were sawn open and the explosive recovered for use in impro-vised munitions. Smaller items, mortars or shells would simply be fitted with command- or victim-operated switches and used in all manner of ways. A captured M14 anti-personnel mine was used in conjunction with a 20-pound block of US explosive and a 105mm shell, all designed to increase the effect when the mine detonated. In another case another M14 mine was set as normal, but Cordtex was used to link the mine to several hidden shell close by. In this configuration detection of the small anti-per-sonnel mine was difficult compared with an anti-tank mine, but a soft-skinned vehicle hitting the fuze of the mine would detonate the surrounding shell, producing a hail of lethal splinters. Tree-mounted mortars or shells were also popular with the Viet Cong. One of their ploys was to place these in the trees above routes which were regularly taken by enemy forces. As they moved underneath the trees the suspended shells were detonated by remote control. This technique was particularly success-ful against troops who did not correctly exercise overhead security.

The Americans were well aware that the Viet Cong recovered failed ord-nance, particularly aircraft bombs, and American EOD personnel spent many hours trekking through the jungle to try to locate and destroy these. Captain Bob Leiendecker served in the 85th Ordnance Detachment sup-porting the 4th Infantry Division in 1969. One of the tasks they regularly had to undertake was searching for unexploded ordnance. Normally this was when a pilot reported 'dud' munitions. Some failures were due to incor-rect loading procedures; in some instances the bombs were dropped too low to arm, and in others they simply failed to detonate. In any event wherever possible these bombs had to be located and destroyed to prevent them being recovered and used by the Viet Cong. This of course was not an easy task. When dropped in the jungle it was normally easier to look up, because most of the bombs had snake-eye fins which would chew up a visible path as they came down through the trees. In tall grass or low vegetation, such methods were impossible, and searchers would almost step into any entry hole before seeing it. Quite often the pilots made errors in reporting the locations where the bombs had been dropped and EOD officers would spend many hours fruitlessly searching for the lost munitions. This was a very dangerous task, as the bombs would have originally been aimed at the Viet Cong, so they too would almost certainly be in the area, possibly also looking for the failed ordnance. Eventually the decision would be made to abandon the search and hope that 'Charlie' would, like them, fail to find the bombs.

The Viet Cong displayed great skill in their use of mines. They were rarely used *en masse* and were most often deployed in the classic nuisance–harassing role. The key to their successful employment was to outwit the enemy into thinking they were safe. Many ploys were used.

One trick used during the mining of earth roads was simply to dig up the road and then leave it. After the Americans had filled in the excavated sections, the Viet Cong would return and mine them. Infuriatingly, the Viet Cong dug many holes in dirt roads but only mined a few. In addition metal fragments were used to deceive detectors. Under such circumstances delays in opening roads were caused because every filled pothole had to be investigated.

In a similar manner the Viet Cong dug potholes in compacted earth tracks and then filled the holes with loose earth. Mine-sweeping teams noticing this disturbed earth would clear these holes. The Viet Cong would then slip in behind them and mine them. To counter this the mine-sweeping teams were instructed to cover the loose earth in cleared holes with oil. On their return if the soil had been disturbed it would be obvious.

Mines were placed above metal culverts that ran under the roads and dirt tracks. The inexperienced mine-sweeper would be deceived into thinking that the road was clear because he would expect a reading from the culvert. The proper procedure was to set the mine-sweeper sensitivity so that it could just detect the culvert, then adjust it so that the culvert could not quite be detected and the surface swept afresh for mines.

Clearly the Viet Cong had to ensure that the mines and booby traps they laid did not cause large numbers of casualties among their own forces. They did in many cases make arrangements for the recording and marking of devices. It was not universal, however, and in some districts no markings were used at all. In areas where they had a strong presence it seems the Viet Cong would have some regard for the local population and their protection, particularly if the people were friendly and helpful to their cause. In these areas, where the Viet Cong were in control, mines and booby traps were used, but it was important that they had freedom of movement and so marking systems were developed. If they were forced to abandon a locality and could do this in an organised manner then most of these markers would be removed. However, if US forces quickly overwhelmed an area it was quite possible that these markers would be left in place, and it was vital therefore that the signs could be identified. The methods of marking varied tremendously and would not always indicate the presence of a mine or booby trap, but recognising the sign was enough to induce caution and possibly prevent injury. Typical signs were arrowheads on paths or trails, bamboo squares or tripods over mines, broken branches or sticks and the use of rocks or stones. In buildings, string hanging down vertically a few inches from the entrances was an indication that it was booby-trapped. Some doctored grenades which had had their delay pellets removed were indicated by coloured paint spots, but this was by no means universal.

The Americans also used mines and booby traps to catch out unwary enemy soldiers. The Viet Cong always made strenuous efforts to retrieve their dead and to recover lost equipment or scavenge items from the battle-field. Thus they could be targeted and trapped. US Special Forces proved particularly adept at this, particularly when they undertook long-range patrols and ambushes. On 11 October 1966, one such patrol led by Captain James Felon set out to watch an area on the border between Laos, Cambodia, and South Vietnam. After many days in the jungle, on 2 November they ambushed a squad of North Vietnamese soldiers pushing bicycles. Using small-arms fire all the soldiers were killed. The saddlebags of the bicycles were each discovered to contain 50 new 'potato-masher'-type grenades. Knowing that other enemy soldiers would come to investi-gate and recover the bodies, the bicycles and the munitions, the grenades were photographed and then booby-trapped using claymore mines and flashlight batteries.[10] Like many traps there is no record of whether or not they were successful.

Alongside their guerrilla operation in the countryside Viet Cong also ran a very successful campaign in the urban areas and made full use of sabotage and improvised devices. These were either covertly introduced into American installations and places frequented by US soldiers or they were deployed overtly in classic hit-and-run attacks on vehicles and against off-duty personnel.

In one instance a foot locker (small trunk) addressed to a US Officer was delivered to a base. This was discovered to contain over 100 pounds of explosives with a clockwork-activated fuze. Personnel working in the base were about to deliver the locker, but became suspicious when the room number it was to be delivered to was noted to be wrong. On opening the locker the charge was discovered and disarmed only minutes before it was due to detonate.

In another case, a fountain pen was found on the floor of a vehicle which had been left unattended. When X-rayed it was discovered that the pen contained a small explosive device which would function when the top of the pen was twisted off and removed. The device contained sufficient explosive to blow a man's hand off. In a similar fashion Zippo-type lighters were discovered left in areas where they would be easily found. They gave the outward appearance of being a common cigarette lighter. However the cotton in the fluid compartment was removed and replaced with a small explosive charge. This would be initiated by a detonator which was itself set off by a fast-burning fuse running down from the wick. Although small, the charge was sufficient to blow off the hand of a man using the lighter. It could easily kill if it was being used actually to light a cigarette. These devices are already familiar and seem to have their origins back in the closing stages of the Second World War.

There was also one interesting booby trap that made use of the fact that American soldiers would often borrow unattended bicycles. The Viet Cong filled the frame under the seat of a cycle with explosive and ran an electrical firing cable to the small dynamo generator, which provided the power for the lights on the bike. It was then abandoned at night in an area where an American serviceman might take it. Fortunately it was discovered. If not, a very nasty injury would have ensued, because when sufficient speed was built up enough current would have been generated to fire the explosive charge under the seat.

Overt attacks included grenades concealed in items being thrown to passing troops. In one incident a loaf of bread was thrown into the back of a US navy truck. The men in the back of the truck, being well-trained, reacted immediately and threw it out just before it exploded. Even so two individuals were wounded by flying fragments. Command-detonated directional mines were also deployed; these were often hidden in the saddlebags of bicycles, or motorbikes, or in the panels of car-doors. These would be detonated as American troops or vehicles passed by. The Viet Cong also employed swimmers to position delayed-action limpet mines against anchored shipping. Swimming Viet Cong sappers also deployed demolition charges against bridges and piers.

The Americans quickly realised that the use of mines, booby traps and sabotage devices created a sense of apprehension and fear which could be both debilitating and demoralising. To counter the Viet Cong mine and booby trap threat the US Army embarked on a massive training program. This stressed that with proper training and strict discipline in the field, many of the casualties could be overcome. Records from 1968 indicated that US forces unintentionally initiated 50 per cent of all the enemy mines and booby traps. This, it was recognised, was unacceptably high. Schools were set up to teach enemy methods and the best and most effective procedures for dealing with them. An understanding of Viet Cong techniques, combined with defensive procedures diligently applied significantly reduced the effectiveness of the mines and traps deployed.

The key to successful training started with the analysis of all reported attacks and then drawing common lessons from them. This produced much valuable information. It was established that almost all the booby traps that were found and not activated were located by visual means. Very few of them, less than 1 per cent were detected by other methods, for example, by using dogs. Therefore it was vital that soldiers were constantly alert and searching the area in front of them for traps. It was concluded that the best mine and booby trap detector was an alert and observant point-man. The rota for this had to have short stints or the stress of the job became unacceptable. The person needed a tactical awareness and the ability to avoid the obvious routes or dangerous areas. In populated districts, this included the ability to observe the movements of civilians; many locals either knew where mines or booby traps were. Other simple measures such as banning the use of sunglasses also helped – these made it much more difficult to detect tripwires. An awareness of typical Viet Cong mine-markers enabled traps to be located before they could be seen. The importance of overhead security was also stressed, particularly because booby-trapped mortar bombs or shell produced very effective fragment patterns when suspended above a trail. 'Kit Carson scouts' could also be used to help detect booby traps and mines. These were former Viet Cong or North Vietnamese Army soldiers (named after the famous frontiersman of the 19th century) who defected to the south. The best and most skilled of these men when properly used and motivated could spot anything odd or unusual well before their new allies.

It was discovered that most of the traps were located at around 11:00 hours in the morning, when troops were fresh and alert. The average time of successful attacks turned out to be around 16:00 hours by which time troops were weary. The majority of all casualties occurred from booby traps during reconnaissance in force missions. When a soldier plodded for hours up to his waist in water in paddy fields in hot humid conditions he became rapidly fatigued and the temptation was always to take the easiest route, which invariably would be trapped. The simple expedient of rotating lead soldiers, and lead units within a formation, did much to reduce the casualty rate.

When the location of traps was investigated it was discovered that just fewer than 50 per cent were laid along trails, rice-paddy dykes and canal or stream banks. Another one-third were laid in the jungle itself. The reason for this was twofold. The Viet Cong often deployed their traps in such a manner that the first would be on a trail but would be surrounded by others. Troops taking cover in the jungle or in a rice paddy after the explosion of one trap would be likely to walk into another. The second reason was that the Viet Cong made use of booby traps in the jungle to protect the perimeters of their permanent and semi-permanent defensive positions. Clearly, then, troops advancing through or attacking such positions had to be aware of the increased risk of traps.

One of the most disturbing statistics was that 46 per cent of all mines and booby traps that detonated resulted in multiple casualties. The bunching up of troops as they moved through hostile areas caused this. One prisoner of war commented on US march discipline as follows:

> US troops were moving fast, so I knew they did not have any idea the booby traps were there. Suddenly I heard some booby traps explode. Five US soldiers in the front element went down and were wounded or dead.[11]

Using more than one trap also often caused multiple casualties. The first would cause a single casualty, and the second, usually with a much larger charge, was designed to kill and maim any personnel going to assist the injured man. The Viet Cong frequently placed booby traps in caches of weapons, explosives and stores that they anticipated would be discovered by US or other forces. In one incident several soldiers were injured while recovering materials from a captured cache. Although the unit involved had initially maintained the correct spacing to ensure casualties were reduced, this had changed while searching for the cache. They had congregated around the hoard to help move all the captured material. It was during this time that a booby trap functioned. In this case it was a grenade with the safety pin removed. When the stores were removed the grenade, which had had its delay pellet removed, exploded. Not surprisingly, the old rule was re-confirmed that one man at a time should be used to search caches to prevent multiple casualties. Even better, remote means such as a hook and line should be used to pull items from the cache.

Many measures were adopted to prevent 'bunching' of personnel and the rush to investigate incidents in the hope of reducing casualties or preventing incidents from being made worse. This required commanders to keep very tight control of their troops and use their tactical knowledge to respond correctly to enemy contacts, for example, being aware of the dangers of an obvious follow-up if Viet Cong showed themselves. This rarely happened unless they wanted to be seen and pursued into a follow-up ambush or trap. The more aggressive soldiers, for example the 1st Battalion (Airborne) of the 503rd Infantry often found this difficult, their ethos was to 'close with and destroy the enemy'. According to First Lieutenant James F O'Brien most of the units casualties were caused by booby traps often after quick follow-ups. He wrote:

> Their escape routes were made secure by the most devastating weapon in the enemy's armoury – the booby trap. Phu My district was saturated with every type of booby trap, ranging from 'toe

poppers' to 155 mm artillery rounds. The vast majority of 1/503d's casualties were from these devices. Their physical damage was equalled by their psychological effect. Once tripped there was a feeling of complete helplessness; except on rare occasions there was no enemy to strike at.[12]

Where grenade traps were used, analysis showed that more often than not the delay pellets in the grenade had not been removed. When the trap was tripped, therefore, there would be a short delay between the striker hitting the initiating cap and the fuse burning through to the detonator. If the man who tripped the trap, or another close by, heard the pop as the cap was initiated then there was a few seconds to take cover. Where a grenade was located at ground level the simple expedient of 'hitting the deck' could prevent casualties. Troops had to be trained to recognise instantly the sound of a grenade cap being struck and, more importantly, to shout a warning to those nearby. Adoption of this simple immediate action helped reduce casualties.

Analysis of wounds from the traps reinforced the need for protective equipment. The use of helmets was strictly enforced to reduce head wounds from flying shrapnel and the widespread introduction of the Kevlar-lined flak jackets, which protected the vital organs, did a lot to reduce the effectiveness of small mines and traps. Good first-aid training also helped save lives, although this could not prevent the loss of limbs or other serious injuries.

When traps were discovered it was important that they were safely dealt with. There could be nothing worse from a morale point of view than a trap being discovered before it detonated and then an injury resulting from attempts to disarm or neutralise it, particularly by self-proclaimed experts. Even when specialists were available it was concluded that the best method of dealing with traps was remotely. As most had some form of tripwire, dragging lines were used. These consisted of a weight, often a filling-plug from a 155 mm shell, which was attached to a line. This could be thrown over the tripwire and could be pulled from a safe location to initiate the trap. It paid, of course, to be wary of an obvious tripwire which when pulled detonated a more cunningly sited trap nearby. Traps and mines using pressure or other initiation systems were best destroyed in place by demolition.

Wherever possible, properly trained personnel dealt with devices that were found. The men from the various Ordnance Detachments (EOD) dealt with thousands of incidents some simple, others very complex.

On 29 July 1969, 25th Ordnance Detachment (EOD) responded to a call from company D, 2nd/503rd Infantry near a landing zone called 'Two Bits'.

They arrived to find a booby-trapped M26 grenade. The normal fuze had been removed and the fuze-well filled with black powder. A fuze that looked almost identical, taken from a smoke grenade, was placed in the M26. This had no delay so when thrown it would immediately spit flame back into the black powder. This, being confined, was possibly enough to detonate the filling in the grenade. One American soldier had recently been killed by another similar grenade.

On 8 April 1970 the same detachment responded to a call from the MACV District Headquarters at An Khe. It was reported that North Vietnamese sappers had entered and booby-trapped a compound after it had been abandoned. Once the area was recaptured, a combat-engineer vehicle led the way back to the compound and promptly had its mine-roller blown off by a device. At this point EOD assistance was requested. On arrival it was discovered that there were two compounds, one large and one small, both of which had been booby-trapped. The larger compound was successfully cleared and two satchel charges connected to Soviet designed pull switches recovered. Disaster struck when the EOD team entered the smaller compound, as one of the members stepped on a partially buried bamboo pressure switch which set off an explosive charge. He suffered burns, eye damage and severe concussion. A team-member close behind him was less seriously injured.

The continuous effort made in training programs to indoctrinate all personnel in defensive measures against such devices went some way to reducing the numbers of casualties. Initially too much information was given and this proved counter-productive. Some considered that teaching the soldiers about the non-explosive traps caused more fear than they actually warranted. Later the principles alone were taught. With a sound understanding of these, more traps could be detected and safely neutralised. But the nature of the war was such that, despite sound training some inevitably would be bound to succeed. It is easy to train; it is another matter putting that training into practice, particularly for the PBI (Poor Bloody Infantry) who had a massive physical burden, debilitating climate and 101 other things to worry about.

Like all wars the clash in South East Asia was won by the side that had the political will and the means to prosecute and continue the fight until the other was exhausted. The Americans and their Allies did not lose the war on the ground in Vietnam; the political will was eroded at home as a result of casualties. Most of these were the result of direct engagements with the enemy, but more than in any other war, booby traps and mines claimed their share of victims. To the watching cameras, the cause of death, or reason for mutilation meant little. It was body bags and wounded that counted. The mines and traps contributed to this figure and added to the political pressure building in USA for the troops to be brought home. On 11 August 1972, the last American ground-combat unit, the 3rd Battalion of the 21st Infantry, packed their weapons and left their base at Da Nang. American bombing of the North continued until December and US advisors remained on the ground for a further month. A cease-fire followed, but the outcome was by now predestined. Two years later, on 30 April 1975, Saigon fell and the last 11 Marines guarding the US embassy departed by helicopter.

Notes

1 Mangold Tom and John Penycate, *The Tunnels of Cu Chi*, Hodder and Stoughton, London, 1985.
2 Cox, Capt James M, US Army Report, 5 October 1968.
3 McNiel, Ian, *To Long Tan: The Australian Army and the Vietnam War 1950–1966*, Allen & Unwin, St Leonards, NSW, Australia, 1993.
4 Chanoff David and Doan van Toai, *Portrait of the Enemy*, Random House, New York, 1986.
5 *op. cit.*, note 3.
6 Marshal, S L A, *Battles in the Monsoon*, William Morrow, New York, 1967.
7 Landmine and Countermine Warfare, US Report 1972 – Vietnam.
8 *op. cit.*, note 1.
9 Rogers, Lt Gen B W, *Vietnam Studies: Cedar Fall – Junction City, A Turning Point*, Department of the Army, Washington DC 1974.
10 Garland, Albert N, *Infantry in Vietnam*, The Battery Press, Nashville, 1967.
11 Ewell Lt Gen J J and Hunt Maj Gen I A Jnr, *Sharpening the Combat Edge - The Use of Analysis to Reinforce Military Judgement*, Department of the Army, Washington DC, 1974.
12 Garland, Albert N, *A Distant Challenge, The US Infantry in Vietnam 1967–1972*, The Battery Press, Nashville, 1983.

CHAPTER ELEVEN

Postscript

As I explained in the introduction, it was never my intention to cover the use of military booby traps up to the present day. There are three main reasons for this. Firstly, booby-trapping today is synonymous with the use of improvised explosive devices. There no longer exists a clear distinction where one ends and the others starts. The beginning of this process started in the campaigns after the end of the Second World War. But as supplies of military switches dried up then improvisation became the order of the day. As the word implies improvisation means using whatever is at hand to make devices. It would clearly be wrong in today's climate to describe how to make such improvised traps, and to indicate which methods of attack are most successful. This would put our own civilians, police and security forces at risk.

Secondly, there is now a range of new military devices. As far as the predominantly military operations are concerned, booby traps have been deployed in most theatres of operation. The Argentinians used them in the Falklands, all sides deployed them in Afghanistan, and they were used in both the Iraqi Wars. These new devices were also deployed in the bloody Balkan wars alongside improvised traps. New technologies have given the booby-trapper, be he a terrorist or conventional soldier, new ways of targeting his prey. Historically most booby traps were set off by the physical actions of the victim or after a time delay. The former at least were tangible. The principles behind the operation of the traps were known and easily understood. With careful observation, simple procedures, and basic equipment they could be detected and rendered safe. Today, although it is still the physical actions that set off a trap, there is now a whole new range of stimuli which can be used as the trigger. These include acoustics, light, laser, vibration, infra-red, thermal, fine-break wires rather than tripwires and combinations of the above, to mention but a few. Much of this technology was developed during and shortly after the Second World War. However, it is only in the last 30 years, with the improvements in reliability, and reduction in cost of electronic components, that these new booby traps have become

259

economically viable and safe and suitable for service. This new range of switches when carefully laid are almost impossible to detect without causing them to function. Furthermore, devices can be designed to discriminate between different targets. For example, in South Africa during the apartheid years railway switches were designed which could be set to differentiate between steam and diesel trains. It would be wrong to describe these new systems in detail.

The final reason for stopping at Vietnam is related to the changing nature of war. Today, even with the advent of precision-guided weapons, civilians still become legitimate targets. This is doubly true where mines and traps are concerned. The reader should now understand that nuisance or harassing mining is in many respects akin to booby-trapping because to be effective thought has been put into where and how the mines are laid. Over the last 40 years a new and terrible form of mining has developed. This can best be described as indiscriminate mining. This atrocious activity, using cheap plastic anti-personnel mines, scatterable mines and sub-munitions, has left large parts of the Third World littered with the deadly explosive remnants of war. They are the new scourge of the Third World and the poor. Altough this problem is recognised, and there is an international campaign to ban such munitions, some countries have still not signed up to the treaty.

While carrying out my research I came across a two-page article which, like the incident with the children at the well in the Arakan, left a lasting impression on me. It said:

The mines in Cambodia are being cleared daily . . .

It was a cause for hope, things were improving I thought. I could not have been more wrong: on turning the page there was a picture of a young man on an operating table, one leg a bloody stump below the knee and the other, clearly shattered, lay abnormally twisted and caked in congealed blood and mud. The caption underneath the picture said simply

limb by limb.

I have no desire to describe this activity.

Select Bibliography

BOOKS

Introduction
Partington, JR, *A History of Greek Fire and Gunpowder*, Heffer, Cambridge, 1960.

Regan, Geoffry, *The Guinness Book of Military Anecdotes*, Guinness, London, 1992.

World War One
Birchall, Peter, *The Longest Walk*, Arms and Armour Press, London, 1997.

Boraston, Lieutenant Colonel JH and Bax, Captain CEO, *The 8th Division in War 1914–18* Medici Society Ltd, London, 1926.

Brown, Malcolm, *The Imperial War Museum Book of the Western Front*, Imperial War Museum, London.

Coppard, George, *With a Machine Gun to Cambrai*, Imperial War Museum, London, 1990.

Dunn, Captain JC, *The War the Infantry Knew*, King, London, 1938.

Edmonds, C, *A Subaltern's War*, Cedric Chivers, Bath, 1966.

Fairlie-Wood, Herbert, *Vimy*, Macdonald, London, 1967.

Fries, Amos A and Clarence West, *Chemical Warfare*, McGraw Hill, New York, 1922.

Gough, General Sir H, *The Fifth Army,* Hodder and Stoughton, London, 1931.

Graham, Captain HW, *The Life of a Tunnelling Company*, JCatherall, Hexham, 1927.

Grieve, Captain W Grant and Bernard Newman, *Tunnellers*, Herbert Jenkins, London, 1936.

Guillan, Captain Stair, *The Story of 29 Division*, Thomas Nelson, London, 1925.

Hutchison, Lieutenant Colonel G Seton, *Warrior*, Hutchinson, London, 1932.

Jünger, Ernst, *Storm of Steel*, Chatto and Windus, London, 1929.

Linman von Sanders, General, *Five Years in Turkey*, Williams and Wilkins, Annapolis, 1928.

McBride, Captain Herbert W A, *Rifleman Went to War*, Small Arms Technical Publishing Company, North Carolina, 1935.

Nagel, Fritz, *Fritz: The WW1 Memoirs of a German Lieutenant*, Der Angriff, Huntington VA, 1981.

Nash, TAM, *The Diary of an Unprofessional Soldier*, Picton, 1991.

Oldham, Peter, *The Hindenburg Line*, Leo Cooper, London, 1997.

Pritchard H L, Major General, *History of the Corps of Royal Engineers, volume V, The Home Front, France, Flanders and Italy in the Great War*, Longmans, London, 1952.

Trounce, H D, *Fighting the Boche Underground*, Charles Scribner's, New York, 1918.

Tucker, John F, *Johnny Get Your Gun*, William Kimber, London, 1978.

Vaughan, Captain Edwin Campion, *Desperate Glory*, Papermac, London 1995.

The Work of the Royal Engineers in the European War 1914–19, Military Mining, Institution of Royal Engineers, Chatham, 1922.

World War Two

Allen, James R, *In the Trade of War*, Parapress, Tunnbridge Wells, 1994.

Boyce and Everett, *SOE the Scientific Secrets*, Sutton, Stroud, 2003.

Brunner, Dr John W, *OSS Weapons*, Phillips, Williamstown NJ, 1994.

Burhans, Lt Colonel R D, *The First Special Service Force - A War History of the North Americans 1942–44*, Washington DC, Infantry Journal Press, 1947.

Carell, Paul, *The Foxes of the Desert*, Bantam Books, New York, 1960.

Cookridge, E H, *Inside SOE*, Arthur Barker, London, 1966.

Cooper, Mathew, *The Phantom War*, Macdonald and James, London, 1979.

Crichton Stuart, Michael, *G Patrol*, William Kimber, London, 1976.

Daniell, A P. de T, *Mediterranean Safari: March 1943–October 1944*, Buckland Publications, London, c. 1990.

Delaforce, Patrick, *Churchill's Secret Weapons*, Robert Hale, London, 1998.

Foot, MRD, *Resistance*, Eyre Methuen, London, 1976.

Foot, MRD, *SOE The Special Operations Executive 1940–1946*, Pimlico, London, 1999.

Halsted, Michael, *Shots in the Sand*, Gooday Publishers, East Wittering, 1990.

Hammerton, Ian C, *Achtung! Minen*, Wild Hawthorne Press, 1980.

Harrison, Gordon A, *Cross Channel Attack,* series *United States Army in*

WW11: The European Theatre of Operations, Office of the Chief of Military History, Washington DC, 1951.

Hart Dyke, Brigadier T, *Normandy to Arnhem,* Green and Thompson, Sheffield, 1966.

Henniker, Mark, *An Image of War,* Leo Cooper, London, 1987.

Hoffman, Major Carl W *Saipan, The Beginning of the End,* USMC Historical Division HQ, US Marine Corps,1950.

Hogben, Major Arthur, *Designed to Kill,* Patrick Stephens, Wellingborough, 1987.

Jackson, Sir William, *The Rock of the Gibraltarians,* Associated University Press, London, 1987.

James, Malcolm, *Born of the Desert,* Greenhill Books, London, 1991.

Jamison, Captain Wallace H, 'Achtung! Mines', *Infantry Journal,* November 1943.

Ladd, J D, *Assault from the Sea,* David and Charles Ltd, Newton Abbott, 1976.

Lampe, David, *The Last Ditch,* Cassell, London, 1968.

Lee Harvey, J M, *D Day Dodger,* William Kimber, London, 1979.

Lewes, John, *Jock Lewes Co-Founder of the SAS,* Leo Cooper, Barnsley, 2000.

Lindsay, Martin Lt Colonel, *So Few Got Through,* Collins, London, 1946.

Lucas Phillips, C E, *Cockleshell Heroes,* Pan Books, London, 1957.

Macrae, Stuart, *Winston Churchill's Toyshop,* The Roundwood Press, Kineton, 1971.

Morris, Eric, *Circles of Hell: The War in Italy,* Hutchinson, London 1993.

Perrett, Bryan, *The Valentine in North Africa 1942–43,* Ian Allan, London, 1972.

Riches, Paul, *The Spirit Lives On,* privately published, [UK], 1992.

Riordan, Thomas M J, 7th Field Company RE, 1939–1946: the 'Shiny 7th', T M J Riordan, York, *c.* 1984.

Rothschild, Lord, *Meditations of a Broomstick,* Collins, London, 1977.

Seaman, Mark, *World War II Secret Agent: Directory of Special Devices,* PRO, London, 2000.

Tucker, Lt Gen Sir Francis, *Approach to Battle,* Cassell, London, 1965.

Post World War Two

Chanoff David and Doan van Toai, *Portrait of the Enemy,* Random House, New York, 1986.

Ewell, Lt Gen J and Hunt, Maj Gen I A Jnr, *Sharpening the Combat Edge: The Use of Analysis to Reinforce Military Judgement,* Dept of the Army, Washington DC, 1974.

Follows Roy and Hugh Popham, *The Jungle Beat,* Blandford, London, 1990.

Garland, Albert N, *Infantry in Vietnam*, The Battery Press, Nashville, 1967.

Grivas, General George, *Guerrilla Warfare and EOKA's Struggle*, Longmans, London, *c.* 1964.

Jones, Tim, *Postwar Counterinsurgency and the SAS, 1945–1952*, Frank Cass, London, 2001.

Mangold Tom and John Penycate, *The Tunnels of Cu Chi*, Hodder and Stoughton, London, 1985.

Marshal, S L A, *Battles in the Monsoon*, William Morrow, New York, 1967.

McNiel, Ian, *To Long Tan: The Australian Army and the Vietnam War 1950–1966*, Allen and Unwin, St Leonards, NSW, 1993

Paget, Julian, *Last Post: Aden 1964–67*, Faber and Faber, London, 1969.

Short, Anthony, *The Communist Insurrection in Malaya 1948-1960*, Fredrick Muller, London, 1975.

Westing, Arthur H, *Explosive Remnants of War*, SIPRI & UNEP/Taylor & Francis, London, 1985.

MILITARY PAMPHLETS

Field Engineering and Mine Warfare, part 1 (all arms), pamphlet no. 4: Mines (individual mechanisms), The War Office, April 1947, WO code 8208.

Mines and Booby Traps Military Training Pamphlet no. 40: Part 1 (all arms) How to Deal With Individual Mechanisms,The War Office, London, May 1943.

Illustrated Record of German Army Equipment 1939–1945 , volume V: Mines, Mine Detectors and Demolition Equipment, MI 10, The War Office, London, 1947.

Enemy Equipment Part I, German Mines and Traps, 1943, The War Office, London, December 1943.

Enemy Equipment Part II, Italian Mines and Traps, 1944, The War Office, London, August 1943.

Japanese Explosive Ordnance, (Bombs, Bomb Fuzes, Land Mines, Grenades, firing Devices and Sabotage Devices), TM 9 1985-4 to 39B-1A-11, Departments of the Army and Air Force, March 1953.

Land Mines and Booby Traps War, FM 5-31, War Department, United States Government Printing Office, Washington DC, 1943.

Palestine Pamphlet, Terrorist Methods with Mines and Booby Traps, HQ Chief Engineer, Palestine and Transjordan, 1946.

The Use and Installation of Booby Traps Department of the Army, Technical Manual FM 5-31 1956, Departments of the Army, Washington DC, 31 January 1956.

Mines and Booby Traps, revised from the 1951 edition by the 584th Engineer Technical Intelligence Team, HQ Eighth US Army, Korea (EUSAK), Office of the Engineer, APO 301.

Guide to Selected Viet Cong Equipment and Explosive Devices, 381-11HQ, Department of the Army, 1966.

US MACV Technical Intelligence Bulletin, HQ US Military Assistance Command Vietnam, 1962.

Landmine and Countermine Warfare, Washington DC, 1972.

Index

References in italics are to illustrations

5

	DATE DUE		
~~5/15/06~~ 9/7/09			